Keeping the peace

The Melland Schill Monographs
in International Law

General editor Gillian M. White

Keeping the peace

The United Nations and the maintenance of international peace and security

N. D. WHITE

Lecturer in Law,
University of Nottingham

Manchester University Press

Manchester and New York

Distributed exclusively in the United States and Canada by St. Martin's Press

Published by Manchester University Press
Oxford Road, Manchester M13 9PL, UK
and Room 400, 175 Fifth Avenue, New York, NY 10010, USA

Distributed exclusively in the USA and Canada
by St. Martin's Press, Inc., 175 Fifth Avenue, New York,
NY 10010, USA

British Library Cataloguing-in-Publication Data
A catalogue record for this book is available from the British
Library

Library of Congress Cataloging-in-Publication Data
White, N. D. 1961–
    Keeping the peace : the United Nations and the maintenance of international peace and
security / N. D. White.
        p. cm. — (The Melland Schill monographs in international law)
    ISBN 0–7190–3766–2 (hard). — ISBN 0–7190–3767–0 (pbk.)
    1. United Nations. 2. United Nations–Armed Forces. 3. Pacific
settlement of international disputes. I. Title. II. Series.
JX1977.W466   1993
341.23—dc20   93–17869

ISBN 0 7190 3766 2 *hardback*
      0 7190 3767 0 *paperback*

Photoset in Linotron Times
by Northern Phototypesetting Co Ltd, Bolton

Printed in Great Britain
by Redwood Books, Trowbridge, Wiltshire

CONTENTS

FOREWORD

The Melland Schill Fund, which supports the publication of the *Melland Schill Monographs in International Law*, was established by the will of the late Olive Schill in memory of her brother, Melland, who was killed in the First World War. Miss Schill wished to contribute to scholarship and learning in international relations and international law, hoping that humanity might increase in wisdom and the likelihood of further armed conflicts decrease. Publication of this study of the United Nations' role and practice in *Keeping the Peace* falls squarely within the intentions of the benefactor.

In mid-1992 the Secretary General of the UN felt able to declare that a conviction had grown among nations, in recent months,

that an opportunity has been regained to achieve the great objectives of the Charter – a United Nations capable of maintaining international peace and security, of securing justice and human rights and of promoting, in the words of the Charter, 'social progress and better standards of life in larger freedom'.

He went on to urge that this opportunity must be seized. The UN 'must never again be crippled as it was in the era that has now passed'.

These positive statements by the Secretary General in his report to the Security Council, *An Agenda for Peace* (June 1992), might be greeted now, in mid-1993, with scepticism if not cynicism, by commentators frustrated and saddened at the UN's apparent impotence to secure cessation of hostilities in Bosnia, and by the continuing strife in other countries such as Angola and Somalia. But the Secretary General reminds us, in his report, that it is 'the sovereign State' which is 'the fundamental entity of the international community', and that the many calls on the security arm of the UN 'will demand the concerted attention and effort of individual States, of regional and non-governmental organisations and of all the United Nations system, with each of the principal organs functioning in the balance and harmony that the Charter requires'. Peacekeeping is essentially consensual and requires cooperation from all parties involved. Enforcement action, and/or peacemaking in the sense of resolving disputes through diplomatic mediation, raise other and more acute problems for the UN and its member States.

Dr Nigel White, in this new and revised edition of his work, offers a sober initial evaluation of the decisions and actions of the political organs, the Security Council and the General Assembly, since the ending of the Cold War in the fundamental areas of international peace and security. His analysis, anchored firmly in the structure of the organisation as envisaged by the founders in 1945 and subsequently developed and modified by the practice of members confronted with numerous threats to or breaches of international peace, contributes positively to informed debate on the UN's achievements and failures, and the prospects for the future as it faces daunting challenges which seem to increase monthly. As I wrote in the foreword to the first edition

It is through increased understanding of past practice, achievements and failures that possible future improvements in the ways in which States use the Charter provisions and the powers of the United Nations may come about.

The Melland Schill Series is indeed a fitting context for the publication of this valuable study.

G. M. White,
Emeritus Professor of International Law,
University of Manchester
June 1993.

PREFACE

It has been only three years since the publication of *The United Nations and the Maintenance of International Peace and Security*, but what momentous years they have been. That work forms the basis of the following text, but great emphasis has been placed on the developments which have occurred at the United Nations since the end of the Cold War and the demise of the Soviet Union. Instead of paralysis in the Security Council and rhetoric in the General Assembly, we have an active Council and a less antagonistic Assembly, although the tensions between the two organs remain.

Full coverage is given to the UN's recent involvement in the Gulf, the former Yugoslavia, Western Sahara, Cambodia, Somalia, Central America, Libya, and South Africa, as well as to the body of practice developed over the forty-five years prior to these recent events.

Although the political climate has changed dramatically at the UN, a development which has primarily affected the Security Council, the legal principles, while being developed and perhaps extended by recent practice, have their origins in the Charter as interpreted by the Council during the Cold War and have therefore remained relatively constant. The increased use of the enforcement mechanisms of Chapter VII as well as the further development of the peacekeeping function in the post Cold War era have added to the body of precedent on the use (and possibly abuse) of those legal powers.

In order to discern the political changes as well as the development of legal powers, this revised and updated version of the original retains the basic division into three parts on the Security Council, the General Assembly and Peacekeeping. Peacekeeping is dealt with separately because of the unique nature of the function and also because the 'blue helmets' can be authorised by either organ, although naturally it is the Security Council which is dominant. Each of the three parts contains a chapter on the historical and political context, followed by a chapter on the legal parameters, and finally a chapter on the practice and effectiveness of the UN. Of course these three elements cannot realistically be considered in isolation from one another, and the influences of law on politics and vice versa is fully considered, but what the basic division hopes to do is to increase accessibility for the reader, whether she or he is interested in politics or law or simply wants an account of the workings of the United Nations in the realm of peace and security.

N. D. White
Nottingham
September 1992

PART ONE
The Security Council

INTRODUCTION

The demise of the League and the creation of the UN

The principal function of the United Nations is to maintain international peace and security.[1] Throughout the complex Great Power negotiations which led to the conference at San Francisco in 1945, the emphasis was on a particular body within the United Nations, the Security Council, performing that role. Indeed, this is reflected within the provisions of the UN Charter, which, *inter alia*, gave the Security Council 'primary responsibility' for the maintenance of international peace, accompanied by comprehensive powers to enable it to fulfil that role.[2] The Great Powers did not foresee the General Assembly having any substantive powers, intending merely to have it as a meeting-place for the representatives of States. However, the smaller powers at San Francisco managed to secure sufficient provisions in the Charter to enable the Assembly to develop an important subsidiary role in the maintenance of international peace. We will examine this development in Part Two; for the moment our emphasis is on the Security Council.

This introduction is mainly concerned with giving a background to the United Nations viewed in the light of the League experience and the Great Power negotiations which preceded the adoption of the UN Charter. It must be remembered that throughout these negotiations it was the UN Security Council which was intended to embody the principal aim of the United Nations, namely the maintenance of international peace through a system of collective security. It is also essential at this stage to explain in more detail the concept of collective security and its relationship with the more traditional concept of collective defence. The importance of these concepts will become apparent, particularly in the detailed discussion of the Security Council's use of enforcement powers.

The League of Nations had failed to keep world peace primarily because the idea of collective security was far weaker than each individual State's desires to protect its national interests. One of the statesmen behind the creation of the League, President Wilson of the United States, saw the Organisation replacing the previous balance of power system with a centralised body comprised of powerful States acting in concert as the trustees of world peace.[3] Paradoxically, it was the United States' refusal to join which could be said to be the first example of a powerful State believing that collective security was not in its best interests.

Although the Covenant of the League of Nations did contain innovative provisions for collective security and provided for the imposition of embargoes and possibly collective military sanctions against offending States,[4] the League was doomed to failure because sovereign States continued to see national interests as paramount over collective interests despite the horror of the First World War, a situation exacerbated by the requirement in Article 5 of the Covenant of unanimity for most substantive decisions of the Council or Assembly of the League. Overriding considerations of national power resulted in the dilution of the League's powers to such an extent that the question of imposition of sanctions under Article 16 became not one for the consideration of the Council or Assembly, but for each individual member, evidenced by the piecemeal and ineffective sanctions imposed against Italy after its invasion of Abyssinia in 1935. The failure to impose any sort of collective measures against aggressors meant the inevitable demise of the League.

The United Nations, in particular the Security Council, represented the world's second attempt at developing a feasible system of collective security. The Organisation had its origins, indirectly, in the 'Declaration by the United Nations' of 1 January 1942[5] which did not refer to any world body, instead it concentrated on spelling out the Allied programme to be pursued against the Axis powers to end the Second World War. Nevertheless, the idea of the United Nations continuing after the war was outlined in the Moscow Declaration of October 1943,[6] in which the Big Four: China, the United Kingdom, the United States and the Soviet Union, recognised 'the necessity of establishing, at the earliest possible date, a general international organisation based on the principle of sovereign equality of all peace loving States, and open to membership by all such States, large and small, for the maintenance of international peace and security'.

The ideal of collective security was behind this statement, though by juxtaposing the notion of a world body with that of State sovereignty, the clash between collective and national interests had not been removed. The major lesson of the League had not been learned. Nevertheless, to give collective interests primacy over national interests would be to have created a world government. In practice, the most that could be done was to give the world body, through the Security Council, greater powers for collective measures which might weigh more heavily on the scales against the counterbalance of national interests.

Comprehensive proposals from the Big Four were discussed by those States at Dumbarton Oaks between August and October 1944, resulting in a far-reaching and detailed agreement concerning the Organisation.[7] They agreed that the Security Council should have the function of maintaining international peace through collective measures if necessary. However, they also decided that the Great Powers, the Big Four plus France, should have a special position on the Council consisting of permanent representation with special voting rights which would ensure that no substantive decisions would be taken by the Council without their unanimous concurrence. The right of veto was further refined at the Yalta Conference in February 1945.

Whether one regards the necessity of Great Power unanimity as an idealistic attempt to continue where the Allies finished after the end of the war, or more cynically, as a recognition by those Powers of each others' and their own national interests being paramount over any collective interests, it is realistic to state that without the power of veto the Organisation would probably not have been born, and even if created, it would not have been able to take enforcement action against the Great Powers, particularly the Soviet Union and the United States, without devastating effects. At San Francisco the right of veto was accepted by the other States with little challenge, possibly because most delegates preferred, at least publicly, to lean towards an idealistic vision of Great Power unity providing future collective security.[8] Furthermore, the voting system on the Security Council, which when adopted required seven votes out of eleven (nine out of fifteen since 1966) 'including the concurring votes of the permanent members',[9] was an improvement on the requirement for unanimity of both permanent and non-permanent members on the League's Council.

Generally the delegates were enthusiastic about collective security but unduly optimistic about permanent member unanimity. President Roosevelt recognised this in a speech made a few months before the conference at San Francisco, in which he said that, 'the nearer we come to vanquishing our enemies the more we inevitably become conscious of the differences among the victors'.[10]

The marriage of convenience which resulted in unanimity during the war was terminated after a brief honeymoon in San Francisco. Within two days of the Council's first meeting the Cold War, in the form of a complaint by Iran of the Soviet Union's presence in its country, was on the Council's agenda, followed two days later by a Soviet complaint of the British presence in Greece. This set the tone which severely restricted the Security Council for over forty years. It was only in the late 1980s when the Soviet Union changed its policy from that of confrontation to that of cooperation with the West that we began to see the Security Council using its teeth in the form of enforcement action under Chapter VII, a process that seems set to continue with the collapse of the Soviet Union in 1991 and the emergence of Russia as the inheritor of the permanent seat.

The concepts of collective security and collective defence

A collective security system entails the centralisation of a society's coercive mechanisms.[11] As a corollary the members of that society, in this case States, give up a great deal of their individual freedom to indulge in self-help, and are generally restricted to a limited right of self-defence, usually until the central authority takes over their protection. As we shall see, the UN Charter contains all the rudiments of such a system, whereas the League of Nations did not. It is true to say that the League did contain a somewhat ambiguous limit on aggression in Article 10 but not on other forms of self-help, except for certain procedural restrictions in Articles 12, 13 and 15. The right of self-defence was not mentioned in the Covenant because at the time it was just one of the permissible ways of using armed force. In addition, the League's provisions for coercive measures were voluntary in that States had the option of deciding whether to impose sanctions or to take military measures against an aggressor when called upon to do so by the League.

The novel, but only partial, institutionalisation of the concept of collective security in the League of Nations gave way to the old system of competing interests and rival alliances. The defeat of the Axis powers by the Allies gave the victorious powers another chance to embed the concept of collective security more firmly in the new Organisation. Although there was agreement on the need for a new and improved collective security system, there was considerable disagreement on its nature. Churchill favoured a regional security system on the basis that only those States close to a conflict would be willing to take action to end it. Roosevelt on the other hand followed Wilson's idea that the victorious powers would act as the world's policemen, protecting the smaller States which would be gradually disarmed. Both of these ideas are to be found in the Charter in varying degrees, but each has within it the potential for dominance of the security system by a State or group of States. The only true global collective security system whereby all States would contribute to the maintenance of peace was suggested by Roosevelt's Secretary of State, Hull.[12]

One of the major problems at San Francisco was the reconciliation of the regional and more universal approaches to collective security. The provisions of Chapter VIII of the UN Charter establish the supremacy of the United Nations over regional bodies in the realm of enforcement action, although a regional organisation or any group of States acting in collective self-defence was permitted to use force without prior Security Council authorisation by the late insertion of Article 51 into the text of the Charter. Self-defence, whether individual or collective, was only permitted until the Security Council had 'taken measures necessary to maintain international peace and security'. States supporting regionalism[13] sought this limited escape clause because they foresaw that the composition and voting of the Security Council, the partial embodiment of Roosevelt's collective security concept, could lead to a stalled Security Council as the permanent members protected their pervasive interests by the often indiscriminate use of the veto.

Nevertheless, the UN Charter contained within it a far greater centralisation of coercive measures and machinery than did its predecessor. As well as containing quite elaborate provisions in Chapter VI for the pacific settlement of disputes, the 'teeth' of the Charter were contained in Chapter VII which granted the Security Council the unprecedented power to take mandatory economic and military action against an aggressor or to combat a situation which simply threatened international peace and security. If the Security Council acted under these mechanisms States would be obliged to take economic measures or to supply military forces under UN control. The potential power in the hands of the Security Council was enormous.

The potential of the Security Council was nullified for over forty years due to the intense ideological rivalry between the United States and the Soviet Union. In the place of a collective security system there was established a system of defensive alliances, principally the North Atlantic Treaty Organisation (NATO) dominated by the United States and the Warsaw Pact dominated by the Soviet Union, based on the concept of collective self-defence, namely that an attack on one party to the alliance was an attack against them all.[14] This rival system, which appeared to give some stability in the world, in the sense of preventing another global conflict, can be traced back to the old balance of power systems. Indeed, as with its predecessors, the post 1945 balance of power collapsed with the disintegration of the Soviet Union and the dissolution of the Warsaw Pact in 1991. The serious global instability that has resulted from these tumultuous events has only begun to be addressed by States, but it has already become apparent in the past few years that the Security Council is attempting to fill the vacuum. Whether it has done so successfully and whether it will do so in the future are issues to be addressed in the next few chapters.

Notes

1 Article 1(1) of the UN Charter.
2 Article 24(1), Chapters VI and VII of the UN Charter.
3 K. P. Sakensa, *The United Nations and Collective Security*, 8–10 (1974).
4 Articles 10, 11 and 16 of the League Covenant. UKTS No. 4 (1919), Cmd 153.
5 For text see R. B. Russell and J. E. Muther, *A History of the United Nations Charter*, Appendix C (1958).
6 For text see World Peace Foundation, *The United Nations in the Making: Basic Documents*, 9–10 (1945).
7 For text see United Nations Conference on International Organisation

(UNCIO), vol. 3, 2–17.

8 See for example UNCIO, vol. 1, 502–3, delegate from Luxembourg.
9 See Article 27(3) of the UN Charter.
10 Message on the State of the Union, 6 January 1945.
11 L. A. Mander, *Foundations of a Modern World Society*, 59, 2nd ed. (1948).
12 Russell and Muther, *A History of the United Nations*, 96, 105.
13 See for example UNCIO, vol. 12, 687.
14 See further L. M. Goodrich, *The United Nations*, 168–76 (1960).

CHAPTER ONE

A geopolitical analysis of the Security Council

Before analysing, in chapter two, the jurisdiction of the Security Council as contained in the Charter it will be helpful to identify the major geopolitical factors affecting the jurisdiction and operation of the Security Council. Factors arising, in particular, as a result of the global and strategic interests of the permanent members often caused a paralysis in the Council in the past, as those interests were protected by the veto during the Cold War between the United States and the Soviet Union of 1945–90. Latterly, however, the concert of Western powers on the Security Council, namely France, the United States and the United Kingdom, has seized domination of the Council and has used the West's economic leverage to secure the support, or at least to avoid the veto, of China and, since 1992, Russia as successor to the Soviet Union's seat.

It must be remembered, however, that the veto, along with another geopolitical limitation – regionalism – are located in the Charter. In this sense they are legal limitations, but they must be viewed realistically as geopolitical limitations because they are manipulated for political motives. In addition the use of the power of veto and of the various regional organisations is often in contradiction to the literal terms of the Charter so that one cannot really say that they are legal as opposed to geopolitical limitations. It is true to say that with the end of the Cold War in the late 1980s these factors have had less of an impact on the Security Council. Free of these powerful limiting factors, the Security Council has been able to use the range of powers provided for in the Charter more readily, and indeed it has appeared in some instances to stretch those powers to breaking point. Moreover, this new-found freedom should not disguise the fact that the Security Council is, as we shall see, still conditioned by political considerations, in that at the moment its actions correspond to the strategic, economic and political interests of the winners of the Cold War, the Western States.

The power of veto

The power of veto is contained in Article 27 of the Charter. After stating in paragraph 2 that 'decisions of the Security Council on procedural matters shall be made by an affirmative vote of nine members', paragraph 3 provides that 'decisions of the Security Council on all other matters shall be made by an affirmative vote of nine members including the concurring votes of the permanent members; provided that, in decisions under Chapter VI, and under paragraph 3 of Article 52, a party to a dispute shall abstain from voting'. Bailey lists those matters that the Council has treated as procedural in its practice, the most important of which are: inclusion of items on the agenda, removal of an item from the list of matters of which the Council is seized, rulings of the President, suspension and adjournment of meetings, invitation to non-members to participate in meetings, and convocation of an emergency special session of the General Assembly.[1] All non-procedural or substantive matters are the potential objects of a permanent member veto, which has been interpreted by the subsequent practice of the Council as requiring a negative vote. On this basis abstention by a permanent member on a substantive vote does not constitute a veto.[2]

The power of veto had its genesis in the desire to prevent the permanent members from being the potential objects of collective measures. However, Article 27(3) was drafted on a much wider basis after the Yalta Conference of 1945. It was clear after Yalta that Great Power unity was destined to be an unachieved ideal with the power of veto extending beyond the enforcement provisions of Chapter VII, to Chapter VI, which granted the Council general, recommendatory powers for pacific settlement, unless one of the permanent members was a party to the dispute.

Indeed, the Yalta formula, presented to the San Francisco conference in explanation of the right of veto, illustrated the permanent members' desire to leave no loopholes to prevent their use of the veto. The Yalta formula introduced the prospect of the 'double veto', which meant that any 'decision regarding the preliminary question as to whether or not such a matter is procedural must be taken by vote of [nine] members of the Security Council, including the concurring votes of the permanent members'.[3]

However, the smaller powers' objections at San Francisco were not directed at the double veto, but at the 'chain of events' theory outlined in the Yalta formula. The smaller powers demanded that the veto should be confined to questions concerning enforcement action. The Australian delegate argued that 'the Council has the duty rather than a right to conciliate disputants' and that it was essential that no member should have the right to veto resolutions aimed solely at pacific settlement of disputes.[4] The major powers stuck to the somewhat fallacious argument presented in the Yalta formula that any pacific measures 'may initiate a chain of events which might in the end require the Council under its responsibilities to invoke measures of enforcement'.[5] It might well be that such a chain of events could occur, but it did not appear necessary to allow the veto to apply at the pacific settlement stage as long as the permanent members could operate it at the enforcement stage. The 'chain of events' theory was, in reality, a mechanism whereby the whole field of Council action would be the subject of the veto. The smaller powers continued to object, but it became clear that Article 27 would have to be accepted as the 'Big Five decided to let it be known that unless the voting provision was accepted, there would be no Organisation'.[6] It was no longer a question of preserving Great Power unanimity but of preserving the Organisation.[7]

The applicability of the double veto and the chain of events theory peppered exchanges in the Council during its first decade. These have been thoroughly reviewed by Bailey[8] and it is not proposed to discuss them as a separate issue here. Such debates have, in any event, petered out in the face of the permanent members developing a practice which enabled them to use the veto to defeat any sort of proposal under Chapter VI or Chapter VII, unless it was clearly procedural.

In stating the chain of events theory the sponsoring powers still deferred to their obligation to abstain if they were parties to a dispute being dealt with by the Council under Chapter VI. In practice the permanent members have disregarded this provision thus destroying the general aim of this aspect of Article 27(3) to separate 'law as it is invoked by the claimants to the dispute and law as it is employed by [the Council] when passing its decision'.[9] The drafting of the provision allows a member to argue, if it wants, that it only has an 'interest' in the dispute which is insufficient to make it a 'party' or that the proposed resolution is only dealing with a 'situation' and not a 'dispute',[10] or does in fact envisage Chapter VII rather than Chapter VI action. In practice the permanent members rarely raise such arguments. The power of veto is exercised according to considerations of interests rather than in accordance with the letter of the Charter.

Permanent member, particularly superpower, interests and influences became so pervasive in the Cold War that the veto effectively debarred the Security Council from taking action or recommending measures of any sort in many areas of the globe. Indeed, in many cases, the superpowers operated the veto not to protect 'vital' interests but in order to curry favour with other States or as a reflex reaction to oppose the other superpower's voting intentions. The Soviet Union's veto of a proposed resolution that would have condemned the Indian invasion of Goa in 1961 and called for a cease-fire and an Indian withdrawal, is an example of the veto being used not for any vital protective purpose but, in this case, to express support for India, the Third World, and anti-colonialism.[11]

Even when a permanent member appears to be a 'party' to a 'dispute' within the meaning of Article 27(3), it has disregarded its obligation to abstain when faced with the possibility of being subject to a recommendatory Chapter VI-based resolution. The French and British could hardly deny that they were 'parties' to the Suez crisis in 1956, but they did not have to as they vetoed draft resolutions proposed by the United States and the Soviet Union calling for Israel to cease-fire and withdraw. The proposers of the draft resolutions deliberately refrained from invoking Chapter VII for fear of justifying the imminent Anglo/French intervention. Nevertheless, the British and French vetoes were not challenged on the grounds of Article 27(3).[12]

During the Falklands crisis in 1982, the Panamanian representative thought that the last operative paragraph of resolution 502 placed it under Chapter VI, in that it called for pacific settlement of the dispute, in which case, he argued, the United Kingdom should be debarred from voting on the resolution. Sir Anthony Parsons, the British ambassador, stated that the resolution came under Chapter VII, namely Article 40, and so the obligation to abstain was not applicable.[13] Although no members challenged Sir Anthony further on this point, the very fact that he had to justify his right to vote was a rarity. Perhaps it can be explained by the fact that the Security Council approached the Falklands free from any overt superpower concern, and consequently discussions and resolutions were more clearly based on considerations of international and Charter law rather than on considerations of power and zones of interest.

Bailey has tabulated the number of vetoes in the period 1946–86.[14] The tally in this period was: China 22, France 16, Soviet Union 121, UK 26, and the USA 57. It is interesting to note that the Soviet Union cast 77 of its vetoes in the first ten years when the UN was Western dominated, whereas the United States cast 45 of its vetoes in the period 1976–86, when the Non-Aligned and Socialist blocs combined successfully in the UN. With the end of the Cold War in the late 1980s, the number of vetoes has decreased dramatically, for instance in 1991 no vetoes were cast by the permanent members. Whilst this trend indicates a new spirit of cooperation amongst the 'permanent five', there is as yet no sign that it is based on a new-found respect for the limitations on the veto contained in Article 27(3). For example, the United States used the veto twice following its military intervention in Panama in December 1989, first to prevent condemnation of the action and a call for a withdrawal of troops, and secondly to prevent a condemnation of its occupation of the Nicaraguan ambassador's residence in Panama in breach of the Vienna Convention on Diplomatic Relations.[15] Neither proposal envisaged Chapter VII action and clearly the United States was a party to the dispute.

The United States' military intervention in Panama clearly continued a pattern of such actions undertaken by the superpowers during the Cold War, and it is to these that we turn first before looking at the period of cooperation between the permanent members. The end of the Cold War unfortunately does not signify the end of geopolitical limitations as the Panamanian vetoes illustrate, although it is true to say that those limitations are much reduced.

Cold War limitations 1945–90

In a world dominated by two superpowers with their own hemispheric or bloc domains there emerged a distinction between intra-bloc and inter-bloc conflicts. In intra-bloc conflicts such as Guatemala 1954 and Hungary 1956, the veto was operated by the relevant bloc leader to allow the dispute to be settled within that bloc, sometimes combined, in the case of the United States, with arguments in favour of the relevant regional organisation.

Inter-bloc conflicts often occurred on the 'power frontiers'[16] between the 'spheres of influence'[17] of the superpowers, usually as a consequence of a miscalculation by one of them as to the ambit of its hemispheric control. Good examples of such disputes were the Berlin blockade 1948 and the Cuban missile crisis in 1962. In these cases, it will be argued, the Security Council did play a significant role. The polarised positions taken by each side before the Council were gradually whittled down behind the scene until a common ground was achieved. In inter-bloc conflicts the stark choice was between annihilation or 'peaceful coexistence'.[18] Both superpowers had to make concessions if peaceful coexistence was to continue.

Intra-bloc situations

During the initial Cold War period (1945–55), the United Nations was dominated by the West[19] which managed to manipulate the whole Organisation to further its political and strategic ends. The American-backed coup in Guatemala of 1954 is illustrative of how that manipulation often occurred to protect American interests. It also shows how the Soviet Union was often forced to use its veto in the early years because of the American dominance of the Council.

The Guatemalan episode involved the question of whether regional bodies should have priority over the world body. As we shall see in this chapter, Articles 52(4) and 103 of the Charter clearly provide a negative answer and yet the Soviet Union was forced to use its veto to uphold this view after Brazil and Colombia had proposed a resolution which would have left the matter to the Organisation of American States (OAS).[20] The United States was in such a strong position in the Security Council that it did not have to use its veto to protect its interests – it merely relied on its allies on the Council to outvote any proposal which was deemed to be against Western interests. Its dominance of the Guatemalan debate was highlighted when the US President of the Council effectively prevented further consideration when he proposed to take a procedural vote on the question whether to keep the item on the agenda. The item was duly removed despite the negative Soviet vote.[21]

As with several of the earlier intra-bloc disputes involving the United States, that country was so confident of its position on the Council that it did not feel it necessary to veto what appeared to be constructive Council resolutions on Guatemala. Resolution 104,[22] proposed by France, called for the 'immediate termination of any action likely to cause bloodshed, and requests all members to abstain from giving assistance to any such action'. It was essentially a neutral, valueless resolution but by voting for it along with the Soviet Union, the United States reinforced the view that it was the upholder of the Charter even where the principles contained therein seemed to be operating against American interests, whereas the Soviet Union was portrayed as only voting for resolutions criticising the United States and as using its veto when there was even a hint of criticism of its own actions. Nevertheless, such illusions should not hide the real fact that the United States was manipulating the Council to protect its hemispheric interests. Its representative made this very clear by instructing the Soviet Union to stay out of the United States' 'hemisphere'.[23] This amounted to a reassertion of the Monroe Doctrine and constituted 'a declaration which reciprocal practice over the next two decades was to stamp with an almost jural quality'.[24]

The tacit agreement between the Great Powers at Potsdam in 1945 that Eastern Europe was within the Soviet Union's sphere of influence was put beyond doubt after the Soviet Union's military intervention in Hungary in 1956.[25] The Western powers were unwilling to help the Nagy government when it announced on 1 November the withdrawal of Hungary from the Warsaw Pact accompanied by a declaration of its neutrality, and requested the United Nations and the four other permanent members to defend its neutral status. The Soviet Union also saw it necessary to protect its interests by using its veto in the Security Council to defeat a United States' sponsored draft resolution calling for Soviet withdrawal and respect for 'the independence and sovereignty of Hungary'.[26] Ambassador Sobolev of the Soviet Union explained the action in terms of defence of the Soviet Union's strategic zone.[27]

Just as the United States saw, and probably still sees, the creation of a 'communist' government – whether created by popular assent or by outside interference – as an attack on Western principles and interests, so the Soviet Union viewed 'capitalism' as an attack on its bloc solidarity. Both powers viewed the removal of each respective threat from their respective zones as a legitimate defence of their strategic interests. This form of defence is not recognised as legitimate under Article 51 of the UN Charter which only allows for self-defence in the face of an 'armed attack'.

Intra-bloc interventions were often challenged by the other superpower in the Security Council to show rhetorical, political support for the people of the country being intervened in. By allowing the other side to vent its anger verbally, it could be argued that the Security Council reduces the chance of that side counter-intervening leading to a global conflict.

The United States complained of Soviet intervention in Hungary in 1956. The compliment was repaid in 1965 when the Soviet Union complained of 'armed intervention' by the United States in the Dominican Republic.[28] The Soviets introduced a draft resolution condemning the intervention and demanding that the United States withdraw.[29] Western support was still strong enough in the Council to ensure that the proposal only secured two votes in its favour.[30] The United States treated the situation on a similar basis to Guatemala a decade earlier by allowing resolutions to be adopted calling for a cease-fire but not prejudicing the OAS's role in the situation.[31] Again the world saw the United States refraining from using its veto in contrast to the Soviet Union's use of its power to block resolutions on Hungary and later on Czechoslovakia.

Nevertheless, it is clear that the United States would have used its veto to prevent criticism of its action, or to prevent proposals for peaceful settlement of the situation, or to prevent the establishment of machinery to facilitate a cease-fire such as UN peacekeeping – in other words anything that would have vaguely hindered or criticised the US/OAS operation. According to Ambassador Stevenson 'the establishment of a communist dictatorship' in the Dominican Republic was a matter for 'hemispheric action only', thereby making it clear that the UN was precluded from taking any positive action.[32]

On 28 August 1968, Western States brought the situation in Czechoslovakia to the attention of the Council.[33] The Soviet Union's military intervention led to the enunciation of the Brezhnev Doctrine of limited sovereignty within the Socialist commonwealth,[34] paralleling the various interventionist doctrines expounded by American Presidents. Ambassador Malik made a weak attempt to justify the intervention by referring to it as defence against an 'imperialist' attack. However, in the same speech the overt political reasons became apparent, in that 'the situation in Czechoslovakia affected the vital interests of the Soviet Union'.[35]

During the Cold War, the Soviet Union viewed the use of the veto in the Council to prevent criticism of its actions as a necessary corollary to the protection of its vital interests by intervention. There was no question even of allowing weak, neutral resolutions to be adopted, an attitude that probably can be explained by a 'knee-jerk' reaction produced by its minority position on the Council. In 1968, the Soviet Union vetoed a Danish draft which condemned Soviet 'armed intervention' as well as a Canadian draft which was aimed at achieving limited measures and took the form of a request to the Secretary General to send a representative to Prague 'to ensure the personal safety of the Czechoslovak leaders under detention'.[36]

The Soviet intervention in Afghanistan in December 1979 was different in geopolitical terms from its previous interventions in Czechoslovakia and Hungary because it represented the first time the Soviet Union had pushed its troops beyond the zone inherited after the Second World War. This was reflected in the large number of States – Non-Aligned as well as Western – which requested the convening of the Security Council to discuss the situation in Afghanistan.[37] A draft resolution was proposed by the Non-Aligned group on the Council which deplored the 'recent armed intervention' and called for 'the immediate and unconditional withdrawal of all foreign troops from Afghanistan'. The vetoed draft resolution also called for respect for Afghanistan's non-aligned status reflecting the Western view that the Soviet Union had stepped beyond its zone as well as the Non-Aligned movement's fear of its members being subjected to superpower intervention.[38]

Afghanistan illustrated the fine line between intra-bloc conflicts in which the other superpower will be content with rhetorical confrontation, and inter-bloc conflicts which may have escalated into a global military confrontation. The Carter Doctrine,[39] which warned the Soviet Union not to advance any further towards the Gulf, drew the line at the Afghan border, suggesting that the United States was treating the intervention as politically allowable. However, President Reagan redrew the power frontier closer to the Soviet Union by authorising material support for the Afghan rebels.[40]

The intervention in Grenada in 1983, which was legally justified on three grounds by the United States, namely the protection of nationals (and wider arguments of humanitarian intervention to protect the whole population), the invitation of the Governor General and regional action by the Organisation of Eastern Caribbean States (OECS),[41] was, in reality, an application of the so-called Reagan Doctrine. This doctrine or policy encompassed support for anti-communists, whether established governments or rebels, not only in the American hemisphere but throughout the world. Consequently, the Reagan Administration supported the Contras fighting in Nicaragua,[42] the Khmer Rouge fighting the Vietnamese-imposed government in Kampuchea (Cambodia), the National Union for the Total Independence of Angola (UNITA) guerrillas fighting the Soviet/Cuban-backed Popular Movement for the Liberation of Angola (MPLA) government in Angola, and the Afghan mujahedin. The Reagan Doctrine was offensive; its aim was to attempt to stand the dominoes back up again.

In the debate over its intervention in Grenada, even the United States' closest ally, the United Kingdom, refused to support it in vetoing a draft resolution condemning the 'armed intervention' and calling for the withdrawal of foreign troops.[43] Unlike the cases of Guatemala and the

Dominican Republic, the United States was unable to avoid using the veto to protect its interests. Indeed, the United States has continued to use its veto to protect its military interventions within its hemisphere as the blocking of a condemnation of its action in Panama in December 1989 shows. However, on this occasion the resolution was blocked by the triple veto of the Western permanent members,[44] indicating an even greater cohesiveness on the Security Council of these States, a group now labelled the 'permanent three' at the UN.

With the Cold War drawing to a close by the late 1980s, the world witnessed a decreased global tension which enabled the UN to become increasingly involved in areas hitherto excluded from its purview. We will examine this period of cooperation among the permanent five later in this chapter but it is interesting to note that the United States has not renounced its policy of intervention within its bloc as the Panamanian intervention shows, although as we shall see it has also allowed the UN to become involved in that region. With the collapse of communism, the political justifications are now concerned with combating drugs and terrorism, and supporting democracy, although the legal justifications remain the same, namely the protection of nationals or wider arguments of self-defence. It appears that whereas the winners of the Cold War reserve the power to intervene, the Warsaw Pact renounced the Brezhnev Doctrine in October 1989 and the Soviet Union refused to intervene within the Eastern bloc to prevent the collapse of communist regimes in that year.[45]

Inter-bloc situations

The superpowers' pervasive global interests during the Cold War meant that there were very few areas in the world in which the Council could have fully utilised the powers at its disposal. It is axiomatic that where there was a case of direct East-West confrontation there was little possibility of a Security Council resolution. Nevertheless, there was evidence to the effect that in these inter-bloc disputes, the Security Council did sometimes play a significant role, although the spotlight was normally on the Secretary General helping a negotiated solution using quiet diplomacy away from the verbal battleground of the Council chamber.

One must not underestimate the role of the Council in one of the most dangerous situations to threaten world peace since 1945. In 1962 the Americans purported to use the forum as a tactical measure with no real intention of using it to negotiate with the Soviets over the withdrawal of missiles from Cuba. The United States convened the Council and introduced a draft resolution which had little chance of being adopted. It reasserted its demand 'for immediate dismantling and withdrawal from Cuba of all missiles and other offensive weapons' and the dispatch to Cuba of a 'United Nations' observer corps to assure and report on compliance'.

Only after the affirmative 'certification of compliance' would the quarantine imposed by the United States be terminated. The call for withdrawal of the missiles was expressly stated to be 'under Article 40', that is a 'decision' of the Council having binding force under Article 25.[46] The Soviet draft resolution was equally uncompromising in that it condemned the actions of the Americans and called for the immediate revocation of the 'decision to inspect the ships of other States bound for' Cuba, and for an end 'to any kind of interference in the internal affairs of' Cuba.[47]

There appeared little chance of settling the issue through these kinds of polarised proposals, but the draft resolutions did overlap in one area; they both called for bilateral negotiations between the United States and the Soviet Union to remove the threat to the peace. Acting Secretary General U Thant seized on this common area in letters to Kennedy and Khrushchev in which he called for the 'voluntary suspension of all arms shipments to Cuba and also the voluntary suspension of the quarantine for a period of two to three weeks'.[48] On 26 October 1962 President Kennedy agreed to the proposal.[49] The Soviets indicated their willingness to accept by stopping the shipments. This eventually led to a tacit agreement by which the Soviets would remove their missiles already emplaced in Cuba in return for the American withdrawal of missiles from Turkey.

It may appear that it was the Secretary General's diplomatic moves which helped to settle the dispute, whereas moves in the Council were a failure. This view is founded on the belief that the Security Council is primarily an adjudicative body. The Council, being a political organ, very rarely acted in this fashion during the Cold War when the political inhibiting factors were strong. In these situations it established the often extreme positions of the parties, which obviously could not be reconciled in the public forum, so necessitating the supplementary aid of 'corridor' diplomacy.

The Cuban missile crisis of 1962 involved an inter-bloc dispute in the form of a direct confrontation between East and West. However, a large preponderance of modern warfare during the Cold War concerned the indirect involvement of the superpowers, in which one or both confronted the other by the use of proxy armies, often in the form of national liberation fronts.[50] In these situations the danger of escalation was less because the superpowers were effectively two steps away from all out war. Thus with this cushion the superpowers were less willing to compromise. As with the situation of direct East-West confrontation, this rendered the Security Council a barren place, but unlike direct inter-bloc disputes, there was often little possibility of diplomacy filling the vacuum. A good example of Council impotence was its paltry involvement in the Vietnam conflict.

The conflict in Vietnam lasted in various forms from 1946 until 1975 when the North took over the South. It was a battle on the edge of the 'zones of influence', in this case the 17th parallel. The United States was determined to hold the line for if Vietnam fell to communism the 'domino theory'[51] suggested that neighbouring countries would fall as communism spread through Indo-China. The United States did not distinguish between the Chinese and the Soviets who both supported the North Vietnamese, but with hindsight, the American defeat was seen as an expansion of the Soviet sphere.

The period 1946–54 saw France fighting the North Vietnamese communist movement until the French were heavily defeated at Dien Bien Phu. Although the French were fighting to maintain their colonial empire in this period, by 1954 the conflict was taking on a Cold War aspect with the United States paying 75 per cent of the French costs in fighting the war. After Dien Bien Phu, a conference was held at Geneva in July 1954 to consider the future of French Indo-China. A cease-fire agreement divided Vietnam at the 17th parallel, while the Final Declaration of the Conference provided for elections to be held leading to a single Vietnamese State.[52] The elections did not occur mainly because of South Vietnamese opposition, and so the scene was set for a conflict between North and South with Sino-Soviet aid to the former and American military commitment to the latter.

The Security Council, indeed the United Nations, had little to do either with the 1954 Conference or the preceding period.[53] After French involvement was replaced by American commitment, the Security Council played a peripheral role. It met inconclusively on four occasions, three of these concerned aspects of the war rather than the whole situation. In 1959, Laos complained of military incursions into its territory by the North Vietnamese.[54] The Security Council, using a procedural vote in the face of Soviet objections based on the 'double-veto' and the 'chain of events' principles, created an investigative sub-committee.[55] This committee reported that the fighting was of a 'guerrilla character' and so did not constitute a crossing of the frontiers of Laos by the North Vietnamese.[56]

In May 1964, the government of Cambodia complained to the Security Council of alleged acts of 'aggression' directed against it by South Vietnamese and United States' forces.[57] These two States denied the charge, and suggested that the non-demarcation of the boundary between Cambodia and South Vietnam was the reason. The United States' representative suggested that the answer would be a role for a United Nations' force, emplaced to observe the integrity of the boundary.[58] South Vietnam indicated its willingness to accept such an observer force on its territory, but Cambodia was opposed to having it on its side of the border. No observer or peacekeeping forces were sent.

In August 1964, the United States requested that the Council consider the attacks on American vessels in the Gulf of Tonkin by the North Vietnamese. The Hanoi regime was unwilling to state its case before the Council and declared via the Soviet Union that consideration of the problem did not lie with the Security Council, but with the members of the 1954 Geneva Conference.[59]

It was not until 1966 that an attempt was made to bring the whole situation before the Security Council when the United States requested a meeting of the Security Council and submitted a draft resolution calling for 'immediate discussions without preconditions', with the priority being the arrangement for a cessation of hostilities.[60] The Soviet representative objected to a Council meeting to discuss the Vietnam war. He stated that the move by the United States was a diversionary tactic to cover the expansion of its aggressive war in Vietnam as evidenced by the resumption of its 'barbaric' air raids on the North.[61] The overwhelming atmosphere of distrust between the superpowers meant that the American proposal was not even voted on.

Although many other complaints and correspondence were directed to the Security Council, Vietnam was only discussed by the body on the four occasions outlined above, in which no concrete measures were adopted. Yet the situation was so grave in Vietnam that although it was not on the agenda of the 21st session of the General Assembly, 107 out of 110 speakers referred to it. It was a virtual poll of international opinion. All of those who spoke on the subject recognised the conflict in Vietnam as a serious threat to international peace and security which had the potential to spread beyond south-east Asia and ignite a Third World War.[62]

There were certain factors which restricted the ability of the Security Council or General Assembly to deal with the threat to the peace which Vietnam posed. At the Geneva Conference in 1954, very few of the participants envisaged United Nations' involvement, particularly the North Vietnamese and Chinese.[63] These two countries maintained a strong desire to exclude the United Nations from being involved, seeing the United Nations as 'a tool for US aggression'.[64]

They had some justification for feeling this in that the West had dominated and, to a certain extent, had manipulated the United Nations in the early years particularly, as regards the Chinese, in the case of Korea in 1950. The United States had also prevented the communist Chinese from taking the permanent seat until 1971. The Chinese and North Vietnamese, not being represented at the United Nations, felt a deep distrust for the Organisation, which when combined with the mutual distrust between the Soviet Union and the United States during the Cold War, had the result of giving the United Nations little possibility of taking positive steps to solve the conflict in Vietnam.

The United States relied on a similarity between the Korean War of 1950–53 and the conflict in Vietnam to justify its support for the South.[65] In the case of Korea, the United States was willing to turn its support for South Korea into a United Nations' action at the outset of the war, whereas in Vietnam, the United States only showed a willingness to involve the United

Nations when the war was going against it, by which time the position of the opposing parties and their respective superpower backers had become too intransigent for the United Nations to intervene. While in the case of Korea, the communist attack from the north was a clear breach of Article 2(4) and a 'breach of the peace' within Article 39, the Vietnamese situation was more complicated, evidenced by the fact that there was considerable support for the Vietcong in the South. There was no discernable initial aggression by the North and no significant event which would have enabled a collective response as in the case of Korea, and certainly the Soviet Union was not going to absent itself and so allow the collective response to become a collective United Nations' response. Vietnam could best be described as a gradually escalating, internationalised civil war which was a 'threat to the peace' rather than a clear 'breach of the peace' as in Korea. The gradual escalation of the conflict in Vietnam severely limited the potential of United Nations' action. It had not really dealt with the situation at its origin, either in 1946 or by participating in the 1954 Conference, and thereafter it was in the untenable position of having to deal with the conflict from the outside.

The Secretary General, U Thant, supported this view. In his New Year message in 1966, he pointed out that just as the parties to the conflict had decided in 1954 to negotiate the end of the war outside the framework of the United Nations, the conflict could not be settled in 1966 under the auspices of the United Nations because only the United States, of all the parties to the conflict, was a Member of the United Nations. U Thant preferred diplomacy rather than open debate in the Security Council and at several points in the conflict made proposals for settlement.[66]

The Vietnam War only involved one superpower directly and so the other, the Soviet Union, was quite content to block any diplomatic moves initiated by the Security Council or in the United Nations as a whole, because by indirectly encouraging the North Vietnamese, it was partly tying up the United States militarily and politically, and also embarrassing it. The North Vietnamese showed considerable independence evidenced by the aid received from both the Soviet Union and the Chinese, whereas the South Vietnamese were to all intents and purposes 'puppets' of the United States. The Soviets did not control the North Vietnamese. The asymmetry of the conflict in Vietnam, in other words the difference in commitment between the two superpowers, meant that it was virtually impossible to solve in the United Nations.[67]

Regionalism

So far we have seen how the influences and interests of the superpowers during the Cold War effectively precluded the Council from taking action in relation to disputes within large areas of the globe. Another *de facto* limitation on the Council's sphere of operation was regionalism, which was often, but not always,[68] related to the spheres of influence claimed by the super-powers.

De jure, however, the United Nations' Charter does not permit regionalism to be paramount over globalism. The Charter, in Chapter VIII Article 52(1), recognises 'the existence of regional arrangements or agencies for dealing with such matters relating to the maintenance of international peace and security as are appropriate for regional action'. It even provides, in Article 52(3), that the Security Council 'shall encourage the development of pacific settlement of local disputes through such regional arrangements'. However, the provisions of Chapter VIII make it plain that the Security Council is supreme in matters relating to international peace and security. In relation to the pacific settlement of disputes, the Council's paramountcy is maintained by Article 52(4), whilst Article 53(1) provides that 'the Security Council shall, where appropriate, utilise such regional arrangements or agencies for enforcement action under its authority. But no enforcement action shall be taken under regional arrangements or by regional agencies without the authorization of the Security Council'.

Articles 52(4) and 53(1), together, mean that the Security Council retains supremacy over matters coming within Chapter VI or Chapter VII. Any lingering doubts about overall United Nations' supremacy are seemingly removed by Article 103, which states that 'in the event of a conflict between the obligations of the Members of the United Nations under the present Charter and their obligations under any other international agreement, their obligations under the present Charter shall prevail'.

However, the compromise between regionalism and globalism attained in Chapter VIII (and Article 103) is itself compromised by Article 51. The insertion of this provision into the Charter at San Francisco arose from 'the fear that the veto power' preserved in Article 53(1) 'might cripple the functioning of regional arrangements'.[69] Consequently regional arrange-ments were granted the right of collective self-defence in Article 51, a right which could be exercised 'until the Security Council has taken measures necessary to maintain international peace and security'. Whereas Article 53(1) allows the Security Council to veto any proposed enforcement action by a regional organisation, Article 51 effectively removes action taken in collective self-defence from being vetoed, at least at the outset of the action.

Writers have tended to concentrate on the difference between regional bodies in the nature of collective self-defence pacts under Article 51 and regional organisations in the nature of 'arrangements' and 'agencies' under Chapter VIII, rather than looking to specific actions to see if they are of a defensive or enforcement nature.[70] This writer takes the view that organisa-tions such as the North Atlantic Treaty Organisation (NATO) and the former Warsaw Pact are not, *prima facie*, regional arrangements under Chapter VIII. Indeed, the treaties establishing these bodies seem to be clear

that they are based on Article 51.[71] Such arrangements are probably confined to those which have similar functions and powers to the United Nations
as regards international peace and perhaps as regards economic and social
cooperation, except that these powers are operated on a regional not a
global basis. Organisations designed primarily to enhance the defence and
military capabilities of power blocs do not fit this concept. This does not
mean that such 'collective self-defence' pacts do not undertake enforcement
action, but if they do, it should be authorised by the Security Council under
Article 53(1). On the other hand, if a regional organisation, which primarily
appears to come within Chapter VIII operates, on occasions, solely in
collective self-defence, it should not require such authorisation for it is
acting under Article 51. Designating that a regional organisation or body
comes within Article 51 or Chapter VIII is only a *prima facie* presumption
that its actions will be based on those provisions, it does not prevent that
organisation from taking collective self-defence action under Article 51 even
if it is a regional arrangement under Chapter VIII; nor does it prevent a
prima facie collective self-defence pact from taking enforcement action
under Article 53(1) as long as it is authorised by the Security Council.

The OAS appears to be a regional organisation for the purposes of
Chapter VIII, not simply because its Charter specifically states that it is, but
also because it is designed to perform similar functions to the United Nations
on a hemispheric level. Nevertheless, it can act solely within the terms of
Article 51 as a self-defence pact, a fact envisaged by its Charter.[72] Be that as
it may, unfortunately the OAS has sometimes been used when it was
dominated by the United States before 1970 to attempt to legalise interventions aimed at purging ideological non-conformity by one of the other
American States.

The United States' intervention in the Dominican Republic in 1965 is
illustrative of the manipulation of the OAS by the United States. Originally
solely a United States' operation, the OAS authorised the use of its own
force,[73] which remained mainly composed of United States' troops. Predictably the Soviet Union took the view that, 'in order to cover up its armed
intervention in the Dominican Republic' the United States was 'once more
trying to retreat behind the screen of the Organisation of American States,
which it long ago placed in the service of its imperialist aims'.[74] The United
States stated that the OAS action did not constitute 'enforcement' action
within the meaning of Article 53(1) and so did not require prior Council
authorisation, arguing instead that the organisation was undertaking a
'peacekeeping operation'.[75] It appears that peacekeeping operations,
which if properly based on basic legal principles of peacekeeping are
conceptually distinct from enforcement actions, can be undertaken outside
the United Nations without authorisation by the Security Council. The fact
remains that, assuming that the OAS force was a true peacekeeping force,

this could not somehow legitimate the initial unlawful intervention by the United States.[76]

The United States has advanced further arguments to attempt to circumvent Article 53(1). The quarantine imposed around Cuba by the United States and rubber stamped by the OAS during the missile crisis of 1962 was not undertaken in response to an 'armed attack', and as such it could not be considered as self-defence within the terms of Article 51. It was therefore enforcement action which, according to the United States, did not breach the authorisation requirement of Article 53(1) because that provision should be interpreted to allow regional enforcement action when the Council has failed to adopt a resolution, in effect allowing a permanent member to veto a resolution forbidding regional action, so freeing such action.[77]

Akehurst suggests that the United States' attempts at circumventing the Charter, attempts that do not appear to stand up to objective scrutiny, are merely designed to give the United States-inspired actions an air of reasonableness rather than legality, making them perhaps *politically* more acceptable to the rest of the world community.[78] However, United States' politicians occasionally seem to go further than this, evidenced by Robert Kennedy, then United States' Attorney General, commenting on the Cuban missile crisis: 'It was the vote of the Organisation of American States that gave the legal basis of the quarantine. It changed our position from that of an outlaw acting in violation of international law into a country acting in accordance with twenty allies legally protecting their position'.[79] This suggests that the United States believes that in American matters the OAS is paramount over the Security Council despite the provisions of the United Nations' Charter.

The relative sophistication of the United States' arguments put forward to attempt to justify the OAS operations during the missile crisis and in the Dominican Republic case in 1965 can be contrasted sharply with the former Soviet Union's quite spurious arguments of self-defence when it intervened within its hemisphere. Its interventions in Hungary in 1956 and Czechoslovakia in 1968 were not even sanctioned by the former Warsaw Pact, and the arguments of self-defence, for instance that Czechoslovakia was under an imperialist attack in 1968,[80] were quite clearly false. Although actions in collective self-defence escape the requirement of Security Council authorisation by reason of Article 51, it is quite clear that the action must be truly one of self-defence at the request of a State the victim of an armed attack,[81] neither of which were present in the case of Czechoslovakia.

The development of quite independent foreign policies by most American States has meant that the United States can no longer use the OAS to purport to justify its actions. Its intervention in Grenada was, as we have seen, accompanied by justifications based on authorisation by the more localised OECS and prevention of formal criticism by the Security Council by using its veto. The United States did not rely on regional machinery in its latest intervention in Panama in 1989. Instead, it paralleled Soviet interventions, by relying on the right of self-defence, embodied in Article 51 of the UN Charter and Article 21 of the OAS Charter,[82] whilst vetoing condemnation in the Security Council. The falsity of this argument was evidenced by the fact that the intervention was not only condemned by the General Assembly of the United Nations but also by the OAS itself.[83]

Cooperation and domination

The political changes in the United Nations in the period 1988–92 coincide with the dramatic changes in Eastern Europe and the Soviet Union that have occurred in the past few years. The coming to power of Mikhail Gorbachev in the Soviet Union in 1985 started a slow, sometimes imperceptible warming in East-West relations, until the dramatic climax which led to the collapse of the Soviet empire in Eastern Europe in the late 1980s, inevitably leading to the demise of the Warsaw Pact in 1991.[84] With the Soviet Union undergoing fundamental changes away from communism we saw a period of cooperation between the United States and the Soviet Union, starting in the late 1980s and ending in December 1991. During this period of cooperation in the Security Council the world saw almost a doubling of peacekeeping operations authorised by the Security Council as well as full-scale military and economic enforcement action taken against an aggressor, Iraq, after its invasion of Kuwait in August 1990.

The intense, hectic and, on occasions, ill-conceived Security Council activity of the past few years is set to continue even as the wind of change that blew through Eastern Europe has continued into the Soviet Union itself, leading to the collapse of that country and the emergence of the former republics of the Soviet Union as twelve new States. The Soviet Union was formally ended on the 21 December 1991. It was replaced by a loose alliance of States known as the Commonwealth of Independent States (CIS). The former republics agreed that the Russian Federation (hereinafter referred to as Russia) should take over many of the functions of the Soviet Union, including the permanent seat on the Security Council, whilst the other republics (except Byelorussia, now known as Belarus and the Ukraine, already members from 1945) would be supported in their applications for UN membership.[85]

In a letter dated 24 December 1991, Boris Yeltsin, the President of the Russian Federation, informed the UN Secretary General, that the membership of the Soviet Union in the Security Council and all other United Nations organs was being continued by the Russian Federation with the support of the countries of the Commonwealth of Independent States. The letter went on to say that Russia remains responsible in full for the rights and obligations of the former Soviet Union under the United Nations Charter.[86]

Russia's claim to the permanent seat led to speculation that this would spark off a reassessment of those States entitled to hold a permanent seat, particularly France and the United Kingdom. However, the three Western permanent members appeared, with the acquiescence of China, skilfully to manage a Security Council summit, attended by Heads of State. The summit was held on 31 January 1992, ostensibly to make a general declaration on greater UN activity and effectiveness, but in reality to endorse Russia's claim to the permanent seat. President Yeltsin duly took part in the deliberations but no mention was made of the permanent seat.[87] The Security Council's acquiescence in this presumably met the requirements of rule 15 of the Council's own rules of procedure, which provides that 'the credentials of representatives on the Security Council . . . shall be examined by the Secretary General who shall submit a report to the Security Council for approval'.[88]

The Security Council thus treated Russia as successor to the Soviet seat rather than as a new member, which would have required a recommendation from the Security Council and acceptance by the General Assembly. The Council's approach, although apparently smooth and avoiding any possibility of Security Council composition being called into question, has two drawbacks. First of all it confirms and enhances the perception of the Security Council by most States as an exclusive club, completely controlling its own membership, and secondly the process does not affect the Charter, Article 23 of which states that the permanent members of the Council include 'the Union of Soviet Socialist Republics'. Presumably any change of Article 23 will require the amendment procedure contained in Article 108 which requires a two-thirds vote in the General Assembly and ratification by two-thirds of the members of the UN, including all the permanent members.

The succession of Russia, and more importantly a Western friendly Russia, to the permanent seat represents a major change in the composition of the Security Council. Even a cooperative USSR in its later years represented a limited check on the dominance of that body by the three Western permanent members. For instance, the Soviet Union insisted on Iraq being given time to withdraw its troops from Kuwait before the US dominated coalition of States could use force under UN auspices. The deadline of 15 January 1991 imposed in resolution 678 of 29 November 1990 was the Soviet price for supporting a resolution authorising the use of force. There is little evidence yet of Russia carving out an independent role in the Security Council, although it is too early to analyse its impact clearly.

One can contrast Russia's succession to the permanent seat with the process by which the People's Republic of China only came to occupy the

Chinese permanent seat in 1971, it being occupied for the first twenty-two years by the 'rump Kuomintang government which had taken refuge on Taiwan'.[89] Western domination of the United Nations, although in decline after the first decade, lingered for a sufficient period to keep the communist Chinese out of the permanent seat. Eventually, the growth in members of the General Assembly enabled that organ to adopt a resolution by the requisite two-thirds majority which resolved to 'restore all its rights to the People's Republic of China . . . and to expel forthwith the representatives of Chiang Kai-shek from the place which they unlawfully occupy'.[90] The Secretary General reported to the Council that he was satisfied under rule 15 of the Rules of Procedure and the Council welcomed the communist Chinese on 21 November 1971.[91] The United States had already started its process of *rapprochement* with the People's Republic earlier in 1971. The Republic of China (Taiwan) is no longer a member of the UN even though Article 23 still refers to the 'Republic of China' and not the 'People's Republic of China'.

With Russia now, at least temporarily, in the Western camp it might be expected that the Chinese would act as stop on Western dominance. However, since its accession to the permanent seat in 1971, the People's Republic has been loath to use the veto, seeing it as a tool of the superpowers. Indeed, it has on many occasion preferred not to participate in the vote at all, a procedure designed to be 'an expression of slight disapproval greater than abstention but not great enough for the veto'.[92] However, in the past few years the number of Chinese non-participations and abstentions has decreased drastically, and it now supports the vast majority of resolutions adopted by the Security Council. Its increased cooperation seems to be the product of Western economic pressure and a desire for political rehabilitation after the Tiananmen Square massacre of June 1989. An exception was the resolution authorising the use of force by the coalition of States gathered in the Gulf against Iraq. China abstained on this vote in that it supported a settlement of the problem by peaceful means but recognised that Iraq was being intransigent despite many overtures, by the Chinese amongst others.[93]

The informal and somewhat secretive way by which the transfer of power from the Soviet Union to Russia was carried out in the UN is indicative of the new order at the United Nations. For instance the Security Council debates are no longer characterised by lengthy Cold War rhetoric by numerous invited non-members as well as the members; instead there are short meetings to approve formally resolutions previously negotiated and agreed upon informally behind closed doors. The absence of debate hides two very important elements: first, the political bargaining that has led to the compromise, and secondly an even greater lack of discussion about the legal basis for a particular Security Council resolution. It has become extremely difficult to gauge the political and legal movements in the Security Council, although it is true to say that the organ is now Western dominated. However, it is also true to say that the Council is working with more efficiency and alacrity than at any time in its existence.

In addition, despite domination by the 'permanent three' of the United States, the United Kingdom and France, it is true to say that the world has been opened up to Security Council action which sometimes takes the form of pacific settlement efforts as in the Middle East and Cyprus, sometimes peacekeeping as in Afghanistan, Namibia, Nicaragua, Angola, Western Sahara, El Salvador, Cambodia, Yugoslavia, Somalia, and between Iran and Iraq and Iraq and Kuwait, and sometimes enforcement action of an economic kind, for example limited embargoes against Somalia and Libya, or more complete embargoes as against Serbia and Iraq, as well as full-scale military action against the latter. The removal of the Cold War limitation has opened up the full range of Security Council powers from pacific settlement to military action. Cooperation amongst the permanent members appears even stronger with a pro-Western and Western dependent Russia occupying the permanent seat. The 'permanent three' seem set to dominate Security Council action, using that body to take action against so called anti-Western, 'pariah' States, for example Iraq and Libya, but also dealing with situations in which Western interests are not as strong, particularly when authorising peacekeeping forces. Although there is a danger of complete Western domination one must not forget that Russia and China will not necessarily follow the Western line, nor will a sufficient number of the non-permanent members. Most States seem economically and politically dependent on the West at the moment but as we have seen in the last few years, dramatic changes in the geopolitical shape of the world are possible. Indeed, relations between the three Western permanent members need not necessarily be so tight, particularly with possibly greater European integration, leading to France and the UK representing the European Community as much as themselves.[94]

One is faced with the paradoxical situation of welcoming the new found Security Council effectiveness, particularly in enforcement action, whilst at the same time remaining cautious of the fact that the Council, in its current period of relative Western domination, is not truly fulfilling the ideal of collective security, which requires the *impartial* enforcement of community norms. Time will tell whether the Security Council will combat aggression and threats to the peace wherever they may occur, or whether the end of the Cold War simply signifies that although there has been a vast increase in Council activity, it is still *selective* action against particular aggressors and situations which threaten peace, not against all such States and situations. Nevertheless, if we look beyond enforcement action, to pacific settlement initiatives and to those peacekeeping operations listed above, we shall see that the Security Council has cast a very wide net in recent years, and that despite its manifest deficiencies, a working collective security system is far better than none at all. [95] Indeed, despite the relative supremacy of the Western States at the moment, they still have to persuade a sufficient number of States in the Security Council to support them, which suggests that Security Council action is fulfilling some of the collective security ideals behind the Charter to the satisfaction of the majority of States.

Whereas in the Cold War, the main problem was the fact that political rivalry between the superpowers restricted the Council's sphere of operations as well as stunting its use of powers, its ending has signified an expansion into new areas of the world, which is to be welcomed if the actions are designed to deal with genuine threats to or breaches of the peace when enforcement action is contemplated, or situations likely to endanger the peace when pacific settlement is foreseen. The ending of the Cold War has also resulted in the Security Council using its powers to their fullest extent. Indeed, it does not require a great stretch of the imagination to see the Council overstepping the limitations imposed upon it by the Charter. With this relatively new problem in mind, we will pass on to the next chapter which deals with such issues.

Notes

1 S. D. Bailey, *The Procedure of the UN Security Council*, 199, 2nd ed. (1988).
2 S. D. Bailey, *Voting in the Security Council*, 69–73 (1969).
3 UNCIO, vol. 11, 713.
4 H. V. Evatt, *The United Nations*, 53 (1948).
5 UNCIO, vol. 11, 714.
6 See R. B. Russell and J. E. Muther, *A History of the Charter*, 766 (1958).
7 UNCIO, vol. 11, 592.
8 Bailey, *Voting*, 18–25, 33–7.
9 R. Higgins, 'The place of international law in the settlement of disputes by the UN Security Council' 64 A.J.I.L. (1970), 1, at 1.
10 But see J. P. Cot and A. Pellet, *La Charte des Nations Unies*, 607 (1985).
11 SC 987–8 mtgs, 16 UN SCOR (1961). UN doc. S/5033 (1961).
12 SC 749 mtg, 11 UN SCOR 31 (1956). UN docs S/3710 (1956), S/3713/Rev 1 (1956).
13 SC 2350 mtg, 37 UN SCOR (1982).
14 Bailey, *Procedure*, 209.
15 SC mtg, 23 December 1989; SC mtg, 16 January 1990.
16 J. Fawcett, *Law and Power in International Relations*, 67 (1982).
17 See P. Keal, *Unspoken Rules and Superpower Dominance*, 7–33 (1983).
18 See G. I. Tunkin, 'Coexistence and international law', 95 *Recueil des Cours* (1958), 49.
19 See E. Luard, *A History of the United Nations: Vol. 1 The Years of Western Domination 1945–1955* (1982).

20 UN doc. S/3232 (1954).
21 SC 676 mtg, 9 UN SCOR (1954).
22 SC Res. 104, 9 UN SCOR Resolutions 4 (1954).
23 SC 675 mtg, 9 UN SCOR (1954).
24 I. Dore, *International Law and the Superpowers: Normative Order in a Divided World*, 55 (1984).
25 See generally the report of the UN Special Committee on the problem of Hungary, 11 UN GAOR Supp. (No. 18) (1956).
26 UN doc. S/3730/Rev 1 (1956).
27 SC 754 mtg, 11 UN SCOR (1956).
28 UN doc. S/6316 (1965).
29 UN doc. S/6328 (1965).
30 SC 1214 mtg, 20 UN SCOR (1965).
31 SC Res. 203 and 205, 20 UN SCOR Resolutions 10 (1965).
32 SC 1196 mtg, 20 UN SCOR 19 (1965); paralleling the Doctrine enunciated by President Johnson, 52 *US Dept of State Bulletin* (1965), 29.
33 UN doc. S/8758 (1968).
34 20 *Current Digest of the Soviet Press*, No. 46, 3–4.
35 SC 1441 mtg, 23 UN SCOR 8 (1968).
36 UN docs S/8761, S/8767 (1968), Denmark, Canada.
37 UN doc. S/13724 (1980).
38 UN doc. S/13729 (1980). SC 2190 mtg, 35 UN SCOR (1980).
39 16 *Weekly Compendium of Presidential Documents* (1980), 197.
40 See W. M. Reisman, 'Critical defence zones and international law: the Reagan Codicil', 76 *A.J.I.L.* (1982), 589.
41 78 *A.J.I.L.* (1984), 645.
42 This support was unlawful according to the International Court of Justice in the *Case Concerning Military and Paramilitary Activities in and Against Nicaragua* hereinafter referred to as the *Nicaragua* case, I.C.J. *Rep.* 1986, 14.
43 UN doc. S/16077/Rev 1 (1983).
44 SC mtg, 23 December 1989.
45 *Keesing's Record of World Events* (1989), 36982.
46 SC 1022 mtg, 17 UN SCOR (1962). UN doc. S/5182 (1962).
47 UN doc. S/5187 (1962).
48 UN doc. S/5191 (1962). SC 1024 mtg, 17 UN SCOR 21 (1962).
49 UN doc. S/5197 (1962).
50 See generally J. F. Murphy, *The United Nations and the Control of International Violence*, 135–206 (1985).
51 See D. D. Eisenhower, *Mandate for Change*, 333 (1963).
52 Misc.20 (1954), Cmnd 9239.
53 See generally M. S. Rajan and T. Israel, 'The United Nations and the conflict in Vietnam', in the American Society of International Law, *The Vietnam War and International Law*, vol. 4, 114–43 (1976).
54 UN doc. S/4212 (1959).
55 SC Res. 132, 14 UN SCOR Resolutions 2 (1959). SC 847 mtg, 14 UN SCOR (1959).
56 UN doc. S/4236 (1959).

57 UN doc. S/5697 (1964).
58 SC 1126 mtg, 19 UN SCOR 11 (1964).
59 UN doc. S/5888 (1964).
60 UN doc. S/7106 (1966).
61 SC 1273 mtg, 21 UN SCOR 3 (1966).
62 See GA plen. mtgs 1411–14, 1416, 1418, 1420–4, 1426, 1430, 1432, 1434–8, 1440–7, 1501, 21 GAOR (1966).
63 See generally, *Documents on International Affairs*, 121–42 (1954).
64 *Peking Review*, 16 April 1965.
65 60 *A.J.I.L.* (1966), 565.
66 See *United Nations Yearbook* (1966), 147, 152. *UN Monthly Chronicle* (1967), 69.
67 For 1973 Paris conference peace agreement, see 67 *A.J.I.L.* (1973), 389.
68 See for example B. Andemichael, *The OAU and the UN*, (1976).
69 E. Berberg, 'Regional organisations: a United Nations problem', 49 *A.J.I.L.* (1955), 166, at 169.
70 H. Kelsen, 'Is the North Atlantic Treaty a regional arrangement?', 45 *A.J.I.L.* (1951), 162. A. L. Goodhart, 'The North Atlantic Treaty of 1949', 88 *Recueil des Cours* (1951), 187. E. W. Beckett, *The North Atlantic Treaty, the Brussels Treaty and the Charter of the United Nations* (1950).
71 See Article 5 of the North Atlantic Treaty 1949, 34 UNTS 243, and Article 4 of the Warsaw Pact 1955, 49 *A.J.I.L.* (1955), 194.
72 Articles 1–3 and 27 of the OAS Charter. 119 UNTS 4.
73 UN doc. S/6333/Rev 1 (1965).
74 UN doc. S/6317 (1965).
75 SC 1200 mtg, 20 UN SCOR 33 (1965).
76 M. Akehurst, 'Enforcement action by regional agencies with special reference to the OAS', 42 *B.Y.I.L.* (1967), 175, at 213. See further SC 1221 mtg, 20 UN SCOR (1965), Cuba, USSR, Jordan, France, Uruguay.
77 A. Chayes, *The Cuban Missile Crisis*, 61 (1974).
78 Akehurst, 42 *B.Y.I.L.* (1967), 222.
79 R. Kennedy, *Thirteen Days*, 121 (1969).
80 SC 1441 mtg, 23 UN SCOR 8 (1968).
81 *Nicaragua* case, I.C.J. *Rep.* 1986, 14, at 104–5.
82 UN doc. S/21035 (1989).
83 GA Res. 44/240, 44 UN GAOR (1989), *New York Times*, 23 December 1989.
84 *Keesing* (1991), 38026.
85 *Keesing* (1991), 38654.
86 UN doc. S/23319 (1991).
87 SC mtg 3046, 47 UN S/PV (1992).
88 UN doc. S/96/Rev. 7 (1982).
89 Bailey, *Procedure*, 156.
90 GA Res. 2758, 26 UN GAOR (1971).
91 SC 1599 mtg, 26 UN SCOR (1971).
92 D. Nicol, 'The People's Republic of China in the Security Council', in Nicol (ed.), *Paths to Peace*, 120, at 128 (1981).
93 SC 2963 mtg, 45 UN S/PV 61 (1990).

94 See Articles B and J of the Treaty on European Union, signed at Maastricht, 7
    February 1992. Text in 31 *I.L.M.* (1992) 247.
95 See further A. Hurrell, 'Collective security and international order revisited', 11
    International Relations (1992), 37.

CHAPTER TWO

The legal competence of the Security Council

Chapter one contained an examination of the geopolitical limitations on the competence of the Security Council. However, it would be wrong to say that these limitations are extra-legal, at least in origin. The pressure of the Cold War in the Security Council led to the exploitation and expansion beyond the literal meaning of the Charter of two legal limitations, namely the veto in Article 27(3) and the competence of regional organisations in Article 53(1). The extensive use and, on occasions, misuse of the power of veto in particular often deadlocked the Security Council when it should have been dealing with disputes and conflicts. With the end of the Cold War in the late 1980s and the demise of the Soviet Union in 1991, the opposing political pressures in the Security Council though not removed are much reduced, with the result that the veto is not so prevalent. The Council has been freed to use (and possibly misuse) the powers granted to it in the Charter. In this new order we are faced with the novel situation of assessing the extent of Security Council powers. We are now looking for the limitations on the maximum extent of the Council's powers rather than with those limitations that prevented it operating at all.

This chapter examines the Charter provisions as to jurisdiction which provide the detail within the framework of the larger-scale, global limitations elucidated in chapter one. The difference is essentially one of scale for it will be seen that many jurisdictional questions examined by the Security Council, for example the determination of a 'threat to the peace' within Article 39, are, in essence, political decisions. That is not to say that legal considerations do not play an important role, on occasions, but such considerations only provide a counter-weight to the permanent members' interests which, if sufficiently strong, will predominate. This is still the case with the ending of the Cold War. The political pressures are different, and they are such that Council action is now more likely, but they still greatly influence the interpretation and development of the jurisdictional issues examined below.

This chapter will consider the relative openness of the Charter system regarding the maintenance of international peace and security through the Security Council; in other words whether there is any equivalence between the norm of *jus cogens* contained in Article 2(4) and the situations contained in Article 39 which give the Security Council jurisdiction under Chapter VII, containing the enforcement provisions. Perhaps this may help us to distinguish between the type of situation, dispute or conflict which gives the Council competence under Chapter VI containing powers of pacific settlement, and the type which gives it jurisdiction under Chapter VII. We may discover that there is no essential difference and that what determines competence under each Chapter are political factors. To elucidate whether there is a distinct type of situation which is dealt with under Chapter VII an attempt will be made to find a consistent practice of the usage of, and perhaps even arrive at definitions of, the terms used in Article 39, namely 'threat to the peace', 'breach of the peace' and 'act of aggression'. The analysis will then be concerned with whether the domestic jurisdiction limitation contained in Article 2(7) has any effect on the Council's competence. Once we have distinguished between the elements which initiate jurisdiction under Chapter VI and Chapter VII, the question of whether there is an essential difference in the nature of resolutions adopted under each Chapter will be examined. In essence, this will involve an examination of the mandatory/recommendatory dichotomy, and the nature of the Council's mandatory powers.

The essence of this chapter is to define the factors which grant, and the limitations upon, the Council's jurisdiction as contained in the Charter. It is not concerned with the powers that are at the Council's disposal once it has jurisdiction. An examination of the powers and effectiveness of the Council is left to chapter 3.

The relevance of Article 2(4)

Article 2(4) is a peremptory norm of international law and a fundamental provision of the Charter. It states that all 'Members shall refrain in their international relations from the threat or use of force'. Since Article 2(4) purports to control the use of force by stating a norm of international law to which States must conform, and the Security Council is concerned with maintaining international peace by taking action against States using force in contravention of Article 2(4), it is plausible to examine the possibility of a correlation between Article 2(4) and the competence of the Security Council. One possible approach is to argue that the Security Council can only deal with actual or potential breaches of Article 2(4). Following from this, Chapter VI may be seen to empower the Council to deal with potential breaches, whereas Chapter VII allows it to deal with actual breaches, of

Article 2(4). Indeed, one could go further and accept a direct relationship between 'threat or use of force' under Article 2(4) and a 'threat to the peace', 'breach of the peace' and 'act of aggression' under Article 39, which grants the Council jurisdiction under Chapter VII. In other words 'threat of force' corresponds with 'threat to the peace' and 'use of force' is equivalent to a 'breach of the peace' and 'act of aggression'. This necessarily would entail limiting the Security Council to situations which are breaches of Article 2(4). Such a thesis envisages that the Charter established a 'closed' rather than an 'open' system. The Security Council's competence would be defined, at its limits, by Article 2(4); to go beyond that and, say, determine that a situation was a 'threat to the peace' when it was not a 'threat of force' would be *ultra vires*.

Certainly the extreme thesis, equating as it does Article 2(4) with Article 39, pushes to one side potential breaches of Article 2(4) which may be caught under Chapter VI, where the general requirement is only a danger to international peace, or under Article 39 itself. The introduction of a wide, discretionary concept such as a potential breach of Article 2(4), weakens the argument beyond repair, because it would allow the Council to deal with a wide range of disputes that may theoretically breach Article 2(4) in time, but in reality, are unlikely to do so.

The main advocate of a closed Charter system by which the Security Council's ultimate competence is defined by international law in the form of Article 2(4) is Arntz.[1] Kelsen, on the other hand, states that it is 'completely within the discretion of the Security Council as to what constitutes a threat to the peace'.[2] Kelsen and Higgins[3] state that because the Council is not fettered in its powers of determination under Article 39, such a determination, in a case where no obligation stipulated by customary international law or Charter law is breached, can create new law as to what constitutes a threat to or breach of the peace. It can be seen from this that the Council has a lawmaking role, but it does not necessarily follow that the Council is completely unfettered by international and Charter law. The issue of whether the international legal system embodies the concept of the rule of law, which would mean that all subjects of international law including international organizations, in particular the potentially powerful Security Council, are controlled by legal principles, is an underdeveloped area which will have to be properly addressed if the Security Council continues to expand its powers.[4]

As is to be expected from a politically orientated body, the Security Council has, in practice, manifested a preference for the open system. In particular it has applied the concept of a 'threat to the peace' in Article 39 to essentially internal situations. Arntz argues that internal situations are not within the ambit of Article 39 because they do not constitute a 'threat of force' against another State within the meaning of Article 2(4). He argues that the text of the Charter, particularly the preamble and Article 1, indicate that 'peace' is the antithesis of war, and so the Charter only deals with threats to or breaches of inter-State or international peace, and not to intra-State or internal peace. However, the evidence is that if an internal situation or civil war is serious enough the Security Council will become involved, subject, of course to political limitations. This is sufficient, in itself, to destroy the closed Charter theory.[5]

For instance, in 1966 the Council determined that the 'situation in Southern Rhodesia constitutes a threat to international peace and security'.[6] It cannot really be denied that the only 'threat or use of force' arose from the activities of the guerrillas infiltrating Rhodesia from the frontline African States. Nevertheless, the Council decided that the situation in Southern Rhodesia itself constituted a 'threat to the peace' evidenced by its policy of imposing sanctions against Rhodesia.

In 1977, the Security Council determined 'having regard to the policies and acts of the South African Government, that the acquisition by South Africa of arms and related matériel constitutes a threat to the maintenance of international peace and security'.[7] It could be argued that the 'acts' referred to were the frequent punitive attacks against the frontline countries of Botswana, Angola, Zambia, Zimbabwe, Mozambique and Lesotho, and so the 'threat to the peace' had the international character that Arntz's formulation requires. Indeed, the resolution made reference to South Africa's 'persistent acts of aggression against neighbouring States'. However, the resolution also referred to the 'policies' of the South African government and called for the elimination of apartheid and racial discrimination within the country. Given that the resolution was adopted against a background of riots and killing in the black townships, it is submitted that it was the internal system of apartheid that constituted the 'threat to the peace' with the border conflicts being manifestations of that threat.

A parallel can be drawn with the arrival of oil tankers at Beira carrying oil for Rhodesia, an event which the Security Council seemed to view, in resolution 221, as being, in itself, a 'threat to the peace'.[8] However, the real threat was the situation in Southern Rhodesia itself, a fact later recognised by the Council in resolution 232. The Council initially made a limited finding of a threat because of political factors.[9] The same can be said of South Africa, where, before the recent reforms, the Western members refused to allow a general finding of a threat.[10]

It is often forgotten that the Council determined that there was a 'threat to the peace' arising from the crisis in the Congo after the situation had deteriorated so badly as to constitute a civil war in 1961.[11] It is arguable whether this was an internal situation as such with Belgian support for Tshombe and Soviet aid to Lumumba. However, there was certainly no direct 'threat or use of force' by one State against another. At the time the

Council determined that there was a 'threat to the peace' in resolution 161, the main foreign element of force consisted of the few hundred mercenaries employed by Tshombe to maintain Katanga's secession. The crisis had international repercussions in that the civil war could suck in outside forces including the superpowers and that was why the internal civil war in the Congo was a threat to international peace. The linkage of the civil war in the Congo and the threat to international peace was emphasised in resolution 161.

The situations in Southern Rhodesia, South Africa and the Congo involved international repercussions of varying degrees, but it must be remembered that these repercussions derived from the internal situations themselves. To be sure, the Council has often refused to find a 'threat to the peace' in situations that seem to fit the Rhodesian model. Portugal's failure to implement the General Assembly's 'Declaration on the Granting of Independence to Colonial Countries and Peoples'[12] is one example. The Council went as far as to adopt a resolution in 1972 which found that the 'situation resulting from the policies of Portugal both in its colonies and in its constant provocations against neighbouring States seriously disturbs international peace and security'.[13] Although this falls short of a finding under Article 39 there is evidence to suggest that a finding of a 'threat to the peace' might eventually have been made as a result of international pressure against Western members had the Salazar regime survived in 1974.[14]

The above analysis suggests that a finding of a 'threat to the peace' is, to a large degree, a political decision on the part of the Council, and so such a finding as regards a wholly internal situation is not precluded. Generally, however, the permanent members are not going to exercise this discretion unless the situation has potential international repercussions which could affect their interests, or even involve them in an escalating conflict. The requirement that the internal situation has international consequences is also a convenient method of allowing the permanent members to hide behind the argument that a situation is purely internal and therefore not a threat when they want to protect their interests. Recent practice suggests that the requirement is something of a formality, and that the Council is in reality concerning itself with purely internal situations. In April 1991, the Council condemned the repression of the Iraqi civilian population, including the suppression of the Kurdish minority rebellion in the north of Iraq following the end of the war between the UN authorised army and Iraq in and around Kuwait. The resolution declared that 'the consequences of [this repression] threaten international peace and security'. In an earlier paragraph the Council elaborated on those 'consequences', namely 'the massive flow of refugees towards and across international frontiers'.[15] Further, in January 1992 it found that the civil conflict in Somalia had 'consequences on the stability and peace in the region' the 'continuation' of which 'constitutes

. . . a threat to international peace and security'.[16] One can perhaps perceive the requirement for the threat to be against *international peace* as opposed to *internal peace* being stretched to breaking point.

Danger or threat to the peace

Articles 33 and 34 of Chapter VI of the UN Charter refer to a 'dispute' or 'situation' which is 'likely to endanger the maintenance of international peace and security'. The remainder of Chapter VI, with the exception of Article 38, relates to the Council's powers of pacific settlement over disputes or situations of the nature referred to in Articles 33 and 34. The title to Chapter VII reads 'action with respect to threats to the peace, breaches of the peace, and acts of aggression'. These terms are repeated in Article 39 which make it clear that the set of circumstances to be dealt with under Chapter VII, containing the Council's enforcement powers, are threats to or breaches of international peace.

This section will be concerned with determining whether there is any objective difference between situations or conflicts dealt with under Chapter VI and those dealt with under Chapter VII, or whether the Security Council treats the powers contained in the two Chapters as one continuum, using them selectively and interchangeably as political factors, including the need for consensus, dictate. The main area of this analysis will concern the fine distinction, if one can be drawn, between a 'danger to international peace' and a 'threat to the peace'.

So close is the relationship between a 'danger' and a 'threat' that it will become clear from the following analysis that there is often no substantive factual distinction between the two. They are, in effect, often merely 'labels' put into the resolutions to indicate the political climate in the Council. Conceptually, however, there is a legal distinction between a 'danger' and a 'threat'. The latter, for example, is often used as a legal tool to facilitate the imposition of mandatory measures under Chapter VII, a function which the label 'danger' is not legally qualified to perform.

To say that there is little practical difference between a 'danger to international peace' and a 'threat to the peace' is not so radical as it may first appear. At San Francisco, the Dumbarton Oaks proposals had provided for a link between Chapters VI and VII. The proposals had a provision at the beginning of what emerged to be Chapter VII of the Charter which empowered the Council to find a 'threat to the maintenance of international peace and security' if the procedures in what is now Article 33(1) or recommendations in Article 36(1) had failed or had been ignored.[17] This implies that the scale or the nature of the conflict need not have altered significantly from when the Council had purported to deal with it under Chapter VI. The factor which converted a danger to international peace under Chapter VI to a threat to the peace under Chapter VII was not necessarily a change in the nature of the conflict (except its prolongation) but a failure by the Council to end it under Chapter VI. The provision was dropped at San Francisco not because it brought the concepts of danger and threat too close together, but because it fettered the Council's operation of its powers,[18] that is, it might have prevented the complete unfettered discretion of the Council in determining whether a situation was a 'threat to the peace' or not. This was despite the fact that the proposed provision would have been of relative insignificance in practice for it was, itself, discretionary.

Nevertheless, in its formative years the Council did seem to develop a jurisprudence purporting to differentiate between a danger and a threat to international peace, revealed most clearly by the Spanish question in 1946. The Council adopted a resolution establishing a sub-committee of five members to determine whether the existence and activities of the Franco regime in Spain endangered international peace and security.[19] The sub-committee reported that the situation was of 'international concern' but not yet a 'threat to the peace' within Article 39. There was a 'potential menace to international peace' and therefore 'a situation likely to endanger international peace' within the meaning of Article 34.

The sub-committee thus created a distinction between a potential threat to the peace which corresponds to a danger within Chapter VI and an actual or real threat within Article 39. There is no further development of the distinction in the report except the factual findings that Spain had no imminent warlike intentions which suggests that the test is the relative immediacy of the war or conflict. However, the probable reason for distinguishing between a potential and an actual threat was that the sub-committee was labouring under an understandable view that Chapter VII was a 'very sharp instrument' which enabled the United Nations to wage war if necessary. This belief meant that it was reluctant to find a threat unless there was a very real and immediate danger to international peace which there was not in Spain.[20]

However, the powers of Chapter VII were not fully exploited during the Cold War, resulting in the relaxation of the distinction between a danger and a threat. In addition, the sub-committee's assumption that a determination of a threat to the peace within the terms of Article 39 necessarily leads to enforcement action was mistaken. Nevertheless, the motivating factor behind the Council's finding or not finding a 'threat to the peace' remains, in most cases, the reluctance by some members to impose economic sanctions under Chapter VII.

The development of the Security Council's arms embargo against South Africa is interesting for it reveals that often the difference between a potential threat and an actual threat or a danger and a threat is not an increase in the level of violence of a dispute or conflict, but the ephemeral motives and interests of the members of the Council. Until the southern African peace process which started in 1988 with the agreement by South Africa to withdraw from Namibia in return for the Cuban withdrawal from Angola followed by a reform process in South Africa itself, the Western permanent members saw the protection of their economic interests in South Africa as vital, and therefore their general aim was the prevention of a mandatory set of sanctions being imposed against the Pretoria government.

Nevertheless, the international pressure on South Africa and consequently on Western governments forced them to grant some concessions. Thus changing political factors affect the Council's jurisdictional finding often to a greater extent than any legal criteria.

In 1963 the Council called upon all States to cease the shipment of arms and military material to South Africa after expressing its conviction 'that the situation in South Africa is seriously disturbing international peace and security'.[21] The call was only voluntary with the phrase 'seriously disturbing' seemingly equivalent to 'likely to endanger'. As we have seen, this was eventually made mandatory in 1977 with a determination that the supply of arms to South Africa constituted a 'threat to the peace'. The finding of a 'threat' accompanied by a specific embargo was delayed by the intransigence of Western States until 1977 mainly because it was not until this time that South Africa had become fully armed. There may have been a change in the nature of the situation due to an increased level of violence within South Africa which may have influenced the Council in its determination of a threat, though by far the most significant factors were the political interests of the Western States. The General Assembly had made its own determination that the situation within South Africa was a threat to the peace in 1965.[22]

The gradual change in the Council's collective will can be traced in the language of its resolutions on South Africa. By 1970, the determination was that, 'the situation resulting from the continued policies of apartheid and the constant build up of the South African military and police forces constitutes a potential threat to international peace and security'.[23] The original draft resolution sponsored by the Non Aligned members of the Council contained the phrase 'serious threat',[24] but with Western opposition the second and final draft amended this to 'potential threat'. The representative of the United Kingdom expressed the West's opposition to the earlier drafts using the language of Chapter VII, whereas the phrase 'potential threat' was not objectionable on those grounds.[25] With the prevention of entry into Chapter VII achieved, the resolution's call for an arms embargo was generally accepted to be only recommendatory, even though it also referred to a 'real threat to the security' of surrounding African States due to the arms build up in South Africa.

'Likely to endanger international peace', 'seriously disturbing international peace', 'threats to the security' of neighbouring States, 'potential threat to international peace' and a 'threat to international peace' are terms used by the Council. They could be said to be arranged here in a scale of ascendancy with the last being the most serious and the only one which is recognised as representing an implied finding under Article 39. The factors which produce a move up or down the scale are a combination of factual and determinable change in the level and nature of the conflict and also political and strategic adjustments by the members of the Security Council, particularly the permanent members. Political factors being the stronger, the phraseology used should be seen as an indicator of a change in political will rather than providing any significant criteria by which one can legally define the difference between a danger to international peace and a threat to international peace. Nevertheless, political factors primarily influence the timing of a finding of a 'threat to the peace'. Once a finding is made it is possible to determine why a situation is a 'threat to the peace' and to construct a legal definition. In doing this one should try to ignore the political factors which influenced the designation of the situation as a threat to the peace at a particular time, for it may well be that, legally speaking, such a threat had existed for many years prior to the finding.

The influence of political factors in finding a 'threat to the peace' in the Rhodesian situation illustrates the influence a solitary permanent member can have. Resolution 216 adopted on 12 November 1965 condemned the Unilateral Declaration of Independence (UDI) and called upon States not to recognise the 'illegal regime' or render any assistance to it. The resolution contained no determination of a danger to international peace nor of a threat to the peace because it arose from the desire to find a compromise between a British draft resolution which determined that the 'continuance of the resulting situation is likely to endanger the maintenance of international peace and security',[26] and a draft resolution proposed by the Ivory Coast which stated that the declaration of independence constituted a 'threat to international peace and security'.[27] The difference in terminology arose principally because of the British and Western view that Rhodesia should not be subjected to immediate punitive sanctions but to a policy of gradually escalating sanctions to urge peaceful change, whereas the Afro-Asian and communist view was that Rhodesia should be the subject of immediate and punitive mandatory sanctions and possibly the use of military force.[28] This divergence was not primarily due to different perceptions of the nature of the situation in Rhodesia. According to the General Assembly a 'threat to the peace' had existed in 1963,[29] and since the Assembly's resolutions are also politically motivated, to a great extent, it may well be that a 'threat to the peace' had existed for some years prior to the Assembly so deciding.

Due to the United Kingdom's hold over the other members of the Council in the form of its veto, the Council's resolutions reflected the British policy rather than that of the Afro-Asian States. The Council gradually moved towards a finding of a threat to the peace with a corresponding move from voluntary to mandatory measures which were eventually made comprehensive. Resolution 217 adopted on 20 November 1965 determined that the 'continuance in time' of the Rhodesian situation 'constitutes a threat to international peace and security'. This phrase appears to be akin to a 'potential threat' and so it was no surprise when the Council found a 'threat to the peace' specifically in relation to the oil tankers arriving at Beira, then a general finding of a 'threat to the peace' as regards the Southern Rhodesian situation as a whole, accompanied by the imposition of mandatory sanctions which were later made comprehensive.

An intermediate finding of a potential threat is generally indicative of the Council members' first consensual step towards an implied finding under Article 39. Ambassador Goldberg of the United States summarised the state of the Council's deliberations when voting on resolution 217, stating that it did 'not mention whether Chapter VI or Chapter VII is brought to bear. My Government agrees with this interpretation of the text'. This bizarre comment merely reflects the mid-point between the polarised views of the other Council members. For example, the Ivory Coast believed that resolution 217 imposed mandatory sanctions, whereas the British viewed it as 'not falling under Chapter VII'.[30]

The phrase 'potential threat', which conceptually appears to be no different to a danger to the peace, is a product of the Cold War which forced members to achieve consensus by appeasing all sides. If some members desired a finding of a threat accompanied by Chapter VII action, whilst others, for equally political reasons, desired only a finding of a danger and a recommendation of peaceful settlement under Chapter VI, in order to produce some sort of resolution a compromise was often achieved by the use of 'potential threat' accompanied perhaps by voluntary measures. If a compromise was not achieved the veto was inevitably used.

In the two examples given, one can perceive a slow march by the Security Council towards a finding of a threat to the peace combined with the undertaking of enforcement action. In other instances, during the Cold War the process was much more likely to halt before the Council reached Chapter VII as the all pervasive political limitations intervened. With the ending of the Cold War, this slow process is less evident, and as we shall see, the Council more freely enters upon Chapter VII, often avoiding any preliminary steps such as the determination of a danger or potential threat to the peace. Indeed, the evidence of the last three years is that the increasingly dynamic Council is not, for the moment, concerned with concepts such as potential threat. Many resolutions appear now to be clearly within Chapter VII, and increasingly contain enforcement measures, others are not within Chapter VII. The jurisdictional phraseology of Chapter VI seems to have become subverted to the general need for the Security Council to react rapidly to situations without the need to consider the legal niceties. The most important jurisdictional distinction in the post Cold War era is that between Chapter VII resolutions, which normally are mandatory and Chapter VI resolutions, which normally are recommendatory.

Occasionally, the Council will find a threat to the peace without taking any mandatory action, as when it found that the consequences of the suppression of the Kurdish rebellion threatened international peace and security in April 1991. Normally, however, it signifies its use of Chapter VII not only by making a finding of a threat to or breach of the peace within the terms of Article 39, but by actually stating that the resolution, or the relevant part of a resolution, is adopted under Chapter VII. For example, in September 1991, the Security Council determined in a preambular paragraph of its resolution that 'the continuation of' the fighting in Yugoslavia and its effects on neighbouring countries constituted 'a threat to international peace and security'. It then decided 'under Chapter VII of the Charter' that all States immediately implement a complete arms embargo against Yugoslavia.[31]

Indeed, unlike the Security Council's laborious approach to the Rhodesian and South African situations, its post Cold War approach generally gives States little chance to prepare themselves for Council action. In January 1992, the Western dominated Council turned its attention to Libya, long seen as a 'pariah' State in the West, and with the end of the Cold War, without many friends either inside or outside the Council chamber. The Council did urge in resolution 731 that the Libyan government effectively respond to the requests of France, the United States and Britain for extradition of the Libyan nationals those States alleged were behind acts of terrorism, specifically the sabotage of the Pan Am flight over Lockerbie in Scotland in 1988. However, the same resolution made it clear that this was not the only action the Council was prepared to take if necessary by stating in the preamble that certain acts of terrorism constituted 'threats to international peace and security'. This effectively opened the door for Chapter VII action in the future if the Libyan government did not respond to the satisfaction of the Council, or more correctly, the Western permanent members. During the Cold War, it may have taken many months, possibly years, for the Council to take further action, if at all. It was just over two months later on 31 March 1992 that the Council adopted resolution 748, in which the Council stated that it was 'acting under Chapter VII of the Charter' in imposing an arms and air embargo against Libya.[31a]

Whereas the Cold War encouraged the proliferation of phrases such as potential threat which may have indicated the general direction of the Council towards Chapter VII, its ending in the late 1980s has removed these nuances in Council language. The new approach is a simple one, namely a clear distinction between a determination of a 'threat to the peace' which, alongside 'breach of the peace' and 'act of aggression', form the gateway to Chapter VII action, and other disputes or situations which are not, at that moment, to be dealt with under Chapter VII but under Chapter VI, or under the Council's increasingly developed declaratory powers. The formal requirement of a finding of a 'danger to international peace' does not now seem necessary for a resolution to bear the mark of a Chapter VI resolution, it simply must lack the necessary finding under Article 39. It is interesting to note that this approach, which is obviously favoured by the dominant Western permanent members on the Council, ties in with their traditional attitude to the question of the Council's mandatory powers, which we will look at later in this chapter.

Threat to the peace

We have seen in the above section that because of a delay caused by political factors in a finding of a 'threat to the peace' there appears to be little factual difference between a situation 'likely to endanger international peace' and a 'threat to the peace'. Undoubtedly, a 'threat to the peace' is a very flexible concept covering anything from intra-state situations to inter-state disputes. Nevertheless, if we ignore for a moment the confusion caused by political delay, it can be seen that, on the limited occasions of its use, the term 'threat to the peace' is taking on a conceptual form.

Earlier practice of the Council does not reveal the same usage of 'threat to the peace' as does later practice, which is probably a reflection of change in the type of dispute or conflict occurring in the post 1945 world order. In early years, a finding of a threat to the peace was viewed as a preliminary to a finding of a breach of the peace. The invasion of Palestine by the surrounding Arab countries after the proclamation of the State of Israel on 14 May 1948, eventually led the Council to classify the situation as a 'threat to the peace within the meaning of Article 39', and to order that 'pursuant to Article 40', there should be a cessation of hostilities which should take place 'not later than three days from the date' of the resolution. Any failure to comply 'would demonstrate the existence of a breach of the peace within Article 39'.[32] The Council was not saying that the Arab countries were threatening to breach the peace for hostilities had already begun, it was the continuance in time of the conflict which would convert a threat into a breach of the peace.

Later practice shows the term being modified to deal with intra-state situations and conflicts rather than the traditional inter-state conflict, for which the other terms in Article 39 are more applicable. The most extensive use of the term, undoubtedly, was during the meetings of the Security Council between 1965 and 1968, although very few of the speakers explained why the situation in Southern Rhodesia was a threat to the peace. Perhaps the decision was a political one requiring no rational or conceptual deliberations by the members of the Council. However, the meeting of 16 December 1966, at which the first mandatory resolution of a more general nature was adopted, reveals that at least some of the representatives had applied their minds as to why an essentially internal situation was a threat to the peace. The representative of Jordan stated that UDI amounted to 'an invasion of the rights of the majority. It is an act of aggression that cannot be condoned. The answer to such invasion and aggression is Chapter VII'.[33] Superficially he appeared to be referring to an inter-state conflict rather than an internal situation; however, the 'invasion of the rights of the majority' clearly shows that the primary reason for the situation being a threat to the peace was the denial of the right to self-determination of the people of Southern Rhodesia, although another element in a threat to the peace is the potential spillover effect, the likelihood of internal violence spreading to become international violence. This writer believes that the spillover element in a finding of a threat is overplayed because any situation where there is a denial of self-determination or a significant deprivation of human rights has the potential to ignite international violence, for example through misconceived or misapplied unilateral humanitarian intervention.

Although recent changes in the direction of the white minority regime in South Africa have raised the possibility of the system of apartheid being dismantled, the fact remains that the denial of the South Africans' right to self-determination has for many years constituted a 'threat to the peace'. The Council has not made such a finding in general terms, although resolutions passed in condemnation of the system of apartheid have said as much without using the term. For example resolution 473 of 13 June 1978 reaffirmed that, 'the policy of apartheid is a crime against the conscience and dignity of mankind and is incompatible with the rights and dignity of man, the Charter of the United Nations and the Universal Declaration of Human Rights and seriously disturbs international peace'. The last phrase appears to be added to keep the resolution within the bounds of Chapter VI. Nevertheless designating apartheid as a 'crime against mankind' and a 'crime against humanity'[34] must surely have brought the whole situation, and not just the acquisition of arms by South Africa, within the concept of a 'threat to the peace'. The decision to keep the situation within the terms of Chapter VI was a political one on behalf of the Western permanent members who were not willing to subject the regime to a more comprehensive embargo.[35]

It appears that a 'threat to the peace' is the term the Council has shaped to use in situations of non-traditional international violence in which the main danger to international peace is not a conflict between two or more States, instead it arises primarily from the internal events in one State, which may, as in the case of South Africa, manifest itself in the form of attacks upon other States.[36] Whereas South Africa and Rhodesia were concerned with the denial of self-determination by racist regimes, the crisis in the Congo was more akin to a civil war situation. The problems of civil strife and human suffering were, in themselves, sufficient to warrant a finding of a threat to the peace, although the Council tended to combine this with the menace caused by Belgian and mercenary military intervention.[37]

In other conflicts the question of civil strife is often overshadowed by foreign intervention. In 1974 a Greek-backed coup against Archbishop Makarios followed by the Turkish invasion of the northern part of Cyprus led the Council to adopt resolution 353, which stated that there was a 'serious threat to international peace and security' and demanded 'an end to foreign military intervention' in Cyprus.[38] The threat to international peace was inherent in the civil strife between the Greek and the Turkish Cypriots, a fact recognised by resolution 186, adopted in 1964, which classified the violent eruptions on the island as 'likely to threaten international peace'. The Turkish invasion in 1974 was a manifestation and realisation of the threat.

The term 'threat to the peace', it can be seen, is being applied increasingly to internal situations. In 1969, Ireland requested a meeting of the Security Council to consider the situation in Northern Ireland with a view to sending a United Nations' peacekeeping force to the province because of the serious disturbances caused by the alleged denial of civil rights to the Catholic community.[39] Although the question was not even adopted on the agenda, it is interesting to note that Lord Caradon was sufficiently perturbed by Irish references to southern Africa that he not only relied on Article 2(7) as would be expected, but also denied that the situation in Northern Ireland was a threat to international peace.[40]

The Northern Ireland situation illustrates that the concept of a 'threat to the peace' is restricted to denials of self-determination or civil wars, which is not the case in Northern Ireland, with the additional requirement that the situation must have consequences for international peace, in terms of destabilising neighbouring States or drawing in outside powers. Recent post Cold War practice when the Council has been more willing to enter Chapter VII illustrates this point. As has been pointed out in the above sections, the civil wars in Iraq, Yugoslavia and Somalia were all designated threats to the peace within 1991–92, not only because of the massive scale of destruction in each of these conflicts but also because of their adverse affects on neighbouring States. The rather nebulous 'consequences' requirement appears to be a method whereby the permanent members can limit the usage of the concept of a threat to those situations which do not affect their interests, or further their interests.

The extension of the concept of a 'threat to the peace' into what are essentially internal situations has not been without controversy. It is interesting to note that resolution 688 of 5 April 1991 which found that the consequences of the Iraqi repression of the Kurds, which mainly took the form of a 'massive flow of refugees' towards and over the Iranian and Turkish frontiers, threatened international peace was the least supported of the Council's resolutions on the Gulf Crisis following Iraq's invasion of Kuwait in August 1990. The resolution received only ten votes in favour, with three against, Cuba, Yemen, Zimbabwe, and two abstentions, China and India. Many of those States who could not support the resolution expressed alarm at the intrusion into another State's internal affairs.[41] On the other hand the resolutions on Yugoslavia and Somalia received unanimous votes. The difference appeared to be that resolution 688 concerned the suppression of a section of the population by the legitimate government of Iraq, a move that clearly would bother members of the Council themselves guilty of suppression, whilst the other states, Yugoslavia and Somalia, were completely factionalised by the time the Council determined that there was a threat to the peace. The resolutions were not directed against an established government and therefore could be supported by all members.[42]

The same cannot be said for recent Council resolutions against Libya, which represent a new development of the concept of a 'threat to the peace' to cover aspects of terrorism. Building on a general resolution of June 1989, which determined 'to encourage the promotion of effective measures to prevent acts of terrorism', and specifically condemned 'all acts of unlawful interference against the security of civilian aviation',[43] the Western members satisfied the Council of the complicity of the Libyan government in acts of air sabotage and gained Council support for their demand that Libya respond immediately and effectively to the requests of the three Western permanent members that Libya cooperate in the 'legal procedures', namely the extradition of alleged terrorists to the West. Resolution 731, adopted unanimously on 21 January 1992, was not mandatory in that there was no reference to Chapter VII within it, but it contained the possibility of further action in the future when it affirmed 'the right of all States . . . to protect their nationals from acts of terrorism that constitute threats to international peace and security'. Little was said in the Council meeting at which this resolution was adopted to explain further this development of the term threat to the peace.[44]

Although Libya did respond by offering to try the alleged terrorists in Libya, and thereby purporting to comply with its obligations under Article 7 of the Montreal Convention on the Suppression of Unlawful Acts against the Safety of Civil Aviation of 1971,[45] this did not satisfy the Council, which on 31 March 1992 adopted resolution 748 by a majority of ten votes to nil with five abstentions – China, Cape Verde, India, Morocco and Zimbabwe. The Council, after recalling Article 2(4) of the Charter, determined 'that the failure of the Libyan Government to demonstrate by concrete actions its renunciation of terrorism and in particular its continued failure to respond fully and effectively to the requests in resolution 731 (1992) constitute a threat to international peace and security'. It then went on to impose enforcement measures under Chapter VII with the aim of obtaining Libya's compliance with the requests and its renunciation of terrorism.

The Security Council debate was inconclusive as to the exact nature of the threat in this case, although at one point the British representative said, 'terrorists . . . have as their objective the undermining of efforts . . . to seek peaceful solutions to international disputes. They represent, in fact, one of the greatest threats to peace around the world, and that includes peace in the Middle East'.[46] The concept of threat to the peace, although expanded from its immediate post 1945 meaning, has generally been restricted to civil wars and denial of the right to self-determination (usually involving some degree of armed struggle). The invocation of Article 2(4) in resolution 748 may have been intended to give the resolution that necessary reference to armed force, which appears essential if the Security Council is to embark upon enforcement action in its collective security role for the maintenance of international peace and security. Extensive support for terrorism can obviously affect international peace, although one might suggest that its impact has to be quite serious to merit the finding of a 'threat to the peace'. Resolution 748 reflected the General Assembly's 1970 Declaration of Friendly Relations[47] when it stated that 'every State has the duty to refrain from organizing, instigating, assisting or participating in terrorist acts against another State or acquiescing in organized activities within its territory directed towards the commission of such acts, when such acts involve the threat or use of force'.

One might have expected such issues to be discussed by the International Court of Justice, when it was faced with a request by Libya for interim measures of protection from coercion pending determination of its claim under Article 14 of the Montreal Convention against the United States and the United Kingdom that it had complied with that treaty despite not extraditing the alleged terrorists. On 14 April 1992, the day before the Security Council's measures were to come into effect, the Court was not prepared to determine definitely the legal effect of resolution 748. It considered that whatever the situation prior to the adoption of the resolution, the rights claimed by Libya under the Montreal Convention were not now appropriate for protection by provisional measures designed to preserve that prior *status quo*. The Court found that resolution 748 was binding in accordance with Article 25 of the Charter and prevailed over the Montreal Convention by virtue of Article 103.[48]

Although a final determination of the case, including the question of whether the International Court was prepared to question the competence of the Security Council, was left to the merits, the tenor of the judgement seems to reflect the Court's presumption against *ultra vires* actions by the organs of the United Nations, an approach more clearly stated in the *Expenses* case. However, some of the judges in the *Lockerbie* case, in separate and dissenting judgements, seemed to suggest that the Court would be prepared to act as guardian of Charter law, which certainly implies the possibility of the Court overruling decisions of the Council.[49] Unfortunately, further clarification appears unlikely unless Libya proceeds to the merits stage. Indeed, the slim possibility of the World Court, which lacks mandatory jurisdiction, having another opportunity in this case or any other in the foreseeable future, signifies that the Court, even if it was prepared to challenge the competence of the Council, cannot be viewed as a practical limitation on the Council's power.

Although the concept of a 'threat to the peace' is flexible, and very much motivated by political factors, which were clearly in play here, the imposition of specific sanctions against Libya following a determination that its alleged support for terrorism was a threat to the peace seems to be a new departure from past practice. It is a development that needs to be entrenched by consistent, subsequent practice by the Security Council. Western States ought to be prepared to see this extension of the concept become embedded in the practice of the Security Council, before developing the term further. Nevertheless, although one may advise the West to be cautious, such is their dominance of the Council at the moment that one can foresee the possible development of the concept even further to enable the West to use the powers of the Security Council to deal with other problems such as drug trafficking, or perhaps the suppression of democratic movements by autocratic governments. However, the extent to which Western policy can become institutionalised in the practice of the Security Council is still limited by the interests of the other permanent members, particularly the Chinese, who presently are certain to veto any extension of the concept of a threat to the peace to cover the suppression of democracy.

Breach of the peace

In practice, a breach of the peace has rarely been found, the recent preference being for findings of aggression. This is surprising for aggression is merely a special case of breach: Article 1(1) of the Charter mentions 'acts of aggression or other breaches of the peace'. Although a finding of aggression is much more condemnatory, often, as shall be seen, it produces little by way of sanctioning measures. 'Breach of the peace', although a much more neutral expression when applied to traditional international violence has, on the four occasions on which it has been found, been accompanied by positive Council action.

The Australian representative attempted a definition of a breach of the peace during discussion of the Indonesian question, when he assumed that it meant 'a breach of international peace and applies to cases where hostilities are occurring, but where it is not alleged that one particular party is the aggressor or has committed an act of aggression'.[50] He advocated such a finding in relation to the conflict occurring in Indonesia.

The Dutch representative objected on the grounds that, 'what happened in Indonesia was not a breach of international peace but rather a breach of internal peace. Breaches of internal peace are and remain the exclusive responsibility of the Members of the United Nations on the territory of which those unfortunate occurrences take place'.[51]

A finding of a threat to the peace may have been more applicable if the situation was indeed a breach of internal peace. As will be seen later a finding under Article 39 generally renders nugatory the application of Article 2(7). However, the Council did not make such a finding, neither at the beginning of the conflict nor at any stage throughout it, in order to gain Dutch consent to its resolutions. Council practice in the late 1940s had not evolved the wider concept of a threat to the peace, which in retrospect could have been applied to the Indonesian question.

There have been four findings of a breach of the peace in conflicts brought to the attention of the Council. The first concerned the conflict in Korea in 1950. On 25 June, the Council was rapidly convened at the request of the United States, after massive North Korean forces had crossed the 38th parallel which had divided the country since the Japanese surrender to Soviet forces north of that line and to American forces south of it.[52] The Soviet Union had been absent from the Council since 30 January 1950 in protest at the failure to install the Chinese communists in the permanent seat instead of the Nationalists. If the Soviet Union had been present any Council moves would probably have been vetoed, possibly on the grounds that the armed conflict in Korea was a civil war or war of national liberation involving only that country. However, the rest of the Council viewed the North Korean attack as a 'breach of the peace'.[53] The resolution referred to the 1949 General Assembly resolution (293) which recognised the government of the Republic of Korea based in South Korea, and so the Council was able to view the attack as akin to an armed attack by one State against another. It is probably correct to say that objectively speaking, the North Korean attack was an act of aggression, a view taken by the United States.[54] The Council drew back from making a damning determination and opted for the more neutral concept of a 'breach of the peace' as sufficient for it to proceed to take military enforcement action against North Korea.

It was not until 1982 that the Council made its next formal determination that international peace had been breached. On 3 April, after Argentina had invaded the Falklands, the British introduced resolution 502 which determined that there was a 'breach of the peace in the region of the Falkland Islands'. The resolution did not condemn Argentinian aggression to ensure that it did not incur the veto of an otherwise indifferent Soviet Union. It then introduced certain provisional measures which although not complied with were, in the circumstances, probably the best that could be expected.

The third occasion upon which the Security Council determined that a breach of the peace existed was on 20 June 1987 when it unanimously adopted resolution 598. The breach was found in relation to the Gulf War between Iran and Iraq which had been continuing for seven years before the Council found that a clear case of inter-state conflict came within Article 39. This illustrates the political nature of such a finding because during those years the Council was unwilling to step into Chapter VII.

The Security Council acted with much greater alacrity when Iraq invaded Kuwait on 2 August 1990. Within hours the Council had convened and had adopted resolution 660 which condemned the Iraqi 'invasion' of Kuwait after determining that 'there exists a breach of international peace and security as regards the Iraqi invasion of Kuwait'. Again the more condemnatory term 'aggression' appeared more suitable to a clear violation of Article 2(4) within the terms of Article 3 of the Assembly's 1974 Definition of Aggression. Although some members of the Council condemned the Iraqi aggression, others seemed to hope that a more neutral determination, whilst giving the Security Council the option of taking further action under Chapter VII, would not make the Iraqis more intransigent, when in the days following the invasion, there appeared to be the possibility of the Iraqis withdrawing voluntarily.[55]

'It would seem logical that any resort to armed force would come within the meaning of the phrase' breach of the peace.[56] Even if the phrase is defined more narrowly as referring to international and not internal peace, it appears, at the very least, incongruous, that a body established with primary responsibility for international peace and security has found a breach of the peace on only four occasions. The conflicts between Ethiopia and Somalia in 1977, Tanzania and Uganda between 1978–79, India and Pakistan between 1947–49, again in 1965 and 1971, Vietnam and Cambodia in 1978, China and the Soviet Union in 1969, India and China in 1962, the Arab-Israeli wars of 1948–49, 1956, 1967, 1973, the Israeli invasions of Lebanon in 1978 and 1982, the Soviet armed interventions in Hungary 1956, Czechoslovakia 1968 and Afghanistan in 1979, the United States' incursions into Guatemala 1954, the Dominican Republic 1965, Grenada 1983 and Panama 1989, are just some of the most obvious breaches of international peace in the sense of direct inter-state armed conflict, on which the Council failed to make a determination under Article 39, or, in some instances, did not even discuss. It is to be hoped that the end of the Cold War will enable the Council to make such determinations and take action much more readily.

Act of aggression

As has been suggested above an act of aggression is a special form of a breach of the peace, in particular it labels or condemns one of the States involved in a conflict as the guilty party. There is also the possibility of individual as well as State responsibility attaching to an aggressor under customary international law as the Nuremberg Trials of German leaders after the end of the Second World War showed.[57] Whilst it is not surprising that the term 'aggression' is used quite frequently in exchanges in the Council chamber, the body as a whole is unlikely to agree to use it on a regular basis. Although the Council is not averse to acting as a quasi-judicial body on occasions, particularly after the ending of the Cold War, the potential consequences of a finding of aggression at the initial stages of a conflict, and the fact that such a determination will not encourage the accused State to withdraw, signify that there has been very limited Council practice on the term 'act of aggression'.

Indeed, before the adoption of a definition of aggression in 1974,[58] there had been no formal findings of aggression; since, there have been several against South Africa[59] and Israel.[60] However, Western members are still cautious about allowing a finding of aggression against two friendly States, only allowing such determinations as long as they are not accompanied by positive measures. They can ease their consciences, as well as deflecting international pressure to introduce sanctions against these countries, by allowing the occasional condemnatory but paper resolution to be adopted. Indeed in the last few years with the peace processes starting in southern Africa in 1988 and in the Middle East in 1991, there have been fewer incidents and no condemnations in terms of aggression from the Council, reflecting the political mood of the Council towards conciliation rather than confrontation with these States.

It is interesting to note that the condemnations so far do relate to quite limited *acts* of aggression, such as the Israeli bombing of the Palestine Liberation Organisation's headquarters in Tunis in 1985, and not to wider *wars* of aggression, in the form of full-scale attacks or invasions. Attempts have been made in the Security Council to make formal findings of aggression in relation to full-scale armed conflicts but none have succeeded. In 1967, during the Six Day War, the Soviet Union submitted a draft resolution condemning Israeli aggression and demanding the immediate withdrawal of Israeli troops from the Arab territories occupied by the Israelis.[61] This attempt to introduce a binding resolution under Chapter VII after an implied finding under Article 39 was too much for the pro-Israeli members of the Council. After much negotiation a consensus was reached on a recommendatory resolution, with no condemnatory overtones.[62] Although obvious superpower competition prevented such determinations, it did not prevent more limited findings of acts of aggression. Furthermore, it seems to be accepted that 'a war of aggression is a crime against international peace', giving rise to individual responsibility as well as State responsibility, whilst acts of aggression simply give rise to State responsibility.[63] This would tend to inhibit a collective finding of a 'war of aggression' because of the more onerous consequences.

During the drafting of the Charter at San Francisco, both Bolivia and the Philippines proposed to include a definition of aggression.[64] The Bolivian definition was similar to the Soviet proposal submitted to the Disarmament Conference in 1933,[65] in that it combined the enumeration of acts of aggression with a recognition of the Council's power to determine that other acts also constitute aggression.

At San Francisco, the committee concerned rejected the idea of a definition, stating that it would not be able to envisage or encompass new developments in warfare, besides which it might lead to the 'premature application of enforcement measures' through 'automatic Council action'.[66] Despite these objections the United Nations struggled for years to find an acceptable definition of aggression. When this finally happened on 14 December 1974 in the General Assembly, the formulation was similar to the Bolivian proposal.

The definition was a compromise between those States who favoured a generic definition and those who favoured an enumerative approach. The problem was resolved by the adoption of a mixed definition. Article 1 contains the generic definition. 'Aggression is the use of armed force against the sovereignty, territorial integrity or political independence of another State, or in any other manner inconsistent with the Charter of the United Nations'. This is similar to Article 2(4) of the Charter. Unlike Article 2(4), the definition makes it clear that for the purposes of a determination under Article 39 of aggression the Council is considering the use of armed force only.

Article 3 enumerates the acts that may qualify as aggression. Invasion, attack, bombardment, blockade and occupation are cases of direct aggression, whereas allowing territory to be used by another State to perpetrate aggression against a third State, and the sending of armed bands to carry out acts of force against another State are really cases of indirect aggression. The latter are additions to the already well-settled cases of direct aggression, and meet to a great extent the objection made at San Francisco that a definition would not be able to encompass modern methods of warfare.

However, although the definition introduces indirect aggression, it has never been found in a Security Council resolution, for as Broms, chairman of the Special Committee on the Definition of Aggression, points out, 'the case of aggression must be exceptionally clear and reprehensive before the term aggression has a chance of being adopted by consensus'.[67] Cases of indirect aggression are more likely to be unclear, although guidance on the interpretation of Article 3(g) of the Definition, which defines indirect aggression, can be found in the *Nicaragua* case.[68]

Articles 2 and 4 of the Definition preserve the discretionary powers of the Council. Article 2 states that the 'first use of armed force by a State in contravention of the Charter shall constitute *prima facie* evidence of an act of aggression' although the Council, in the light of all the evidence, may decide otherwise. Article 4 further states that acts enumerated in Article 3 'are not exhaustive and the Security Council may determine that other acts constitute aggression under the provisions of the Charter'.

Although the use of the term aggression in Council resolutions has increased since 1974, the definition has not resulted in a consistent and objective use of the term. The findings are mainly motivated by selective, discretionary and political factors and so the fears expressed by some[69] that the Definition would lead to a proliferation of unhelpful, condemnatory resolutions have not been realised. The loopholes provided in the Definition by retaining a balance in favour of the discretion of the Council have proved sufficient to save the Council the embarrassment of making an objective finding of aggression.

Although the Council may appear to be acting within the definition when it condemns South Africa and Israel, it is being somewhat selective because, irrespective of their treatment of blacks and Palestinians within their countries or territories under their occupation, they too are being subjected to armed force of an indirect nature which the Council ought to examine to see if it amounts to indirect aggression. However, although formal findings of 'aggression' are sparse, the appearance in Council resolutions of terms which are used to define aggression in Article 3 of the Definition have an increased significance since 1974. When the Council condemned the Iraqi 'invasion' of Kuwait on 2 August 1990 in resolution 660, it was, in effect, determining that Iraq was the aggressor. Given this implicit determination, it can be argued that the Council should no longer be afraid of making formal declaration of aggression.

The relevance of Article 51

It has been stated by the Chairman of the Special Committee on the Definition of Aggression, that most members thought that in defining armed aggression they were also providing a definition of 'armed attack' in Article 51.[70] This view is reinforced if one looks at the French text of Article 51 which uses the term 'agression armée'.[71] Article 51 is, alongside Article 2(4), one of the most important provisions concerning the use of force in international law. It states that 'nothing in the present Charter shall impair the inherent right of individual or collective self-defence if an armed attack occurs against a Member of the United Nations, until the Security Council has taken measures necessary to maintain international peace and security. Measures taken by Members in the exercise of this right of self defence shall be immediately reported to the Security Council . . .'.[72] It is this provision which attempts to define the competence of the Security Council *vis-à-vis* the traditional right of self-defence and to a certain extent it parallels municipal systems which outlaw the use of force by members of that society except in limited self-defence combined with a centralisation of coercive powers. It is quite clear that the Charter admits only two exceptions to the use of force in international law, first the right of self-defence in response to an armed attack, and secondly the authorisation of the use of military measures by the Security Council under Chapter VII of the Charter in response not only to aggression but to wider situations that threaten or breach international peace. It follows that it is important to determine the relationship between the two exceptions *in the case of an armed attack or armed aggression occurring against a State*.

The truncation of the Council's powers signified that there was no real or potential overlap between the two exceptions during the Cold War. The rivalry between the two superpowers led to a system of defensive alliances, whilst the collective security system was frozen. The military option was only used once in the Cold War period in response to an armed attack, in the case of the North Korean invasion of the South in 1950. This illustrates how close the two exceptions are on occasions in that the United States sent troops to the aid of the South immediately, an action obviously in collective self-defence although not stated as such.[73] This response was then transformed into a UN operation by the Security Council recommendation, in the absence of the Soviet Union, that States assist the South to resist the attack. Collective self-defence became collective security in this instance. The complications this caused will be looked at in chapter three.

The significant phrase in Article 51 in this context, is the requirement that the right of self-defence exists until the Security Council has taken 'measures necessary to maintain international peace and security'. Article 51 was inserted at a late stage at San Francisco in order that action in collective self-defence by regional organisations should not require Security Council authorisation under what was to become Article 53 of the Charter. However, the delegates were not prepared to allow a completely decentralised right of self-defence and so the phrase was inserted that would permit self-defence until the Security Council took over the role of combating the aggression.[74]

The problem remained mainly theoretical during the Cold War and only surfaced in the Gulf Crisis which started with the Iraqi invasion and occupation of Kuwait in August 1990. In the Falklands conflict of 1982, Argentina did argue at one point that the United Kingdom was precluded from acting in self-defence following the adoption of Security Council resolution 502 on 3 April which contained a mandatory demand that Argentina withdraw from the islands.[75] The resolution was clearly based on Article 40 of the UN Charter, but it would appear unacceptable that a demand for compliance with a mandatory provisional measure has the effect of precluding a State from acting in self-defence, since such a resolution cannot by itself be a sufficient alternative to the victim State's right to meet and repulse the aggression. Although a resolution containing 'measures', it did not contain 'measures necessary' to restore international peace and security. It is clear that 'measures' within the meaning of Article 51 must be either the authorisation of armed force or the imposition of mandatory sanctions (or both), by the Security Council. Furthermore, there are doubts about whether the imposition of sanctions by the Security Council can constitute measures that can be said to be 'necessary' to maintain, or more properly restore, international peace and security.

Measures within the meaning of Article 51 must be those that can effectively replace the State's right of self-defence, that is they must stop the aggression and remove the aggressor from the victim State's territory. Whereas, self-defence is generally restricted to a proportionate response to the armed attack, military action in pursuit of collective security objectives can extend further, possibly to remove the source of the aggression. This issue was raised both in the Korean war of 1950–53 and in the Gulf Crisis of 1990–91. A realistic interpretation of Article 51, and one that does not leave the victim State defenceless, is to say that only those measures that will be effective[76] in removing the aggression can be said to *suspend* the right of self-defence. The right must revive if the measures prove ineffective for to argue otherwise would again leave a victim State defenceless and still occupied. In the absence of collective security machinery which acts effectively to combat aggression, the system must permit States to protect themselves. International law has advanced to the stage where the wider doctrine of self-help has been reduced to a quite limited right to self-defence. It would appear premature, even with the recent resurgence in effective activity at the UN, to limit that right even further.

The Charter, in Article 39, states that the Council 'shall . . . decide what measures shall be taken in accordance with Articles 41 and 42, to maintain international peace and security'. Articles 41 and 42 contain the express power to decide on economic measures and military measures respectively. Obviously if the Security Council undertakes military action to repel aggression then the right of self-defence is lost, unless the action proves ineffective. In this respect, the United Nations effectively replaced the right of self-defence on behalf of South Korea in 1950 and Kuwait in 1991 when it authorised the use of force against North Korea and Iraq.

The major problem, which was highlighted for the first time during the

Gulf Crisis of 1990–91, was the question whether the right of self-defence can be said to be suspended when the Council has taken 'measures' in the form of mandatory economic sanctions within the terms of Article 41, Chapter VII of the UN Charter. By resolution 661 of 6 August 1990, the Security Council imposed mandatory economic sanctions against Iraq with the aim of forcing Iraqi compliance with the terms of resolution 660, which had demanded Iraqi withdrawal. In other words the 'measures' were imposed to remove Iraq from Kuwait, which would have been the objective of an action in self-defence of Kuwait. However, the United States-led Coalition forces from Western and Arab States were gathering in the Gulf in August to act in collective self-defence of Saudi Arabia if the Iraqi expansion continued, and in collective self-defence of the occupied State of Kuwait, at the request of the rulers of those countries.[77] The two main Coalition States, the United States and the United Kingdom, argued that their right of self-defence was not curtailed by the adoption of a resolution imposing sanctions, in particular one that affirmed 'the inherent right of individual or collective self-defence, in response to an armed attack by Iraq against Kuwait, in accordance with Article 51'.[78] The other permanent members, although far less vociferous, seemed to insist that Article 51 signified that the right of self-defence was lost as long as the Council was purporting to deal with it under Article 41, and that the only way that armed force could be used against Iraq was for the Security Council to take the next step up its ladder of powers and authorise military action.[79] Eventually, the United States sought the authorisation of the Security Council for limited force to be used against vessels suspected of breaching the embargo against Iraq,[80] and eventually the use of full-scale force to evict the Iraqis from Kuwait.[81] However, in doing so, the United States seemed to imply that it was seeking authorisation in order to make the operations politically acceptable to the world community, not out of any legal requirement in the Charter. Both the United Kingdom and the United States thought the authorisations were unnecessary, they simply gave the operations an 'additional' legal basis.[82]

It is a difficult to see an answer to these views, particularly in the light of the limited debate in the Council on such issues. The answer depends to a great extent on the effectiveness or otherwise of sanctions in removing aggression. An empirical analysis of sanctions and their impact will be left until chapter three. If it is concluded that they are an effective alternative to military coercion in removing an aggressor then they are 'measures' within the meaning of Article 51 and the right of self-defence ceases. However, the *prima facie* evidence is not strong. One can see, without looking in detail, that sanctions are a blunt instrument, perhaps more suitable to addressing threats to the peace within countries rather than acts of aggression, in that they are directed at the aggressor State's economy which will only very slowly effect its military capacity to hold on to the victim States's territory. It then becomes a question of how long the world community is prepared to wait for the possible withdrawal of an aggressor whilst all the time the victim State is under military occupation. On the other hand to allow self-defence as well as sanctions might end in an even more devastating conflict. There is no simple solution, although it is a problem we will return to in the next chapter.

The domestic jurisdiction limitation

Article 2(7) of the Charter provides that 'nothing contained in the present Charter shall authorise the United Nations to intervene in matters which are essentially within the domestic jurisdiction of any state or shall require the Members to submit such matters to settlement under the present Charter'; 'but this principle shall not prejudice the application of enforcement measures under Chapter VII'. The meaning of Article 2(7) is unclear. It has been argued that the limitation was intended to exclude all Security Council review, whether discussion or resolution, either under Chapter VI or by its recommendatory powers under Chapter VII when the situation it is faced with is essentially internal.[83] The provision expressly allows for enforcement measures which as we have discussed above would be economic and military measures under Articles 41 and 42.

An examination of the drafting process of the provision in Article 2(7) whereby enforcement action is expressly permitted, shows the delegates intended a wider exception. In the immediate aftermath of the Second World War and the atrocities committed against civilian populations by Germany, the French had proposed to confine the domestic jurisdiction limitation further by proposing that it would apply 'unless the clear violation of essential liberties and human rights constitutes itself a threat capable of compromising peace'.[84] The problem was finding the correct words to express the view that 'it would be proper in the interests of peace and justice, and in the preservation of human rights to interfere in the internal affairs of Member States'.[85] The Australian amendment that the domestic jurisdiction principle 'shall not prejudice the application of enforcement measures under Chapter VII' was rather clumsy. It did not fully express the views of the delegates and has given rise to technical difficulties.

In practice, the Security Council has developed its own interpretation as to what constitutes intervention and domestic jurisdiction. Of course a finding under Article 39 accompanied by the application of enforcement measures under Article 41 or Article 42 is exempt by the terms of Article 2(7) itself. The Council has taken the next logical step by adopting the practice that any finding under Article 39, whether or not combined with enforcement measures, is sufficient to internationalise the situation and so escape the grasp of Article 2(7). In fact this probably does no more than the delegates at San Francisco had in mind for Article 2(7).

For example, it has been argued that if it is accepted that the UN Force in the Congo (ONUC) was authorised pursuant to Article 40 (which is the non-enforcement provision of Chapter VII) it should have been the subject of the domestic jurisdiction limitation.[86] It must be remembered that the Council eventually made a finding of a threat to the peace in relation to the situation within the Congo.[87] Resolution 169 referred to resolution 161 which contained the finding of a threat while authorising the Secretary General to take vigorous action including the requisite measure of force in order to 'apprehend all foreign troops and mercenaries'.[88] The resolution also declared that 'all secessionist activities against the Republic of the Congo are contrary to the *Loi Fondementale* and Security Council decisions' and specifically demanded 'that such activities which are now taking place in Katanga shall cease forthwith'. This certainly appears to be interference in the internal affairs of the Congo which is the sort of activity *prima facie* prohibited by Article 2(7). Certain members expressed reservations about setting a dangerous precedent for the future, by putting the United Nations 'at the beck and call of any State faced with a problem of a dissident minority within its own borders'.[89]

The International Court advised that ONUC was not an enforcement measure under Article 42,[90] which leaves open the question considered in chapter eight whether it came instead within the terms of Article 40. If Article 40 is the correct Charter base for ONUC, according to a literal reading of Article 2(7), the exception to the domestic jurisdiction limitation for enforcement measures is inapplicable. However, this ignores the fact that when a situation is designated a threat to the peace it is inevitably taken out of the domestic realm and put into the international sphere. Any action within Chapter VII, whether enforcement or not is not limited by Article 2(7).

It is also true to say that the limitation contained in Article 2(7) is circumvented not only by a finding of a threat to the peace, but also by the finding that the situation is one of 'international concern'. 'This doctrine of international concern has seen service in the guise of a potential threat to the peace'.[91] Thus a finding of a potential menace can be seen not only as a link between Chapters VI and VII, but also as a means by which the Council can utilise the provisions of Chapter VI and the power to ask for voluntary measures in the face of the provisions of Article 2(7).

Indeed, as early as 1946, the Council interpreted Article 2(7) as allowing it to establish a Commission of Investigation under Article 34 in order to report on aspects of the Greek civil war.[92] Further, in the Spanish question, the Security Council set up a sub-committee to investigate the situation in Spain.[93] These two early examples highlight the fact that an investigation to ascertain the facts and, in the latter case, to make substantive recommendations, do not constitute examples of intervention. The sub-committee found the situation in Spain to be of 'international concern' and a 'potential menace to international peace'. It recommended action under Chapter VI in the form of a voluntary termination of diplomatic relations. Although no such resolution was adopted, the view that Article 2(7) was inapplicable in cases of international concern prevailed, the proposed resolution being vetoed by the Soviet Union on the ground that the situation was a threat to the peace and should have been dealt with by mandatory measures.[94]

A more recent example of the Council using its recommendatory powers in a superficially domestic situation is as regards South Africa. The Council has not found a general threat to the peace in relation to the system of apartheid in South Africa. However, it has adopted many resolutions of a recommendatory nature including a call for selective voluntary measures[95] after 1985 witnessed killings in the townships, further political detentions, suppression of freedom and the declaration of a state of emergency. South African objections based on Article 2(7) proved fruitless, because by characterising apartheid as a 'crime against humanity', the Council has recognised the situation as one of sufficient international concern to warrant collective humanitarian intervention using recommendatory measures.

Article 2(7) was a rather clumsy attempt to reconcile the doctrine of State sovereignty with the need to intervene in cases of international concern, which historically connotes the gross deprivation of human rights. However, it has been pointed out that the concepts of international concern and domestic jurisdiction are 'incapable of capture and crystallisation for all time. What is truly domestic today will not necessarily be so in five years time'.[96] Human rights abuses certainly appear to be of international concern, but even with the ending of the Cold War, there is still a disinclination to intervene within States guilty of quite serious human rights abuses. The doctrine of State sovereignty has been relatively unaffected by the end of superpower rivalry.

One exception to this reticence occurred in the aftermath of the war between Iraq and the Coalition acting under Security Council authority. The rebellion by the Kurds in the north and the Shias in the south was put down with extreme brutality by the still powerful Iraqi army. As we have seen the Security Council adopted resolution 688 on 5 April 1991 which was not supported by five members including China and India on the grounds that it constituted interference in the internal affairs of Iraq. This was despite the fact that although the resolution found that the repression threatened international peace, it did not impose sanctions. However, the Security Council maintained sanctions against Iraq under the auspices of the permanent cease-fire resolution, 687 of 3 April, which provided for a review every sixty days of the continuance of most sanctions 'in the light of the policies and practices of the government of Iraq'.

Resolution 688 on Iraq can be contrasted with the refusal of the Council even to have a meeting over the strife in Haiti in September 1991 after the elected government in that country had been overthrown by a military dictatorship. The ambassador of Haiti, a representative of the deposed government, had requested a meeting under Article 35 of the UN Charter. Members of the Council decided that it was an internal affair in which the Council should not become involved.[97] Admittedly there was a great difference in scale between the two situations in Iraq and in Haiti, with the latter being much smaller. However, this would mean that strife within relatively small countries cannot be of sufficient international concern or threaten international peace for Security Council involvement. One can also point to the large influx of refugees into Iran and Turkey during the Kurdish crisis, but again the difference was only one of scale with thousands of Haitian refugees fleeing the new regime in the days and months following the coup.

The Kurdish issue suggested greater UN involvement in internal affairs, particularly when the Western troops in northern Iraq to protect the Kurds in April and May were replaced by UN guards. However, whereas the Iraqis did not consent to the Western troops they gave formal consent to the UN guards,[98] illustrating the UN's fundamental respect for the sovereignty of a State. The exceptional nature of the Kurdish crisis was underlined in the special summit meeting of the Security Council on 31 January 1992 at which heads of State and government issued a general declaration on the future role of the Council. It was anticipated that the statement would contain mention of greater humanitarian intervention by the Security Council, but consensus requirements led to a bland statement, the only controversial aspect of which was the identification of the need to deal effectively with international terrorism. Western members of the Council, in the individual speeches, made references to human rights and democracy as being the bedrock of the international community, but other members, including Russia, concentrated on other areas, including disarmament. The Chinese Prime Minister made a pointed reference to the importance of the principle of non-intervention in internal affairs of States.[99] The summit accurately encapsulated the extent of the West's dominance of the Council. The other members have assented to the Council facing terrorism but have drawn the line on the issue of internal affairs, in particular they have not consented to the Council being used to promote democracy or human rights beyond those of a very basic nature such as self-determination in a colonial or racist context, and possibly those prohibiting acts of genocide.

The Council's mandatory power

One of the major improvements on the League of Nations was the investment of the primary UN organ with mandatory powers. A resolution

adopted in pursuance of these powers creates an international legal obligation on all members of the United Nations. Article 25 of the UN Charter
provides that 'the Members of the United Nations agree to accept and carry
out the decisions of the Security Council in accordance with the present
Charter'. Although the provision of mandatory powers is unusual, it is
clearly a binding treaty obligation for those States that are members of the
United Nations. Given that most States are members of the Organisation, a
mandatory decision of the Security Council can have a wide-ranging impact.
Treaty law would *prima facie* prohibit treaty obligations extending to non-
party States. However, Article 2(6) of the Charter provides that 'the
Organization shall ensure that states which are not Members of the United
Nations act in accordance with these Principles so far as is necessary for the
maintenance of international peace and security'.

It is possible to reconcile Article 2(6) of the Charter with general treaty
law by concentrating on the Principles of the UN Charter in Article 2 which
in particular contain the now customary provisions banning the use of force
in international relations. A State violating these principles is not only in
breach of its Charter obligations which may result in mandatory measures by
the Security Council, but is also in breach of customary international law
binding on all States. All States therefore are under an obligation to refrain
from recognising or assisting in the illegal act. In this respect non-member
States of the UN are bound to follow the Security Council's decisions if they
are concerned with enforcing the basic provisions of customary law concerning peace and security. The World Court recognised this in the *Namibia* case
in 1971. In discussing the obligations imposed by Security Council resolution
276 of 1970 which terminated South Africa's mandate, declared the South
African occupation of South West Africa/Namibia illegal, and called on 'all
States' to refrain from any dealings with South Africa which were
inconsistent with its illegal presence, the Court opined that although non-
member States were not bound by virtue of Articles 24 and 25 of the
Charter, 'the termination of the mandate and the declaration of the illegality
of South Africa's presence in Namibia are opposable to all States in the sense
of barring *erga omnes* the legality of a situation which is maintained in
violation of international law'. Given that the resolution of the Security
Council was furthering international law and it was adopted pursuant to the
UN powers as supervisory authority over mandated territories as successor
to the League, it was for non-member States 'to act in accordance with those
decisions'.[100]

A similar approach can be taken to the mandatory sanctions imposed by
the Security Council against Iraq following its invasion of Kuwait in resolution 661 on 6 August 1990. The resolution was legally binding on member
States by virtue of Article 25 of the UN Charter. Non-members were obliged
by customary international law not to recognise as legal the Iraqi invasion

and subsequent annexation and not to take any action which would encourage the Iraqis in their illegal acts.[101] One could go further and argue that since Iraq's aggression was breach of a customary obligation *erga omnes*, customary international law required all States to take measures to remove it, or at least to not to take action which would undermine measures taken by other States and by the UN to remove it. This argument comes close to making Security Council resolutions binding on all States, which was certainly the *prima facie* purpose of resolution 661 which called upon 'all States, including States non-members of the United Nations, to act strictly in accordance with the provisions of the present resolution'. However, few States on the Security Council thought that this imposed a legal obligation on non-member States, others seemed to opine that it was simply an encouragement for those States to comply.[102] Customary law obliges non-members *not* to take measures that would encourage the illegal acts. If the circumstances so require, this may oblige the non member State to take economic sanctions if they are necessary to fulfil this customary requirement, but these sanctions may be much more limited than those required by the Security Council. For instance in the case of Iraq, non-members were probably only obliged to take measures that would have ensured that there was no tacit recognition or encouragement of the Iraqi annexation such as not dealing with oil produced in Kuwait while under Iraqi occupation and not allowing Iraq to use any of Kuwait's assets overseas. Further measures, designed for wider purposes as may be set by the Security Council would appear to be optional for non-members under international law.[103]

Having looked at the external impact of the mandatory decisions of the Security Council we need to turn now to the constitutional issue of the extent of those mandatory powers. We are now concerned with the issue of whether the Council's use of mandatory decisions is limited to Chapter VII. Article 25 itself is not found within the confines of Chapter VII but is located in Chapter V of the Charter containing the general powers of the Council in Article 24(1), which confers on that body primary responsibility for the maintenance of international peace and security. Furthermore, a close reading of the specific powers of the Security Council will illustrate that although Chapter VI powers, concerning the pacific settlement of disputes, are mainly recommendatory, provision is made for 'decisions' in Article 37(2), while within Chapter VII we find provision for non-binding 'recommendations' in Article 39 amidst the more frequent provisions for binding 'decisions'.

Different factions of the Security Council have interpreted Article 25 in varying ways. The situation in Namibia has highlighted the controversy over Article 25. During a Council debate on the situation, the British representative stated that 'as a matter of law, my Government considers the

Security Council can only take decisions generally binding on Member States only when the Security Council has made a determination under Article 39', 'only in these circumstances are decisions binding under Article 25'.[104] In this statement he was disagreeing with the advisory opinion of the International Court of Justice on Namibia. The Court opined that Article 25 was not restricted in its application to Chapter VII since it was not located in Chapter VII, besides which Articles 48 and 49 of Chapter VII secured a binding effect for resolutions adopted under its auspices.[105] The Council resolution to which the British objected was resolution 269 of 12 August 1969 which 'decided' that 'the continued occupation of the Territory of Namibia by the South African authorities constitutes an aggressive encroachment on the authority of the United Nations' after reminding Members of the content of Article 25. The resolution did not contain an express or implied determination under Article 39 in spite of the suggestion that the United Nations was in some way the object of some sort of aggression. An express determination would, for example, be 'an act of aggression within the meaning of Article 39'. An implied finding would merely refer to an 'act of aggression'. Similar language, for example, 'an aggressive encroachment' is not usually sufficient to constitute an implied finding. Nevertheless the resolution invoked Article 25. All the Western powers on the Council abstained on this resolution indicating that the collective view of the West is to equate Article 25 with Chapter VII. Nevertheless, the World Court, in advocating an approach of careful scrutiny of Security Council resolutions to discover whether they are binding, opined that resolution 269 was 'adopted in conformity with the purposes and principles of the Charter and in accordance with its Articles 24 and 25' making it binding on all members of the United Nations including those States either abstaining or voting against.[106]

The views of the United States were also enunciated in the initial Council dealings with Namibia after the termination of South Africa's mandate by the General Assembly.[107] Initially, the Council concerned itself with the essentially peripheral matter of the trials by the Pretoria government of members of SWAPO. Although resolutions 245 and 246 originally contained references to Article 25,[108] these were deleted on the insistence of the United States, whose representative explained that 'among these changes is the omission of the reference to Article 25 of the Charter which we would have regarded as inappropriate for a resolution which was to be adopted under Chapter VI'.[109]

The Western view is probably based on the desire to provide a rough and ready, convenient and simple guide to the drafting of resolutions, which through constant reiteration by its adherents has taken on, for them, the status of international law.[110] Other States seem to adopt a more flexible, position more in line with the World Court's approach. The former Soviet

Union adopted this approach in 1973 during the debates of the Council on the Yom Kippur War. The East-West deadlock which had prevented the Council acting at the beginning of the war was overcome by the invitation of Secretary of State Kissinger to Moscow. The result was a resolution virtually forced through the Council by the superpowers which simply called on the parties to the conflict to 'terminate all military activity' no later than twelve hours after the adoption of the resolution, followed by the implementation of resolution 242 of 1967.[111] Non-compliance with the cease-fire resulted in another joint superpower sponsored resolution which confirmed the Council's 'decision' in the previous resolution and urged the combatants to 'return to the positions they occupied at the moment the cease-fire became effective'.[112] Although both resolutions had the appearance of being provisional measures under Article 40, an application of the Western view would mean that without a finding under Article 39, there can be no decision within the meaning of Article 25 and consequently the resolution can only be a recommendation adopted within the parameters of Chapter VI. The Soviet Union, while not actually citing Article 25, seemed to view both the resolutions as binding decisions,[113] although it must be pointed out that it was in the political interests of the Soviet Union to refer to 'decisions' in order to put pressure on Israel to comply because at the time the Arab States, favoured by the Soviet Union, were in retreat.

Professor Higgins has pointed out that the British view of Article 25 would effectively retitle Chapters VI and VII as 'Recommendations for the settlement of disputes' and 'Decisions with respect to the breakdown of peace' respectively. She suggests that although this may provide a good working basis, an equally good working basis would be 'achieved by looking to see whether a resolution was intended as a recommendation or a decision'.[114] If a resolution simply 'calls upon', 'urges' or generally is asking for voluntary cooperation or compliance then it is probably a recommendation, whereas in the Middle East crisis in 1973, the Council, particularly the sponsors, intended resolutions 338 and 339 to be binding without aggravating the situation by making a determination of a threat to or breach of the peace. Often political compromise will not allow a finding to be made under Article 39 of Chapter VII. However, this absence, does not, on occasions, prevent the production of a resolution which is a binding decision. Similarly a recommendation can be made under Article 39. This is expressly provided for in that provision.

Nevertheless, Western States seem to have maintained their position and with their current dominance of the Council many recent resolutions bear the mark of their approach to Chapter VII. Many of the resolutions dealing with the Iraqi invasion of Kuwait, whilst referring to the initial resolution, 660, which determined that the invasion was a breach of international peace within the meaning of Article 39, then simply state that the Council is 'acting under Chapter VII of the Charter'. While this meets the formal requirements of the Western approach, an examination of the contents of the resolutions reveals the development of the Council's powers beyond the literal meaning of Articles 39–42. Although as we shall see in chapter three, the Council used its economic and military powers as well as demanding a withdrawal under Article 40, it also adopted resolutions 'under Chapter VII' which demanded that Iraq release third State nationals from Iraq and Kuwait,[115] demanded that Iraq comply with its obligations as regards foreign diplomats,[116] reminded Iraq of its international responsibility for its invasion and occupation,[117] condemned Iraq for its attempt to alter the demographic composition of Kuwait,[118] as well as imposing far reaching cease-fire conditions upon Iraq after the war ended in April 1991.[119]

The Western insistence that only Chapter VII resolutions are binding has resulted in an artificial approach to the Charter. The resolutions listed above are really examples of the Council's general powers to maintain and restore international peace and security derived from Article 24 which are clearly intended to be binding by Article 25. The Western States may have been advised to have used the Council's general mandatory powers as identified by the World Court in the *Namibia* case rather than attempting to squeeze the resolutions into Chapter VII.

Notes

1 J. Arntz, *Der Begriff der Friedensbedrohung in Satzung und Praxis der Vereinten Nationen* (1975).

2 H. Kelsen, *The Law of the United Nations*, 727 (1951).

3 R. Higgins, *The Development of International Law through the Political Organs of the United Nations*, 266 (1963).

4 See dissenting opinion of Judge Weeramantry, *Case Concerning Questions of Interpretation and Application of the 1971 Montreal Convention arising from the Aerial incident at Lockerbie (Libyan Arab Jamahiriya v USA)*, hereinafter referred to as the *Lockerbie* case (provisional measures) I.C.J. *Rep.* 1992, 114 at 163–81. The Court delivered an almost identical judgement in the Libyan case against the UK, I.C.J. *Rep.* 1992, 3.

5 J. P. Cot and A. Pellet, *La Charte des Nations Unies*, 655 (1985).

6 SC Res. 232, 21 UN SCOR Resolutions 7 (1966).

7 SC Res. 418, 32 UN SCOR Resolutions 5 (1977).

8 SC Res. 221, 21 UN SCOR Resolutions 5 (1966).

9 J. C. Nkala, *The United Nations, International Law and the Rhodesian Independence Crisis*, 77–90 (1985).

10 UN doc. S/18785 (1987), vetoed on 9.4.1987; see SC 2747 mtg, 42 UN SCOR (1987).

11 SC Res. 161, 16 UN SCOR Resolutions 2 (1961).

12 GA Res. 1514, 15 UN GAOR Supp. (No. 16) 66 (1960).

13 SC Res. 312, 27 UN SCOR Resolutions 10 (1972).

14 See SC 1639 mtg, 27 UN SCOR 14 (1972), India.
15 SC Res. 688, 46 UN SCOR Resolutions (1991).
16 SC Res. 733, 47 UN S/PV (1992).
17 UNCIO, vol. 3, 13.
18 R. B. Russell and J. E. Muther, *A History of the United Nations Charter*, 669–70 (1958).
19 SC Res. 4, 1 UN SCOR Resolutions 8 (1946).
20 Report of the Sub-Committee on the Spanish Question, 1 UN SCOR Special Supp. (No. 2) 4–5 (1946).
21 SC Res. 181, 18 UN SCOR Resolutions 7 (1963).
22 GA Res. 2054, 20 UN GAOR Supp. (No. 14) 26 (1965).
23 SC Res. 282, 25 UN SCOR Resolutions 12 (1970).
24 UN doc. S/9882 (1970).
25 SC 1549 mtg, 25 UN SCOR 3 (1970).
26 UN doc. S/6928 (1965).
27 UN doc. S/6929 (1965).
28 H. Strack, *Sanctions: The Case of Rhodesia*, 23–36 (1978).
29 GA Res. 1889, 18 UN GAOR Supp. (No. 15) 46 (1963).
30 SC 1265 mtg, 20 UN SCOR 15, 6, 16 (1965).
31 SC Res. 713, 46 UN SCOR Resolutions 1991.
31a For texts of SC Res. 731 and 748, see 31 *I.L.M.* (1992), 732, 750.
32 SC Res. 54, 3 UN SCOR Resolutions 22 (1948).
33 SC 1340 mtg, 21 UN SCOR 4 (1966).
34 SC Res. 556, 39 UN SCOR Resolutions 4 (1984).
35 UN doc. S/18087 (1986), vetoed at SC 2686 mtg, 41 UN SCOR (1986).
36 See SC Res. 567, 571, 574, 40 UN SCOR Resolutions 16–18 (1985).
37 SC Res. 161, 16 UN SCOR Resolutions 2 (1961).
38 SC Res. 353, 29 UN SCOR Resolutions 7 (1974).
39 UN doc. S/9394 (1969).
40 SC 1503 mtg, 24 UN SCOR 1 (1969).
41 SC 2982 mtg, 46 UN S/PV (1991).
42 SC 3009 mtg, 46 UN S/PV (1991); SC 3039 mtg, 47 UN S/PV (1992).
43 SC Res. 635, 44 UN SCOR Resolutions (1989).
44 SC 3033 mtg, 47 UN S/PV (1992).
45 UKTS No. 10 (1974), Cmnd 5524.
46 SC 3063 mtg, 47 UN S/PV 72 (1992).
47 GA Res. 2625, 25 UN GAOR Supp. (No. 28) 121 (1970).
48 *Lockerbie* case (provisional measures), I.C.J. *Rep.* 1992, 114 at 126.
49 For example, *ibid.*, at 142 (Judge Shahabuddeen). See further T. M. Franck, 'The powers of appreciation: who is the ultimate guardian of UN legality', 86 *A.J.I.L.* (1992), 519. For the presumption against *ultra vires* see *Certain Expenses of the United Nations Case*, I.C.J. *Rep.* 1962, 151 at 168.
50 SC 171 mtg, 2 UN SCOR (1947).
51 SC 417 mtg, 4 UN SCOR (1949).
52 SC 473 mtg, 5 UN SCOR (1950).
53 SC Res. 82, 5 UN SCOR Resolutions 4 (1950).
54 SC 473 mtg, 5 UN SCOR 3–7 (1950).

55 SC 2932 mtg, 45 UN SCOR (1990).
56 L. M. Goodrich, E. Hambro and P. S. Simons, *The Charter of the United Nations*, 296, 2nd ed. (1969).
57 41 *A.J.I.L.* (1947), 172.
58 GA Res. 3314, 29 UN GAOR Supp. (No. 31) 142 (1974).
59 Three examples are: See SC Res. 387, 31 UN SCOR Resolutions 10 (1976) re Angola; SC Res. 466, 35 UN SCOR Resolutions 17 (1980) re Zambia; SC Res. 568, 40 UN SCOR Resolutions 20 (1985) re Botswana.
60 SC Res. 573, 40 UN SCOR Resolutions 23 (1985) re PLO base in Tunis; SC Res. 611, 43 UN SCOR Resolutions (1988), re assassination of Abu Jihad.
61 UN doc. S/7951/Rev 2 (1967).
62 SC Res. 242, 22 UN SCOR Resolutions 8 (1967).
63 Article 5(2) of the 1974 Definition of Aggression.
64 See UNCIO, vol. 3, docs. 577–9, 535–42.
65 See 5 Records of the Conference for the Reduction and Limitation of Armaments, League of Nations publication, Ser.D, 535–42.
66 UNCIO, vol. 12, doc. 505.
67 B. Broms, 'The definition of aggression', 154 *Recueil des Cours* (1977), 299, at 378.
68 *Case Concerning Military and Paramilitary Activities in and Against Nicaragua*, I.C.J. *Rep.* (1986), 14, at 103–4.
69 For example, J. I. Garvey, 'The UN definition of aggression: law and illusion in the context of collective security', 17 *Virginia Journal of International Law* (1977), 177, at 178.
70 Broms, 154 *Recueil des Cours* (1977), 370.
71 Cot and Pellet, *La Charte*, 772.
72 On the reporting requirement see D. W. Greig, 'Self-defence and the Security Council: what does Article 51 require?', 40 *I.C.L.Q.* (1991), 366, at 367, 387.
73 Statement by President Truman, 27 June 1950, *United States Policy in the Korean Crisis*, 18 (1950).
74 Russell and Muther, *History of the UN Charter*, 699–706. UNCIO, vol. 12, 687.
75 SC 2360 mtg, 37 UN SCOR (1982).
76 *Ibid.*, Sir Anthony Parsons, UK.
77 UN docs S/21492, S/21501 (1990).
78 See for example, Prime Minister Thatcher's statement in the House of Commons, *Hansard*, H.C., 6th series, vol. 7, 737. For US position see SC 2937 mtg, 45 UN S/PV 33 (1990). See also *Oppenheim's International Law*, 9th ed. vol. 1, p. 423 n. 22 (1992).
79 *The Independent*, 9 November 1990, USSR; *The Observer*, 11 November 1990, France and China. See also *The Independent*, 9 November 1990 for statement to this effect by the Secretary General.
80 SC Res. 665, 45 UN SCOR Resolutions (1990).
81 SC Res. 678, 45 UN SCOR Resolutions (1990).
82 SC 2938 mtg, 45 UN S/PV 26, 47 (1990).
83 D. R. Gilmour, 'The meaning of intervene within Article 2(7) of the United Nations Charter' 16 *I.C.L.Q.* (1967), 330, at 349.
84 UNCIO, vol. 3, 386.

85 Report of the Conference held at San Francisco by the Rt Hon. Peter Frazer, Chairman of the New Zealand delegation, NZ Dept of External Affairs publication, No. 11, 28.
86 N. T. Kasser, 'The legal limits on the use of international force through United Nations practice', 35 *Revue Egyptienne de Droit International* (1979), 163, at 207.
87 SC Res. 161, 16 UN SCOR Resolutions 2 (1961).
88 SC Res. 169, 16 UN SCOR Resolutions 3 (1961).
89 SC 976 mtg, 16 UN SCOR para. 15 (1961), UK.
90 *Certain Expenses of the United Nations Case*, I.C.J. *Rep*. 1962, 151.
91 Higgins, *The Development of International Law*, 77.
92 SC Res. 15, 1 UN SCOR Resolutions 8 (1946).
93 SC Res. 4, 1 UN SCOR Resolutions 8 (1946).
94 SC 47 mtg, 1 UN SCOR (1946).
95 SC Res. 569, 40 UN SCOR Resolutions 8 (1985).
96 Higgins, *The Development of International Law*, 61.
97 SC 3011 mtg, 46 UN S/PV (1991).
98 UN doc. 20 May 1991.
99 SC 3046 mtg, 47 UN S/PV (1992).
100 *Legal Consequences for States of the Continued Presence of South Africa in Namibia (South West Africa) Notwithstanding Security Council Resolution 276 (1970)*, I.C.J. *Rep*. 1971, 16, at para. 126.
101 SC Res. 662, 45 UN SCOR Resolutions (1990), para. 2.
102 SC 2933 mtg, 45 UN S/PV (1990).
103 UN doc. S/21585 (1990).
104 SC 1598 mtg, 26 UN SCOR 5 (1971). France expressed a similar view at 2.
105 *Namibia* case, I.C.J. *Rep*. 1971, 16, at para. 113.
106 *Ibid*., paras. 114–15.
107 GA Res. 2145, 21 UN GAOR Supp. (No. 16) 2 (1966).
108 SC Res. 245 and 246, 23 UN SCOR Resolutions 1–2 (1968).
109 SC 1397 mtg, 23 UN SCOR (1968).
110 R. Higgins, 'The advisory opinion on Namibia. Which UN Resolutions are binding under Article 25 of the Charter?', 21 *I.C.L.Q.* (1972), 270, at 283.
111 SC Res. 338, 28 UN SCOR Resolutions 10 (1973).
112 SC Res. 339, 28 UN SCOR Resolutions 11 (1973).
113 SC 1751 mtg, 28 UN SCOR 8–10 (1973).
114 Higgins, 21 *I.C.L.Q.* (1972), 283.
115 SC Res. 664, 45 UN SCOR Resolutions (1990).
116 SC Res. 667, 45 UN SCOR Resolutions (1990).
117 SC Res. 674, 45 UN SCOR Resolutions (1990).
118 SC Res. 677, 45 UN SCOR Resolutions (1990).
119 SC Res. 687, 707, 715, 46 UN SCOR Resolutions (1991).

CHAPTER THREE

Powers, practice and effectiveness of the Security Council

Having examined the limitations on the competence of the Security Council, both in terms of politics and law, we will now examine the development and use of the Council's powers, within those limitations. As has been suggested in chapter two, there has been some blurring of the distinction between Chapters VI and VII and this will be reflected in the analysis below. Nevertheless, the basic structure of the Charter in terms of the Council's powers remains intact after forty years of that body's practice. The array of powers available to the Security Council has been described in terms of 'une gradation d'intensité des pouvoirs',[1] culminating in the provisions of Chapter VII.

The development of the Charter provisions concerning collective measures was the main preoccupation of the sponsoring powers at San Francisco in their quest for collective security. As we have seen, the contents of Chapter VII were not greatly questioned by the smaller powers. The only significant amendments to the Dumbarton Oaks proposals were the removal of the provision linking Chapter VI to Chapter VII; and to accept readily a Chinese proposal for the insertion of a provision enabling the Council to call for the adoption of provisional measures. The proposals regarding pacific settlement were to prove more novel and problematic both to the sponsoring powers and to the other delegates at San Francisco.

Chapter VI of the United Nations' Charter arose out of Chapter VIII A of the Dumbarton Oaks proposals. The latter had 'the doubtful distinction of being regarded as one of the most poorly drafted sections' which necessitated a multitude of amendments.[2] In fact the amendments probably created more confusion than the untouched proposals. The proposals were firmly based on the concept of the Security Council as a policeman. This was emphasised in the proposals by placing the Council's powers of investigation at the head of the section containing powers of pacific settlement.

The main action the Council could take under the proposals for pacific settlement was primarily to call on the parties to the dispute to settle it by the peaceful means enumerated in the third paragraph of Chapter VIII A. If the dispute continued the Council could then utilise its powers in paragraph 5 to 'recommend appropriate procedures or methods of adjustment' or move into the enforcement powers contained in section B by means of paragraph 1 of section B.

The original proposals did recognise a 'situation' as well as a 'dispute' but the possible measures outlined above only applied to 'disputes'. The amendments to the proposals extended to the Council powers to give it a somewhat quasi-judicial or arbitral role. One of the amendments to this effect was to empower it to 'recommend appropriate procedures and methods of adjustment' to 'situations' as well as 'disputes' in Article 36(1) of the Charter. Theoretically it is the Council only which can recognise a 'situation likely to endanger the maintenance of international peace and security' in Article 34, for the obligation placed on Members to settle their disputes by peaceful means contained in Article 33 only applies to 'disputes'. This extends the Council's powers of determining the nature of events that endanger peace and hence is an enhancement of its judicial powers. Practically, however, States will often refer situations as well as disputes to the Council under Article 35, and although the Council could, by itself, determine jurisdiction under Article 34, it rarely does so, nor has it attempted to distinguish between a dispute and a situation.

Goodrich, Hambro and Simons summarise the major changes in the Dumbarton Oaks proposals for pacific settlement made at San Francisco.[3] The proposals were rearranged so as to 'give pride of place to the obligation of the parties to seek a solution to their disputes by peaceful means'. The primary emphasis of the Members' obligation to settle in Article 33(1) not only recognises that without some cooperation by the parties to the dispute settlement will be hard to obtain, it also illustrates the greater emphasis on the envisaged judicial role of the Council. If the parties fail to settle out of the Council, they may be subject to settlement not necessarily by the Council but with the (perhaps unwelcome) help of the Council; a process broadened by the second major amendment of enabling the Council to recommend 'terms' as well as 'procedures' for settlement embodied in Article 37(2). In fact, the addition of Articles 37 and 38 to the proposals were intended to invest the Council with quasi-judicial powers. The confusion is created because the change of emphasis from policeman to judge did not involve a wholesale revision of the Dumbarton Oaks proposals, instead the judicial provisions were tacked on so that the fundamental role the Council should play in relation to international disputes is unclear. Only an examination of the Council's practice will help us to understand the role it has created for itself.

Supervision of the obligation to settle peacefully

Article 33(1) of the Charter imposes upon members an obligation to settle disputes 'the continuance of which' are 'likely to endanger the maintenance of international peace and security', by peaceful means. It lists some examples of methods whereby this obligation could be fulfilled such as negotiation, mediation, arbitration and resort to regional arrangements. Article 33(2) states that, 'the Security Council shall, when it deems necessary, call upon the parties to settle their disputes by such means' as contained in paragraph (1). Despite the inclusion of the word 'shall' instead of 'may', this provision does not purport to impose a mandatory obligation on the Council to enforce in some way the provisions of Article 33(1), for it only operates when the Council deems it necessary, which in theory should be when it has found the basic requirement of a danger to international peace and security. The Council's role under Article 33 is one of supervision of the obligation to settle placed on members.

The effective use of this power would not only act as a reminder to States of their duties under the Charter, but also as a warning of future Council action under the other provisions of Chapter VI or, if the States concerned continue to be in breach of their obligation, of the possibility of Council action under Chapter VII. A Presidential statement, made with the unanimous support of all the Council, is often preferable, for it can be made quickly and is illustrative of the mood of the Council towards a continuance of the conflict, or if the Council is purporting to take preventative measures, towards future breaches.

In 1982, with an Argentinian invasion of the Falklands imminent, the President of the Council made a statement on the same day that the Council was convened at the request of the United Kingdom.[4] It called upon Britain and Argentina 'to exercise the utmost restraint at this time and in particular to refrain from the use or threat of force in the region and to continue to search for a diplomatic solution'.[5] Although a balanced reminder, the statement was a warning to Argentina not to invade. The Argentinians needed a fair degree of international support if they were to maintain their hold on the islands, but the statement reflected unanimous Council opposition to invasion. The Argentinians misread the signs and carried out their threat to the almost unanimous condemnation of the Council.[6]

The Council then found a breach of the peace and demanded withdrawal,[7] which although not complied with, effectively put Argentina in the wrong, helped to isolate it internationally, and contributed to Argentina's defeat in that it tacitly supported the British stance in support of principles of international law, though not necessarily the use of force in defence of those principles.

During the Cold War, the use of Article 33(2) was sometimes the only measure available to the Council. In 1983, the United States' objection to any Security Council interference in the Central American region relaxed slightly with the introduction of the OAS-supported Contadora group's peace efforts. This proved to be sufficient regionalisation to enable the United States to support resolution 530 which expressed the Council's concern at 'the danger of military confrontation between Honduras and Nicaragua'.[8] Although the resolution was similar to the previously vetoed draft resolution,[9] it put more emphasis on the efforts of the Contadora group and so represented a particular application of the Council supervising the obligation imposed by Article 33(1), namely of 'resort to regional agencies or arrangements'. It represented a minimum measures resolution aimed at securing the support of the United States.

Sometimes this attitude was taken to extremes, most notably during the horrific and prolonged Gulf War between Iran and Iraq. Although the initial Council call in 1980 to Iran and Iraq within the meaning of Article 33(2)[10] was supplemented by other recommendatory Chapter VI resolutions,[11] it took seven years of bloody conflict before the necessary consensus could be achieved to enable the Council to adopt unanimously resolution 598 on 20 July 1987 which contained a mandatory demand for a cease-fire within the terms of Chapter VII.

With the Cold War over one may hope that such procrastination will cease. The obligation to settle disputes peacefully is primarily to be fulfilled before conflict breaks out, when there is a danger to the peace but not yet a breach of the peace.[12] To extend the Council's supervision of the obligation into the conflict stage would appear to be an abrogation of the Council's responsibility to deal with a breach of the peace, unless it is a prelude to more positive action. A recommendation that belligerents settle their disputes by peaceful means is going to be ignored. Such a call *before* the outbreak of hostilities could act as a warning to States not to use force, which may be particularly powerful with the current cooperation between the permanent members which may more readily indicate that the call will be followed by enforcement measures.

It may be hypothesised that such a veiled warning on 1 August 1990, when the talks between Iraq and Kuwait on oil quotas and disputed territory broke down and the Iraqis massed 100,000 troops and 300 tanks on the border between the two countries, might have indicated to Iraq the consequences of any invasion. Unfortunately, the Council only met after the invasion and immediately adopted a resolution 660 within the terms of Articles 39 and 40. Interestingly the resolution also called upon Iraq and Kuwait 'to begin immediately intensive negotiations for the resolution of their differences and supports all efforts in this regard, and especially those of the League of Arab States'. This call would have had a greater impact if it had been made one day earlier. The Gulf crisis revealed a new edge to the Council's resolve

to combat aggression, but it did not reveal any great development in post
Cold War preventive diplomacy.

Investigation

The Council's preventative function would be greatly increased if it was
supplied with a constant update of information on potential conflict zones
and if it met without relying on one of the disputants bringing the matter to
the attention of the Security Council under Article 35 of the UN Charter.
Alternatively the Secretary General could more readily use his powers
under Article 99 of the Charter 'to bring to the attention of the Security
Council any matter which in his opinion may threaten the maintenance of
international peace and security'.

Investigatory bodies established by the Security Council to ascertain the
facts of a dispute are relatively rare. The Charter basis for such bodies is to
be located in a combination of Articles 34 and 29, although they are rarely
cited in the enabling resolutions. Often the body's function will go beyond
mere fact finding and enter the realm of good offices and peacekeeping. In
this section an attempt will be made to keep the discussion centred on
investigatory bodies, the true basis of which is Article 34. Good offices
committees and peacekeeping bodies have different constitutional bases
and are discussed later. Article 34 provides that 'the Security Council may
investigate any dispute or any situation in order to determine whether the
continuance of the dispute or situation is likely to endanger the maintenance
of international peace and security'.

During the early years of Council practice, some confusion arose from the
fact that this provision did not confer a general power of investigation on the
Council. The power appears to be confined to ascertaining whether the
dispute or situation came within the parameters of Chapter VI. Indeed, the
sub-committee on the Spanish question established in 1946 was directed to
ascertain whether the activities of the Franco regime constituted a situation
within the meaning of Article 34 or Article 39.

However, very soon after, the Council showed its willingness to go
beyond a strict interpretation of Article 34 when, in 1946, it established a
Commission of Investigation to examine certain frontier incidents on the
Greek borders.[13] The Commission not only ascertained the facts but made
several wide-ranging recommendations,[14] which were not adopted by the
Council because of Soviet opposition.[15]

A method used to circumvent the superpower veto in the Cold War was by
applying a procedural vote to the establishment of such a body. This was
done in 1959 to establish a sub-committee to investigate a complaint by Laos
despite the negative Soviet vote. The legality of this method is doubtful and
it has not become an established feature in the practice of the Security

Council.

Another problem as regards fact finding during the Cold War was that even in the areas beyond the superpowers' interests where Council investigation was possible, the body established to undertake the task was often faced with a *fait accompli*. After alleged attacks by Portuguese forces on the independent African States of Guinea in 1970 and Senegal in 1971, the Council established Special Missions to ascertain whether such attacks had occurred.[16] The Mission's report on Guinea led to the Council determining that the attack constituted a threat to the peace.[17] However, since the attacks were over, the Council could only condemn them, warn Portugal against further attacks, and demand that Portugal pay compensation to Guinea.

Often in these cases where the aggression was short-lived and the *status quo* has been re-established, the investigation's only purpose was to find the guilty party which proves virtually impossible in the case of mercenary aggression and difficult in the case of guerrilla activities. After a mercenary attack in 1977 aimed at overthrowing the government of Benin, a Special Mission could only report that the attackers worked for pecuniary motives and that the financiers could not be found.[18] This resulted in a general Council condemnation of mercenary aggression.[19]

Although there were other examples of fact finding during the Cold War, they can be characterised generally as being selective and often ineffectual,[20] although on other occasions they did form the basis of a later peaceful settlement or at least a stabilisation of the conflict with the assistance of a UN peacekeeping force.[21] As early as 1988, with superpower relations beginning to thaw, there was an indication of greater fact finding by the Security Council, when a mission was sent to Nicaragua,[22] and was a foretaste of the regional settlement process started by the Guatemala Accords of 1987 and culminating in the UN supervision of peaceful elections in Nicaragua in 1990.

Nevertheless, fact finding by the Security Council is not undertaken as a matter of course; it often relies on a patchwork of sources including established peacekeeping or observation teams, the Secretary General and his staff, and the occasional formal fact finding body mandated by a Security Council resolution. Whatever the source, fact finding can only be undertaken with the consent of the State or States involved in the dispute. The Security Council has not attempted to invoke a mandatory power to send a fact finding mission into a State, although we shall see that in the Gulf Crisis, after the conflict between Iraq and the Coalition forces ended in March 1991, Iraq was subjected to very intrusive missions. Although Iraq consented to them when it agreed to the permanent cease-fire in Security Council resolution 687 on 3 April 1991, it really had little choice given the threat of further military actions against it.

Without a mandatory power to order a State to accept a fact finding mission, and in view of the fact that the Gulf Crisis was exceptional in the sense that military action *preceded* the missions when normally they should be one of the first steps taken by the Council, fact finding is not going to be properly institutionalised. If all members of the Security Council accepted that it did have the power to oblige States to accept a fact finding mission by making it clear in the enabling resolution that it was a binding resolution under Articles 34 and 25, there does not appear to be any legal limitation on this power. Article 34 itself is not restricted to recommendations, although if one accepts the Western view that it is only under Chapter VII that binding decisions can be made then such a power is not contained in the Charter.

As we have seen from the introduction to this chapter, the Security Council has an inherent quasi-judicial power, one that it has used sparingly for most of its life as the political pressures of the Cold War led to resolutions based on compromise rather than on judicial-type rulings. However, with the end of the Cold War the Council has increasingly used this power to condemn States for breaches of international law, rather akin to the practice of the General Assembly. Any basic judicial process would commence with a determination of the facts before moving on to the judicial decision,[23] yet in the Security Council, the facts are often not clarified, or if they are, the Council has already condemned.

Following disturbances in Jerusalem on 8 October 1990 which resulted in the deaths of several Arabs, the Security Council unanimously condemned the acts of violence committed by the Israeli Security forces while calling on Israel to abide by the Fourth Geneva Convention Relative to the Protection of Civilian Persons in Time of War of 1949,[24] as well as supporting the Secretary General's decision to send a mission to examine the circumstances surrounding the events in Jerusalem and to report on ways to protect Palestinian civilians under Israeli occupation.[25] Not surprisingly Israel refused consent and was duly condemned for its intransigence by the Council.[26] Indeed, the judicial process seemed to be completely reversed when nearly one month after the shootings and the Council's condemnation of Israel, the Security Council watched an amateur video tape submitted as evidence that the shootings were unprovoked.[27]

It is questionable whether this rather summary approach to justice will be improved as a result of a recent General Assembly resolution, supported by all member States, entitled the Declaration on Fact Finding by the United Nations in the Field of the Maintenance of Peace and Security, adopted without a vote on 17 January 1992, following a report of the Sixth Committee which in turn was based on work by the Special Committee on the Charter.[28] Although the resolution recognised 'that the ability of the United Nations to maintain international peace and security depends to a large extent on its acquiring detailed knowledge about the factual circumstances of any dispute or situation', and that the competent organs of the UN should endeavour to undertake fact finding activities that should be 'comprehensive, objective, impartial and timely', it still recognised that 'the sending of a United Nations fact finding mission to the territory of any State requires the prior consent of that State'. Although the Assembly encouraged States to adopt 'a policy of admitting . . . fact finding missions to their territory', the UN's respect for the sovereignty of its members undermines the proper institutionalisation of fact finding, whether it be by the Security Council, the General Assembly, or the Secretary General. The fact is that even when States consent to such missions, they are often too late to contribute to prevent a conflict breaking out, and if a conflict is already under-way, they do little towards its peaceful settlement. The sending of a fact finding mission in May 1992 to the disputed enclave of Nagorno Karabach, which is in Azerbaijan but is claimed by Armenia, was endorsed by the Security Council months after the dispute, which had been a long-running dispute between Soviet Republics, had become internationalised with the breakup of the Soviet Union in December 1991.[29]

The settlement of disputes

Article 36(1) of the Charter provides that 'the Security Council may, at any stage of a dispute of a nature referred to in Article 33 or of a situation of a like nature, recommend appropriate procedures or methods of adjustment'. Paragraph 2 of the Article directs the Council to 'take into consideration any procedures for the settlement of the dispute which have already been adopted by the parties'. This is a reversal of the procedure envisaged by Article 33 but it is also a recognition that the Security Council can recommend 'appropriate procedures or methods of adjustment' to 'situations' as well as 'disputes'.

The terms of Article 36 can be applied to a variety of situations in the absence of any statement in the resolution of its Charter base. Nonmandatory resolutions calling for a cease-fire and withdrawal of troops can be seen as 'appropriate procedures or methods of adjustment' as can recommendations of settlement. This latter power can also be derived from Article 37(2) which empowers the Council to recommend 'such terms of settlement as it may consider appropriate'. When the Council makes a recommendation for settlement it does not state which provision in the Charter it is using and so one must assume that, in practice, the Council's powers as regards settlement have been amalgamated. However, it could be said that Article 36 empowers the Security Council to establish the modalities for settlement or the framework within which a settlement process may be undertaken, whereas Article 37 enables it to recommend directly the terms of settlement.

Before examining the Council's use of these powers, it is worth mentioning the little utilised but potentially wide power conferred on the Council by Article 38, which provides that the Council 'may, if all the parties to any dispute so request, make recommendations to the parties with a view to a pacific settlement of the dispute'. The dispute does not have to cross the threshold of being a danger to international peace and security. However, despite the fact that by means of this provision the Council could involve itself in any kind of dispute as a mediator or conciliator, at the parties' request, it has not been used in this way. During the Indonesian question, the Council appeared to have Article 38 in mind when it adopted resolution 31 on 21 August 1947, which resolved to tender the Council's 'good offices' in the form of a Committee of Three if the parties so requested. There can be little doubt, however, that the Indonesian situation was, at the very least, a danger to international peace and security, although the Council did not make such a determination, nor did it make one under Article 39.

Good offices

The phase of the Indonesian question which ended with a truce between the Netherlands and Indonesia with the signing of the Renville Agreement[30] in 1948 represented a relative early success for the Council in its role as a peacemaker. Resolution 27 of 1 August 1947 called for a cease-fire and called on the parties 'to settle their disputes by arbitration or by other peaceful means'.[31] The Council then began to build on the fragile cease-fire that ensued. Resolution 30 noted with satisfaction the steps taken by the parties to implement resolution 27, steps which included a Dutch statement that it intended to implement the Linggadjati Agreement.[32] It also noted the request by Indonesia for the creation of a commission of observers. On this last point the Council acted quickly by requesting, in the same resolution, that governments with consuls in Batavia jointly prepare reports on the state of the cease-fire for the Council. Then came the creation of the Committee of Three by resolution 31. The Council was creating the machinery to facilitate the reaching of an agreement; it did not, at this stage, recommend one itself, although its resolutions implicitly favoured the implementation of the Linggadjati Agreement. After clarifying the meaning of the earlier resolutions, the Council urged the Committee of Three (alternatively called the Committee of Good Offices) to help the parties reach an agreement.[33]

On 24 December 1947, the Committee of Good Offices addressed an informal message to the parties containing suggested terms for a truce agreement. The Renville Agreement between the Netherlands and Indonesia provided for an immediate cease-fire, the establishment of demilitarised zones, and the supervision of arrangements by the military assistants of the Committee of Good Offices. It also contained principles governing negotiations towards a political settlement. The effectiveness of the Council depended, to a great extent, on the participation and coop-eration in good faith of both parties to the dispute. The Dutch, although still denying the Council's jurisdiction, viewed use of the Council as the only viable means of achieving a peaceful solution.[34] Good offices resolutions do not work when the parties refuse to cooperate or give only token coop-eration. This may be a truism, but it illustrates the inherent and unavoidable weakness of the Council in its pacification role as a whole.

Sometimes the parties to a dispute may appear willing to reach an agreement with the help of the United Nations. In the Cyprus question the two main disputants, Greece and Turkey, have consented, as has the Cypriot government, to the good offices of the Secretary General.[35] How-ever, ever since the Secretary General commenced his task, the Turkish government has gone about consolidating its grip on the northern part of the island. 'Good offices' implies that the Secretary General should help the parties to reach an agreement. In the Cyprus case, it is the Secretary General who has, so far, made proposals for settlement. Several plans have failed. The disputants have so far displayed token, not genuine, consent to the settlement process.

In 1964, the Security Council emplaced a peacekeeping force in Cyprus to stabilise the situation whilst encouraging the Secretary General in a good offices mission to seek a peaceful solution.[36] This was quite usual during the Cold War and as we shall see when examining peacekeeping in Part Three of this book, it can lead to a stalling of the peace process as parties are reluctant to change the *status quo* for something that could possibly be worse. The increase in peacekeeping forces since 1988 has been remarkable as the UN penetrates areas of the world hitherto denied to it by superpower political and economic hegemony. The has led to a new approach to old disputes where peacekeeping and pacific settlement are combined, so that the State or States involved not only accept the peacekeeping force to maintain a cease-fire and if necessary supervise a withdrawal of foreign troops, but also accept a peace plan which may involve, if the situation is internal, the supervision of elections in that country. Such an approach has been successful in Namibia and Nicaragua, and is being attempted in several other States.

However, in other situations or disputes the old approach has persisted with the Secretary General being urged to seek a solution to disputes or conflicts in which the UN may or may not have emplaced a peacekeeping force. Peacekeeping was not linked to peacemaking in the conflict between Iran and Iraq and is not linked to peacemaking in Yugoslavia. Iran and Iraq finally accepted the Security Council's mandatory demand for a cease-fire in August 1988,[37] over a year after the demand had been made, and nearly eight years after the conflict had broken out. A peacekeeping force was emplaced under the provisions of the cease-fire as mandated in resolution

598 of 1987. The same resolution encouraged the Secretary General to find a permanent peaceful solution to the conflict. For several years it appeared that the peacekeeping force was having a stalemating effect on peace talks. Fortuitously, Iraq's invasion of Kuwait in August 1990 and the build-up of Coalition forces against it in the Gulf, signified that Iraq had to concede to Iranian terms on 15 August 1990,[38] to enable its forces to be concentrated in and around Kuwait. In Yugoslavia, the Security Council authorised the emplacement of a peacekeeping force between Croatia and Serbia in resolution 743 adopted on 21 February 1992. In the same resolution the Security Council could only encourage the European Community's attempts at negotiating a peaceful breakup of Yugoslavia.

The quasi-judicial role of the Security Council
Although it has been stated above that some of the provisions of Chapter VI and the general principles contained in Article 1(1) create a quasi-judicial role for the Council, an examination of most Council debates leading to the adoption of a recommendation towards the pacific settlement of a dispute illustrates that it is often arrived at by political consensus, and that law·is often merely a 'tactical device' and a 'weapon in the armoury of rhetoric'.[39] The law of nations could be said to play a residual role in the work of a political body such as the Security Council, although the ending of the Cold War has witnessed an increase in judicial-type determinations by the Security Council.

The contention that although the Council does not decide cases in accordance with international law as does the World Court, it is constrained by a 'broad framework of legally acceptable solutions',[40] did appear to be flawed during the Cold War, in that some Security Council inspired pacification attempts sought solutions which appeared to contradict the tenets of international law. For example, the Council supervised negotiations on the Gulf War between Iran and Iraq were premised on the non-identification of the aggressor, namely Iraq.[41] Indeed, this neutral approach has persisted with Security Council inaction as regards the Iran-Iraq Gulf War despite the fact that the Secretary General apportioned responsibility to Iraq for its attack on Iran in 1980 in a report to the Security Council in *1991*.[42] This attitude appears even more inexplicable in the light of Iraq's new-found 'pariah' status since its invasion of Kuwait in 1990, although it may be that the West has not yet fully accepted Iran into the international community. One can see from this that despite the ending of the Cold War political influences can still cloud the Council's judicial judgement.

Alternatively, it may be argued that the Security Council fails to identify breaches of international law but it does not adopt resolutions which are themselves in breach of international law. However, this is a long way from the position that law plays an important role in the Council's pacification function.

The Council's failure to establish a solution is mainly due to it often being faced with the situation of an aggressor country gaining, with little possibility of it handing back its gains when faced with a Council recommendation. This is an inevitable flaw in any system based on recommendation and voluntary acceptance. Nevertheless, in order to ensure that the recommendation has a chance of success, it should be clear and unambiguous. Unfortunately, the necessities of consensus dictate that clarity is often unattainable. Resolution 242, adopted on 6 November 1967, five months after the Israeli victory in the Six Day War, is an example of an ambiguous recommendation. The resolution stated, *inter alia*, that the Council,

Affirms that the fulfilment of Charter principles requires the establishment of a just and lasting peace in the Middle East which should include the application of both the following principles:
 (i) Withdrawal of Israeli armed forces from territories occupied in the recent conflict;
(ii) Termination of all claims or states of belligerency and respect for and acknowledgement of the sovereignty, territorial integrity and political independence of every State in the area and their right to live in peace within secure and recognised boundaries free from threats or acts of force.

This appears to be a reasonable framework for the settlement of the Middle East problem, although the two principles outlined in the resolution miss the root of the problem, namely the homeless Palestinians. Nevertheless, the resolution is based on legal principles, namely the implication that Israel has the right to exist, the non-use of force, and the return of territories occupied by Israel in the Six Day War. However, the fact that the resolution does not state whether this means 'all' or 'some' of the territories detracts from its value. Law and justice point to the former interpretation, otherwise the Israelis would be gaining by the use of force, although it could be argued that the occupied territories, or at least some of them, are essential for the security and defence of Israel. Although Perry argues that if an advisory opinion of the International Court were sought, there would be no doubt that resolution 242 would be interpreted to mean 'all' the territories,[43] the doubt and confusion created by the British proposed text has not helped to end the conflict. Besides although the World Court may opt for this solution, it is not unforeseeable that the Council may promote peace on the basis of Israel handing back some of its territories but not all. One must not forget that international law is greatly tempered by political considerations in the Council forum.

Generally, when attempting to settle a dispute the Security Council tends to adopt recommendations which are aimed at not causing offence to either party in order to induce them to come to an agreement. Determinations of legal guilt may come later if the parties remain recalcitrant. The initial recommendations are usually based on broad principles of international law and justice centred around the *jus cogens* contained in Article 2(4) and the principle that a State should not gain from its breach. It may be argued that more concrete legal determinations should be made even under purely recommendatory Chapter VI resolutions. There are both pitfalls and advantages in this approach. A 'once and for all' legal determination may make a State more intransigent and so work against the settlement process, and at the same time it may mobilise international opinion which will work in its favour.

However, with the end of the Cold War, the Council has been more willing to make legal determinations even if they might inhibit the settlement process by branding one of the disputants as the guilty party. Part of the reason for this is that the Council is more willing to enter into the enforcement provisions of Chapter VII if the parties do not comply with the determination. Although this approach is somewhat selective and is mainly directed at the so-called 'pariah' States, one must not forget that these States have usually breached international law.

The 'balanced' approach to the situation in the Israeli Occupied Territories evidenced in resolution 242 of 1967, was maintained in the Security Council right up until the end of the 1980s by Israel's ally, the United States, using its veto to prevent consistent declaratory resolutions condemning Israel's actions of repression as a breach of the Fourth Geneva Convention of 1949.[44] However, since mid-1989 the Security Council has consistently condemned such acts in a series of resolutions which may have led, in part, to Israel entering into negotiations, albeit tentative ones, on settlement in the Middle East. At first the United States abstained on these condemnatory resolutions,[45] but now it votes for them.[46] Although, as we have pointed out, there are defects in the Council's judicial approach, in that it is of a somewhat selective and summary nature, in the Middle East, where settlement without consistent condemnations has not occurred, there is a strong argument for supporting the Council's new approach.

The post Cold War practice of the Council has not only taken on greater judicial overtones, but has increasingly extended to enforcement of its determinations utilising the powers of Chapter VII of the UN Charter. This has particularly been the case as regards Iraq following its aggression against Kuwait in August 1990, Libya for its support for terrorism, and finally the remnants of the Yugoslavian State (Serbia and Montenegro) for its intervention in the neighbouring former Yugoslav Republic and emerging State of Bosnia in May 1992. In these instances, as we shall see in subsequent sections, the Security Council condemned the State in question and then went on to enforce that decision using its economic, and in the case of Iraq, its military powers under Chapter VII of the Charter.

Binding settlement

Articles 36 and 37 are firmly premised on the Security Council simply having the ability to recommend terms of settlement. There has been little suggestion that the Council has the power to impose a mandatory settlement by a combination of Article 25 and Chapter VI. Nevertheless, on occasions, the Council's recommendations for settlement based on a combination of Article 24 and Chapter VI, are more comprehensive and detailed so that they suggest a more intense and concerted effort by the Council to achieve a settlement than in other instances. However, they are not binding on non-complying parties.

The conclusion of the Renville Agreement of 1948 between the Netherlands and Indonesia represented a success for the Security Council and its Committee of Good Offices. However, although the truce arrangements were put into effect, the political discussions broke down despite the efforts of the above mentioned Committee. In December 1948, a Dutch surprise attack enabled it to capture most of the principal cities in the territory of the Republic, which when combined with a more intransigent approach by the Dutch, signified that the Council could no longer persevere with its good offices approach. Nor did it venture into Chapter VII. Instead it adopted resolution 67 on 28 January 1949 which represented a much more comprehensive approach by the Council aimed at achieving a political solution.

The resolution uses, in its preamble, the language of Article 24, and then goes on to outline a more detailed recommendation for settlement presumably with Article 36 or Article 37 in mind. The use of Article 24 is possibly to impress upon the intransigent parties the desire of the Council to fulfil its primary responsibility. By the resolution the Council established the United Nations' Commission for Indonesia in the place of the Good Offices Committee, a move which indicated the Council's increased commitment to a more comprehensive settlement. In operative paragraph 3 the Council recommended the establishment of an interim federal government which was to have internal powers until the transfer of sovereignty by the Netherlands which was to be achieved by 1 July 1950. Elections for the Indonesian Constituent Assembly were to be completed by 1 October 1949. The Commission was established to help the parties to implement the resolution.

The resolution was recommendatory only but it had the value of being so comprehensive that it was almost 'decision like' in its content. Nevertheless, the Belgian representative made it clear that the resolution remained a recommendation under Chapter VI.[47] However, the combination of Article 24 and the obvious commitment of the Council to the independence of Indonesia led to the Dutch government notifying its general acceptance of the resolution with a few exceptions.[48] On 27 December 1949 the Netherlands transferred sovereignty to the Republic of Indonesia.

In the Namibian case, the Council 'decided' in 1969 that the 'continued occupation of the Territory of Namibia by the South African authorities' was illegal and that its mandate over the territory was terminated.[49] However, this was only a decision on legality, it was not a political solution, although it provided a basis for the United Nations' plan for Namibia contained in Security Council resolution 435 adopted on 29 September 1978, which endorsed the proposals in the Secretary General's report providing for internationally supervised elections leading to the independence of the disputed territory,[50] a plan which after over a decade of South African inspired frustration, came to fruition on 21 March 1990 with the independence of Namibia. It took an accord negotiated outside the United Nations and containing concessions towards South Africa, particularly by linking Cuban withdrawal from Angola with South African withdrawal from Namibia, before South Africa would agree to the United Nations' plan.

The Security Council, itself, was unable to coerce the South Africans into implementing the plan because Western members were unwilling to back the UN plan with anything more than voluntary measures of a limited nature called for in resolution 566 of 1985.[51] The original text supported the implementation of mandatory sanctions against Pretoria if the Namibian Independence Plan had not been put into operation by a certain date, but the United Kingdom and the United States could not support this and they later vetoed a Non-Aligned draft which would have determined that the 'continued illegal occupation of Namibia by South Africa constitutes a breach of international peace and an act of aggression', and would have imposed mandatory sanctions against South Africa under Article 41, Chapter VII.[52]

The use of Chapter VII action to enforce the provisions of a settlement proposal ostensibly made under Chapter VI and Article 24 would have represented the most effective method of operation for the Council short of the use of force. The two Western powers did not commit themselves to this, when, paradoxically, they were two of the original drafters of the Namibian Plan for Independence.[53]

Although the provisions of Chapter VI do not allow for the Council to impose a mandatory settlement, it is able to use a combination of powers under Chapters VI and VII to the same effect if it determines that the situation or conflict is a threat to or breach of the peace. Indeed, the gateway to Chapter VII, Article 39, provides that the Security Council can 'make recommendations' for settlement 'or decide what measures shall be taken in accordance with Article 41 and 42'. This appears to allow the Council to propose pacific settlement, and if it is not accepted, to take economic or military action. Such a combination of powers amounting to the attempted enforcement of a settlement is tantamount to a *binding* settlement. In Part Three we shall see the Security Council using a combination of powers in order to make the emplacement of a peacekeeping force conditional on the parties accepting the terms of a settlement, but it has not yet fully utilised a combination of settlement and mandatory sanctions. However, it has come close to this in the breakup of Yugoslavia, when it imposed sanctions against the Serbian-led remnants of that State for interfering in the emerging neighbouring State, and former Yugoslav republic, of Bosnia, by imposing quite restrictive sanctions in May 1992.[54]

The Security Council has effectively imposed terms of settlement on Iraq in 1991 following the successful prosecution of a UN authorised war against it to counter the Iraqi invasion of Kuwait in August 1990. This is the reversal of the normal process whereby the Council proceeds in a faltering incremental fashion from settlement proposals to enforcement action. The Iraqi aggression, as we shall see later in this chapter, was met with economic and military enforcement action authorised by the Security Council. With the Iraqis in Kuwait defeated in March 1991, the Security Council imposed the most draconian measures seen in the organ's lifetime. Resolution 687 was adopted on 3 April 1991 by twelve votes to one (Cuba) with Yemen and Ecuador abstaining. Its preamble contained, *inter alia*, an affirmation of the 'sovereignty, territorial integrity and political independence of Kuwait and Iraq' and called on States taking military action under UN authority to 'bring their military presence in Iraq to an end as soon as possible'.

Although this statement satisfied sufficient members that the Council's intention was not to overthrow the Iraqi regime, the thrust of the resolution was to oblige Iraq to compensate for its aggression, to curtail severely that regime's ability to wage further aggressive wars by intrusive disarmament provisions, and also, by maintaining the sanctions regime, to gradually undermine its grip on the country. It also demanded that Iraq and Kuwait respect the 'inviolability of the international boundary and the allocation of islands' as agreed by them in 1963.[55] It authorised the Secretary General to make arrangements to demarcate the boundary between Iraq and Kuwait, and finally decided to guarantee the inviolability of the demarcated international boundary. This, as with the rest of the resolution, was a measure taken under Chapter VII and therefore binding on Iraq. The disputed boundary had been used as an excuse by Iraq for its invasion and so the Council was coercing the Iraqis into settling their dispute with Kuwait to prevent it being so used again. The Iraqis had no choice but to accept this and all the other aspects of the resolution.[56] A Boundary Commission was established in May 1991 with three independent experts and a representative each from Iraq and Kuwait. Despite Iraq's complaints about the legality of the Council's imposition of a boundary,[57] the Commission has agreed on a final plan for surveying and mapping the border area.[58]

On the issue of responsibility, resolution 687 reaffirmed that Iraq 'is liable under international law for any direct loss, damage . . . or injury to foreign

Governments, nationals and corporations, as a result of Iraq's unlawful invasion and occupation of Kuwait', reaffirming its resolution 674 of 29 October 1990. This clearly shows the Council acting in a judicial capacity. It also decided to establish a fund to pay compensation and a Compensation Commission to administer it. The Secretary General was requested to report with a recommendation for 'mechanisms for determining the appropriate level of Iraq's contribution to the fund based on a percentage of the value of the exports of petroleum and petroleum products . . . taking into account the needs of the people of Iraq'. In resolution 705 adopted on 15 August 1991, the Security Council decided that the figure should be that suggested by the Secretary General of 30 per cent.[59]

It is clear from the above that Iraq's ability to comply with its obligation to compensate depended upon it resuming exports of oil, which it could not do since resolution 687 maintained the sanctions regime, first imposed by resolution 661 of 6 August 1990. On 15 August 1991 the Security Council adopted resolution 706, which authorised States to allow the import of petroleum products from Iraq for a period of six months to an amount not exceeding $1.6 billion.[60] The purpose of this resolution was to allow Iraq to purchase foodstuffs and medicines under the exceptions to the sanctions regime, but also to pay 30 per cent of that amount into the Compensation Fund. Iraq so far has refused to sell any oil, not on the grounds that it refuses to comply with its obligations under resolution 687 but on the basis that because it is willing to fulfil its obligations under that resolution, sanctions should no longer be applied against it.[61]

Apart from a continuing arms embargo against Iraq, resolution 687 included a decision that 'Iraq shall unconditionally accept the destruction, removal or rendering harmless, under international supervision' of its chemical and biological weapon, development and support systems, as well as 'all ballistic missiles with a range greater that 150 kilometres'. Iraq was put under an obligation to report fully, within fifteen days, on its weapons systems and to undertake not to develop ones in the future. A Special Mission was created to inspect and verify the destruction of these weapons as well as to develop a plan for the ongoing monitoring of the state of Iraqi armament. Furthermore, resolution 687 decided that 'Iraq shall uncon-ditionally agree not to acquire and develop nuclear weapons' and to report to the International Atomic Energy Authority (IAEA) within fifteen days on its nuclear weapons facilities. Iraq was also obliged to allow the IAEA to remove, render harmless or destroy such facilities and weapons, and to develop a plan for the ongoing monitoring of Iraq's nuclear programme.

The disarmament of Iraq pursuant to resolution 687 has been a long and so far uncompleted task. It has involved a slow process, with the Special Commission's inspectors and the IAEA officials gradually gaining access to weapons facilities not revealed in Iraq's initial response to resolution 687.

Destruction and removal of some weapons and facilities has been achieved but neither the Special Commission nor the IAEA has yet fulfilled their tasks.[62] The Secretary General has pointed out that a three stage process is involved, namely 'inspection and survey, disposal of weapons of mass destruction and the facilities for their production, and ongoing monitoring and verification of Iraq's compliance with its obligations under' resolution 687. In January 1992, the Secretary General reported that progress had been made on all three stages but significant work was yet to be done and pointed to Iraqi intransigence and lack of cooperation.[63] The Security Council has adopted further mandatory decisions in order to obtain Iraqi compliance with its disarmament demands. The Security Council condemned Iraq's failure to comply fully with its obligations contained in resolution 687, in resolution 707 adopted on 15 August 1991, and demanded that Iraq allow the Special Commission and the IAEA inspectors access to all weapons facilities and demanded that Iraq cease concealing some of those facilities. It also determined that 'Iraq retains no ownership interest in items to be destroyed, removed or rendered harmless pursuant to' resolution 687.

As regards future monitoring of Iraq's compliance with resolution 687, the Security Council adopted a mandatory resolution on 11 October 1991. Resolution 715 approved the plan submitted by the Secretary General and the IAEA and demanded that Iraq meet unconditionally all the obligations under that plan. The plan provides for inspections, aerial overflights of Iraq and submission of reports by Iraq so that the Special Commission and the IAEA will be able to monitor and verify that no nuclear, chemical or biological weapons or ballistic missiles or other items prohibited by resolution 687 are acquired anew by Iraq.[64] Iraq has not yet fully accepted the plan as required by resolution 715, instead it has adopted an approach of arrogating to itself the power of determining what it considers to be its obligations under resolution 687.

Despite the problems the Security Council has encountered in trying to remove the threat to the peace constituted by the high level of Iraqi armament, it has achieved a remarkable success in gradually wearing down the Iraqi resistance to its disarmament programme. Whether the programme will be fully completed remains to be seen, but the progress so far has been astounding. Iraqi compliance has been faltering but has been eventually given as it suffers from continuing sanctions and from the threat of further devastating military action. The Council has a general power to formulate plans for disarmament in Article 26 of the UN Charter, but there is no evidence that this was intended to be a mandatory power. Ironically if one accepts the West's view that it is only under Chapter VII that mandatory resolutions can be adopted, there appears little room to imply such a power. However, if one adopts a more flexible attitude, mandatory resolutions can be adopted outside the confines of Chapter VII if the resolution clearly shows such an intention and the implication of such a power does not breach the express provisions of the Charter. Resolution 687 and those adopted to further its aims were expressly stated to be adopted under Chapter VII, and Article 26 is not expressly confined to recommendations. It therefore appears that the Council has this power.

However, if one looks at its imposition of a settlement as regards the issues of compensation and the frontier dispute, it appears more difficult to impute a mandatory power to the Security Council. Those provisions of Chapter VI that allow the Council to propose terms of settlement, namely Articles 36 and 37, allow for recommendations only, yet resolution 687 is expressly adopted under Chapter VII. One may point to the Iraqi acceptance of resolution 687 as pushing to one side the problem of the binding nature of the resolution, but this does not overcome the fact that the Council intended the resolution to be binding, and it may have been for this reason that Iraq accepted it. It appears unavoidable to conclude that whereas the Council's disarmament programme for Iraq is a legitimate implied power derived from Article 26 to fulfil the Council's primary responsibility for international peace and security under Article 24, its development of its quasi-judicial powers to punish Iraq and determine its border with Kuwait appear more problematic.

It may be that such a development will be entrenched by consistent subsequent practice on the part of the Council. It is perhaps possible to reconcile this approach with the International Court's doctrine of implied powers as stated in the *Reparation* case of 1949 when it stated 'the rights and duties of an entity such as the Organization must depend upon its purposes and functions as specified or implied in its constituent documents and developed in practice'.[65] Or it may be that States, particularly the permanent members, have adopted a more open, 'living instrument', approach to the Charter, allowing it to evolve to cope with changes in international relations leading to the development of powers which fulfil the purposes of the UN even if it is not possible to imply such powers from the particular provisions of the instrument.[66] This approach is more akin to the controversial doctrine of 'inherent' powers. Seyersted states that

. . . while intergovernmental organizations, unlike States, are restricted by specific provisions in their constitutions as to the aims for which they shall work, such Organizations are, like States, in principle free to perform any sovereign act, or any act under international law, which they are in a factual position to perform to attain these ends, provided that their constitutions do not preclude such acts . . . Thus, it is not necessary to look for specific provisions in the constitution, or to resort to strained interpretations of the text and intentions, or to look for precedents or constructions to justify legally the performance by an intergovernmental organization of a sovereign or international act not specifically authorised in its constitution. As an intergovernmental organization it has *inherent power* to perform such acts.[67]

Whether one accepts the 'implied' or 'inherent' approach, it is possible to see the imposition of mandatory settlements under Chapter VII as a development of the Council's express powers to recommend settlement under Chapter VI and not as a breach of those provisions.

Reference to the International Court

Article 36(3) of the Charter states that 'in making recommendations under this Article the Security Council should also take into consideration that legal disputes should as a general rule be referred by the parties to the International Court'.

Many factors act against increased reference by the Council to the International Court. Many countries are not willing to gamble losing a dispute in an all or nothing legal ruling; they prefer, if anything, political compromises. In addition a strict delineation between the Council and the International Court on the basis of whether the dispute is political or legal fails to take account of the fine and often blurred distinction between law and politics and the fact that the Council has, by other provisions in Chapter VI, a quasi-judicial role anyway.

In fact the Council has made little use of Article 36(3). In the dispute between Albania and the United Kingdom over aspects of passage through the Corfu Channel in 1947, the Security Council recommended that the parties 'immediately refer the dispute' to the International Court.[68] That the Council, under Article 36(3), can do no more than make a recommendation which the parties are free to accept or reject was made clear by the World Court. The United Kingdom argued that the Council's resolution had established the Court's jurisdiction. Although the Court found it unnecessary to rule on this point, a majority pointed out that Article 36(3) did not introduce a new case of compulsory jurisdiction.[69]

The only other use of Article 36(3) by the Council occurred in 1976 when Greece complained of 'flagrant violations by Turkey of the sovereign rights of Greece on its continental shelf in the Aegean' which has 'created a dangerous situation threatening international peace and security'.[70] Resolution 395 was adopted on 25 August 1976 by consensus; it called for negotiations and invited the parties to refer the question to the International Court.[71]

Article 36(3) is really an example of settlement by pacific means and so should be associated with Article 33(1). It is not generally used by the Security Council because it only entails a recommendation. If the parties are willing to refer their dispute to the International Court they do not generally need the Council to remind them to do so. The infrequent use of Article 36(3) is a consequence of the limited use of the World Court in resolving conflicts and also the wider consideration that both these organs of the United Nations, the International Court and the Security Council, seem to prefer not to interfere in the other's perceived competence.[72]

Provisional measures

Article 40 provides that,

In order to prevent the aggravation of the situation, the Security Council may, before making the recommendations or deciding upon the measures provided for in Article 39, call upon the parties concerned to comply with such provisional measures as it deems necessary or desirable. Such provisional measures shall be without prejudice to the rights, claims, or positions of the parties concerned. The Security Council shall duly take account of a failure to comply with such provisional measures.

By placing this provision in Chapter VII which deals mainly with mandatory measures, there has been a tendency to view recommendations of provisional measures (usually a call for a cease-fire and withdrawal) as coming within Chapter VI, usually Article 36, with Article 40 measures being exclusively mandatory following a finding under Article 39 or by the invocation of Article 25.[73] However, as we have seen, provisional measures can be binding without references to Article 39 or Article 25 if the language of the resolution is peremptory and the discussions in the Council so indicate.

Once one accepts some degree of flexibility in the nature of provisional measures as developed in the practice of the Security Council, one can see that Article 40 is the natural basis for them whether their invocation is recommendatory or in the form of a decision under Article 25, just as Article 41 is the basis for sanctions whether voluntary or mandatory.

The reason why the Council so often has to resort to cease-fire calls is due to the fact that it is badly prepared. Often the cease-fire resolution is the first Council action in a conflict whereas if it had heeded the warnings it could have attempted to defuse the situation at an earlier stage. The Middle East is again illustrative of the Council's poor crisis management. In the build-up to the outbreak of the Six Day War on 5 May 1967, the Council showed an unwillingness to prevent what appeared to be at least 'a very serious potential threat to the peace'.[74]

The withdrawal of UNEF and the military build-up of Egyptian, Syrian and Jordanian forces appeared to be a threat to the peace but pro-Arab members of the Council blocked any attempted move to prevent war.[75] Yet when the war broke out the Council managed to adopt a unanimous resolution which called upon 'the Governments concerned as a first step to take forthwith all measures for an immediate cease-fire'.[76] This was disregarded so on 7 June the Soviet Union, concerned about Arab losses, proposed a more forceful draft which was adopted as resolution 234. In it the Council demanded a cessation of hostilities. A similar resolution was adopted when fighting intensified on the Syrian front.[77] By 10 June all the disputants had accepted the cease-fire.

These latter resolutions appear to have been more effective, perhaps because of the greater use of peremptory language. However, this is deceiving for the Israelis only accepted the cease-fire when they had gained the Sinai, the West Bank and the Golan Heights, whereas the Arabs were in no position to refuse when their armies started losing severely. Cease-fire resolutions are often combined with or are followed by a call for the withdrawal of occupying troops. In the case of the Six Day War it was some months before the Council adopted resolution 242, which, *inter alia*, called for Israeli withdrawal.[78]

The Middle East illustrates how the Council is often unable to step beyond the establishment of a cease-fire. Even compliance with such a call is illusory of Council effectiveness, in that it will only be accepted when both sides are simultaneously ready because of their relative military positions. Withdrawal calls are not generally complied with because the party in the strongest position will lose most. Settlement in terms of international law or justice is unlikely while countries are able to benefit territorially by the use of force.

Potentially, the Security Council's role in a conflict, if one excludes mandatory enforcement measures, can be summarised as calling for or demanding a cease-fire, then a withdrawal to prior positions and then an outline of settlement. The first two stages may be facilitated by the inter-positioning of a peacekeeping force. On several occasions the Council has been unable to go beyond a cease-fire call. For example, the sole Council resolution on a post-colonial armed clash between France and Tunisia in 1961 concerning the remaining French base at Bizerta, was a recommendatory call 'for an immediate cease-fire and a return of all armed forces to their original positions'.[79] Similarly, for many years the Council called on Iran and Iraq to cease firing in the Gulf War.[80]

On 20 July 1987 the Council finally adopted a mandatory demand for a cease-fire between Iran and Iraq in resolution 598 after expressly referring to Articles 39 and 40 of Chapter VII, as well as determining that there existed a 'breach of the peace as regards the conflict between Iran and Iraq'. The evidence is that a mandatory call for provisional measures was more effective since a cease-fire was established in August 1988. However, the cease-fire was as a result of the failure of the Iranian offensive and of economic exhaustion which led it to accept the cease-fire, Iraq having already accepted resolution 598 because of its tenuous position. The mandatory call may have provided the necessary diplomatic handle for both parties to grasp, but they were only prepared to grasp it when they both realised that the war was truly stalemated.

Mandatory resolutions may be marginally more successful than their recommendatory counterparts, but they still have the same inherent flaw when they are successful; they do not provide any basis for a permanent solution nor, if they are simply cease-fires, do they always secure a return to the *status quo ante* as they are intended to do. A simple cease-fire call if complied with will tend to freeze the dispute and usually to the advantage of one of the parties, that is the one which has gained by the use of force. Even fairly rapidly arrived at resolutions, although sometimes effective, work to the advantage of one of the parties. When violence erupted between the two Cypriot communities in 1974, the Council was rapidly convened on 16 July. With a Turkish invasion occurring, the Council adopted resolution 353 which found a 'serious threat to international peace and security' and demanded an 'end to foreign military intervention'.[81] The resolution called for both a cease-fire and for the cooperation of the parties with the peacekeeping force present since 1964. The cease-fire was eventually complied with after the call had been reiterated.[82] Further measures created a security zone between Turkish forces in the north of the island and Greek Cypriot forces to the south.[83] The effect of this was to cement the solution sought by Turkey and the Turkish Cypriots by the partition of the island, and seemed to be contrary to the non-prejudicial nature of provisional measures.

The drafters of the Charter inserted the provisional measures provision as an optional stopgap before the application of enforcement measures under Articles 41 and 42. The Security Council has mainly used Article 40 more in the way of a holding measure while pacific settlement is sought. The Secretary General's attempts at mediation in the Cyprus situation have been mentioned. In the Falklands War, the Council speedily adopted a call for provisional measures after a finding of a breach of the peace and then encouraged the Secretary General in his good offices mission.[84] Although the call for provisional measures was quickly adopted in the Falklands War, it was ignored by Argentina. This is probably because the Council's past record showed that it usually had not taken further measures to ensure compliance.

The one exception to that during the Cold War was in the case of the North Korean invasion of the South in 1950. The Council quickly found a breach of the peace and called for a cessation of hostilities and a withdrawal of North Korean forces to the 38th parallel.[85] This call was also ignored, but was backed up, as we shall see, by the Council recommending military action against North Korea. The end of the Cold War, whilst not revealing any greater preventative peacemaking by the Council, has shown it willing to back up calls for provisional measures with enforcement action if necessary, and so in this respect acting closer to the intention of the drafters of the

Charter. Immediately after Iraq had invaded Kuwait in August 1990, the Council demanded that Iraq withdraw from Kuwait in a mandatory resolution expressly adopted under Articles 39 and 40 of the Charter.[86] Iraqi non-compliance was resolutely met with first economic sanctions under Article 41 and then military action. Similarly on 15 May 1992, the Security Council unanimously adopted resolution 752 which demanded an end to the fighting in the former Yugoslav Republic of Bosnia-Herzegovina, in particular by the remnants of the Yugoslav National Army, dominated by Serbia. When this demand was not complied with the Security Council imposed a range of quite hurtful mandatory sanctions against it.

The current willingness of the Security Council to enforce its demands for provisional measures may increase States' willingness to comply with the demand more immediately in the future instead of calling the Council's bluff as happened in the past. Furthermore, the end of the Cold War has increased the effectiveness of the Council's provisional measures not only because of the greater use of enforcement action but also, as we shall see in Part Three, by an increased use of peacekeeping to facilitate the adoption of provisional measures in combination with peacemaking in the form of a settlement of the dispute.

Sanctions

Article 41 of the United Nations' Charter reads,

The Security Council may decide what measures not involving the use of armed force are to be employed to give effect to its decisions and it may call upon the Members of the United Nations to apply such measures. These may include the complete or partial interruption of economic relations and of rail, sea, air, postal, telegraphic, radio, and other means of communication, and the severance of diplomatic relations.

The powers contained in Article 41 were intended to allow for the imposition of mandatory enforcement measures following a finding of a threat to or breach of the peace under Article 39. However, on many occasions, the Council has been unwilling to take mandatory action with the consequence that it has settled for a call for voluntary measures or sanctions. Such action can be viewed as a reinterpretation of Article 41 to allow for recommendations, or as merely a recommendation under Chapter VI, or a recommendation of enforcement action under Article 39. Although the Charter base for such powers is inconclusive there is no doubt that the Council has developed such a power, the evolution of which lies in political compromise. In almost every case in which voluntary measures have been called for, the Western powers have objected to a finding under Article 39 combined with mandatory sanctions. Voluntary sanctions, as the term implies, are breached with impunity and so are relatively ineffective except for a certain symbolic role.

In the Rhodesian situation the Council called for an arms, oil and petroleum embargo to be imposed against the Smith regime in 1965.[87] The Western powers viewed this as a voluntary call, although others thought that it was 'only under Chapter VII that economic sanctions are mentioned'.[88] With at least two of the permanent members regarding the call as voluntary, the resolution must be regarded as recommendatory.

International pressure sometimes has the effect of turning voluntary measures into mandatory ones. In the case of Rhodesia this happened relatively quickly when the Council first imposed selective mandatory sanctions in 1966 and then more comprehensive sanctions in 1968.[89] Nevertheless, over two years elapsed between the call for voluntary measures and the call for comprehensive mandatory measures, a fact that decreased the effectiveness of the sanctions for it allowed the Rhodesian economy time to prepare. It was almost as if certain members were dragging their feet to allow this to happen. The same can be said as regards the arms embargo placed on South Africa. This was originally a voluntary call made in 1963,[90] but fourteen years later it was made mandatory,[91] giving the Pretoria regime ample time to stockpile and to work out alternative supply routes.

Including Southern Rhodesia and South Africa, the Security Council has deployed the mandatory sanctions weapon on six occasions, the other four being: comprehensive regimes against Iraq from 1990 and Yugoslavia (Serbia and Montenegro) from 1992, a more selective regime against Libya from 1992, and an arms embargo against Somalia from 1992.[92] It is clear from this list that during the Cold War until the end of the 1980s the Council was greatly reluctant to use its full powers under Article 41, but with the freeing of the Council from the chains of superpower control, the Council has entered into Article 41 quite frequently. The fact that the Council has increased the use of its mandatory powers to impose sanctions indicates that it feels that they are effective in a collective security role. It will be the aim of the remainder of this section to assess the level of effectiveness of sanctions, in particular to attempt to assess whether they are an effective alternative to military coercion.

There have been varying assessments of the effectiveness of the mandatory economic measures imposed against Rhodesia. The figures produced by the Security Council's Committee established to monitor reports on the effect of the sanctions regime suggest that, after initially struggling, from 1968 the Rhodesian economy improved.[93] This data provides *prima facie* evidence to deny the effectiveness of economic measures.[94] Nevertheless, there is evidence to suggest that after 1974 with the combined effects of Mozambique's independence (Portugal, the colonial power, was a major sanction breaker), the guerrilla war and the sanctions regime, the Rhodesian domestic situation as a whole began to decline. Although the application of sanctions did not immediately achieve the primary goals of the Security Council, of either ending UDI by forcing Smith to negotiate, or ruining the Rhodesian economy and thus forcing internal change, it did achieve certain subsidiary goals which must be viewed as a success. These were, namely the prevention of an all out civil war in Rhodesia after the proclamation of UDI, the prevention of foreign military intervention to end UDI, and the inducement, as opposed to the coercion, of the white regime to negotiate.

Nevertheless, in the Rhodesian case, sanctions were mandatory and so binding on Member countries. The question remains as to why the Rhodesian economy was not affected more rapidly. One major reason for this is the poor timing of the imposition. Pokalas summarises the effect of this in the case of Rhodesia.

Such anticipatory actions as stockpiling materials, developing alternative supply sources to obviate over-dependence on any one source, diversifying domestic production, planting crops that were readily exportable, conserving key commodities and establishing new trade routes were utilised by Southern Rhodesia even prior to Security Council action.[95]

Comprehensive economic sanctions were imposed several years after the Unilateral Declaration of Independence by the Smith regime in 1965, which in terms of the United Nations was relatively quickly. However, it was six years since the United Nations had taken cognisance of the situation,[96] giving the regime ample time to prepare. For sanctions to be given the chance of being effective they must be immediate, mandatory and comprehensive. In other words a resolution should have been adopted by the Council on the day of UDI or even before containing a determination of a threat to the peace and the imposition of mandatory, comprehensive measures. In the Rhodesian situation sanctions were applied in a 'gradual crescendo of severity' creating many loopholes which the Security Council gradually filled in a piecemeal fashion.[97] Above all, for sanctions to be effective, they must have the full support of the Members of the United Nations, in particular the permanent members of the Security Council.

Furthermore, the sanctions in the Rhodesian situation were by no means watertight, and sanction breakers went unpunished in many instances which led the Council to adopt resolution 333.[98] This called for the 'enactment and enforcement of legislation providing for the imposition of severe penalties on persons natural or juridical that evade or commit breach of sanctions'. Admittedly, in the case of Rhodesia the two countries which openly defied sanctions, South Africa and Portugal, were, at the time, international pariahs, over which the rest of the international community had little hold. In addition to South Africa and Portugal, other prominent sanction breakers during the Rhodesian crisis were the multinational corporations. These proved to be the most difficult to prevent because of their diverse locations and their economic and political power. Multinationals are mainly based in the West and so it is natural that they should have been the responsibility of Western members of the United Nations. In particular, supervision of compliance with the sanctions regime should have been coordinated by the three Western permanent members on the Council.[99]

Another main sanction breaker during the Rhodesian situation was the United States which in 1970 defied the Security Council by passing the Byrd Amendment enabling it to trade with Southern Rhodesia in strategic materials.[100] The Council, with the United States merely abstaining, censored that country in resolution 320 of 1972.[101] The Rhodesian economy could not but benefit from such illegal activities evidenced by its economic growth in conjunction with the reported number of sanction violations. By 1968 there had been 13 violations; this had increased to 73 by 1970 and 346 by 1976. The United States had committed 46 violations by 1978.[102] The United States had ignored a mandatory decision of the Security Council and had therefore abrogated its treaty obligations and breached Charter law. The lead given by the United States led to the initial vigilance of other States being relaxed with the result that the mandatory measures were then treated like voluntary measures, as a token gesture to be ignored with impunity.

Despite the weaknesses of the sanctions regime, the Smith government eventually negotiated majority rule and the Security Council lifted the sanctions in 1979.[103] Sanctions had an effect although Rhodesia was relatively strong in an economic sense. It was self-sufficient in agriculture, had abundant minerals including gold and a strong industrial base, but it still needed trade and investment. This is why the Council should have implemented a total embargo against the country, for as Pokalas points out that 'had the embargo been properly implemented by States' legislation, strictly enforced by States' administration and judicial sectors, and diligently coordinated by the Committee, the Rhodesian economy would have floundered and ultimately collapsed'.[104]

The Rhodesian experience was not a conclusive 'experiment' in the use of sanctions to remove a threat to the peace. The rather ambiguous attitude to sanctions shown by member States undermined their effectiveness. In the case of Iraq, sanctions were first imposed by resolution 661 of 6 August 1990, following Iraq's refusal to comply with the Council's mandatory cease-fire call in resolution 660 of 2 August 1990, the day of its invasion of Kuwait. Immediately we can see that sanctions in this case were imposed very quickly and, as the terms of resolution 661 show, they were comprehensive. Resolution 661 prohibited the import of goods from, and the export of goods to, Iraq and Kuwait, except in the latter situation for 'supplies intended strictly for medical purposes, and, in humanitarian circumstances, foodstuffs', as well as a freeze on financial arrangements with Iraq and its overseas assets.

The Council also decided to establish 'a Committee of the Security Council consisting of all the members of the Council', to examine reports on the progress of implementation of sanctions by member States. In analysing these reports, Bethlehem concludes that support for resolution 661 reached well over 80 per cent of the membership of the UN. Many non-members responded positively, although at least one, Switzerland, stated that it was not under a legal obligation to impose sanctions against Iraq.[105]

The sanctions regime against Iraq appeared relatively watertight. As Bethlehem states,

From the outset, Iraq appeared to be uniquely placed to be influenced by sanctions: it was a one product economy that had recently emerged from a punishing war against Iran; the movement of its principal export commodity, oil, was relatively easy to track and interdict; Iraq imported between 60–70% of its basic food requirements; with the possible exception, in the early stages of the crisis, of Jordan, it could not count on support from any of its immediate neighbours to circumvent sanctions; in an unprecedented show of solidarity, virtually the entire international community had condemned the Iraqi action which had been the cause of the crisis. In short, if sanctions as a means of enforcing international law were not to succeed here, they would not be likely to succeed elsewhere.[106]

Indeed, the Security Council adopted a series of resolutions to fine tune the embargo,[107] including, as we shall see in the next section, the authorisation to navies in the Gulf to intercept suspected sanctions breaking ships. Sanctions were imposed in August 1990; by January 1991, when the UN authorised military campaign started against Iraq, sanctions did not appear to have weakened Iraq's resolve to hang on to Kuwait, although they may have affected Iraq's military capacity to resist the overwhelming military action launched against it. Nevertheless, question marks must be raised against the effectiveness of sanctions and their capacity to act as an alternative to military action. Sanctions were continued against Iraq by resolution 687 of 3 April 1991 after military action successfully ousted Iraq from Kuwait. The purpose of the continuing sanctions regime was to secure Iraq's compliance with the resolution's provisions on disarmament and compensation, although the hidden agenda must have been to undermine the regime of Saddam Hussein. Resolution 687 provides for a review of the sanctions regime against Iraq 'every sixty days in the light of the policies and practices of the Government of Iraq'. At the time of writing (September 1992) the sanctions regime remains in place.[108]

If we look to the effectiveness of sanctions, a fundamental flaw can perhaps be perceived. The aim of sanctions was expressly stated not to be to starve the people of Iraq into submission, but initially to weaken Iraq's hold on Kuwait and then, following its defeat in Kuwait, to force it to comply with its obligations to disarm and to compensate States and individuals for its aggression. This was made clear from the outset by resolution 661 adopted on 6 August 1990 and elaborated upon by resolution 666 of 13 September 1990. The latter resolution outlined a mechanism whereby the Sanctions Committee would monitor the food situation in Iraq and make determinations of how particular needs ought to be met. The Committee struggled to achieve the aim of not using 'starvation as a weapon'.[109] Nevertheless, whereas some States, including the United States, thought that the sanctions regime prohibited foodstuffs unless there was clear evidence of humanitarian need, other States on the Council, particularly Cuba, argued that there was a general humanitarian need in Iraq and therefore all foodstuffs should be allowed into Iraq without any particular proof being required.[110] It appears that the direct affect of sanctions was not on the regime's grip on Kuwait, and when removed from that country in March of 1991, on its grip over its own people, but upon the Iraqi people, significant elements of which, it appears from independent reports, suffered and continue to suffer from malnutrition and an increase in diseases.[111]

The Security Council was not unresponsive to these negative effects.[112] In resolution 687, 3 April 1991, which contained the terms of settlement imposed on Iraq, the Security Council formalised the 'no-objection' procedure which had come to replace the necessity for proof of humanitarian need in the Council's Sanctions Committee. This meant that the export of foodstuffs or other materials or supplies for essential civilian needs was permitted as long as the Committee was notified, and there were no objections to the cargoes in that Committee. In addition to this *prima facie* right to export foodstuffs to Iraq, the Council permitted, by resolution 706 of 15 August 1991, Iraq to sell $1.6 billion of oil to allow for the purchase of foodstuffs and medicine for its civilian population in general, including those segments of its people who revolted against the regime as soon as the ground offensive against Iraq in Kuwait had finished. The Security Council established the mechanisms for the sale and the transfer of funds in resolution 712 of 19 September 1991, but Iraq has so far (September 1992) refused to export any oil, complaining of violations of its economic sovereignty. Without this income Iraq is unable to purchase the foodstuffs it requires and must depend on the provision of charitable aid.

Iraq must blame itself for the suffering of its people, not only by the fact that it has not taken advantage of the Security Council's offer, but also by its unwillingness to comply fully with resolution 687. In addition, one must not forget that it was Iraq which had clearly violated international law in August 1990. Nevertheless, it appears that the sanctions regime is not a sufficiently sharp weapon to point directly at those responsible for the invasion, namely the Iraqi regime of Saddam Hussein. The ordinary Iraqi citizens appear to be the ones suffering, more particularly those elements, the Kurds in the north and the Shias in the south, that revolted against the regime and are now suffering themselves from an internal embargo imposed by the Iraqi government as punishment.

It can be argued that the sanctions weapon, although a blunt instrument and not capable of removing aggression, is more suitable to remove threats to the peace in that sanctions are directed at those who must change the internal situation, both rulers and ruled. However, the Iraqi experience shows that the people who suffer the most are those who are not responsible for the unlawful acts, namely the ordinary citizens. Whether or not sanctions provoke a change in the Iraqi regime, either by fostering discontent in the population, or by eventually forcing the regime to change the system fundamentally in a way acceptable to the Security Council, the experience of sanctions against Iraq, appears to suggest that economic coercion is not an effective alternative to military coercion *per se*, and that sanctions alone are not a sufficiently adequate weapon on which to base a system of collective security. Sanctions should be given time to work, and should suspend the taking of military action in self-defence in response to *aggression*, but if unsuccessful after a reasonable period of time the Security Council ought to consider the use of armed force, or if not, allow States their right of self-defence. If no aggression has been committed but the situation is a *threat to the peace*, then the Security Council alone has the right and the duty to consider whether to use military force to supplement the imposition of sanctions. It may decide that military action is unnecessary or it may not find the political consensus to authorise military action, in which case sanctions will continue in the hope that they will eventually help to remove the threat to the peace as in the Rhodesian situation. This approach accords with the wording of Article 42, which, in the original Charter plan, was the basis for military action. Article 42 opens with the words 'should the Security Council consider that measures provided for in Article 41 would be inadequate or have proved inadequate' it may consider taking military action.

Before moving on to examine the Council's practice as regards military coercion, it is necessary to mention some recent sanctions regimes imposed to combat threats to the peace. Although the evidence on the effectiveness of these embargoes is preliminary it might be suggested that the sanctions experiences against Rhodesia and Iraq show that the only effective method of ensuring that the weaknesses of the target State's economy are exposed is to impose a comprehensive embargo. Limited embargoes are insufficient because even if they are aimed at those areas of weakness the other unsanctioned areas of the economy will develop to compensate. The use of an arms embargo against South Africa was questionable because South Africa's strong economy and natural resources supply have enabled it to produce its own weapons. However, an effectively policed arms embargo may be successful against a country totally dependent on outside States providing arms, particularly when there is no real prospect of that country being able to produce its own arms, as with the arms embargo against war-torn Somalia imposed by the Council in resolution 733 of 23 January 1992. However, the resolution contained no machinery for the monitoring of arms shipments, and without that the Council is relying on members' sense of obligation towards a mandatory decision of the Council.

The Council has also imposed sanctions regimes against Libya and Yugoslavia in 1992. On 31 March 1992, the Security Council imposed a mandatory arms and air embargo against Libya in resolution 748, after determining that that country's support for terrorism was a threat to international peace. A more comprehensive embargo was imposed against the remnants of the war-torn State of Yugoslavia by resolution 757 of 30 May 1992. The Council condemned the continued intervention by Yugoslavia (Serbia and Montenegro) and Croatia in the former Yugoslav Republic, and emerging State, of Bosnia, and determined that the situation there constituted a threat to international peace and security. Despite the fact that both Serbia and Croatia were intervening in Bosnia in support of the factions there, the Security Council implicitly blamed Serbia when it imposed mandatory sanctions against it on the import or export of commodities except for 'supplies intended for medical purposes and foodstuffs' notified to the Council's Committee on sanctions against Yugoslavia, established by resolution 724 of 15 December 1991, as well as a freeze on financial and other transactions with Yugoslavia (Serbia and Montenegro). It can be seen that we have a sanctions regime similar to that imposed against Iraq, illustrating that the Council is prepared to use different levels of regimes depending on a combination of factors, one of which must be the seriousness of the threat, although a more important factor will be the willingness of the permanent members to use this potentially costly weapon.

Military measures

The Organisation's collective security role was premised, in 1945, on the ability of its primary organ, the Security Council, ultimately to use military measures to enforce the peace. The Council's ultimate weapon and deterrent was contained in Article 42, which states,

Should the Security Council consider that measures provided for in Article 41 would be inadequate or have proved to be inadequate, it may take such action by air, sea, or land forces as may be necessary to maintain or restore international peace and security. Such action may include demonstrations, blockade, and other operations by air, sea, or land forces of Members of the United Nations.

Article 43 then details the mechanism whereby armed forces are to be made available, namely by 'special agreements' made by members of the UN, detailing the numbers, location and the state of readiness of such forces. These agreements were to be reached as soon as possible.

The agreements foreseen by Article 43 were not arrived at because the Second World War unity of the Allies soon collapsed into a bitter ideological struggle between East and West. Nevertheless, the Security Council did manage to instruct the Military Staff Committee, established under Article 47 of the UN Charter and consisting of the Chiefs of Staff of the permanent members, to report to the Council by April 1947 on the basic principles that should govern the UN's armed forces.[113] The Committee's report did contain draft articles detailing such basic principles. Unfortunately, only half of these had been accepted by all the permanent members.[114]

The major areas of agreement were that the initial contributions of armed forces should come from the permanent members, with other members contributing at a later stage. It was also agreed that the members' forces should be under the command of the contributing nation except when they were being utilised by the Security Council, when they would come under the overall political control of the Security Council, and under the operational and military command of the Military Staff Committee. Although these were indeed significant initiatives towards the collective security ideal concerning the control of UN forces which has been singularly lacking in the UN military operations to date, there were disagreements on practical issues such as the size of the force, and the contributions from each permanent member, with the Soviet Union preferring a small force with equal contributions.

Furthermore, the Soviet Union was of the opinion that the UN armed forces could not be used against any of the permanent members, an argument which though undermining the collective security ideal as well as the ideal of the rule of law, seemed to be supported by the practical consideration that the voting system agreed upon by the permanent members at Yalta and embodied in Article 27 of the Charter, allowed any permanent member to veto a proposed military action, including, and especially, one aimed at the permanent member in question. Yet the United States, as well as preferring a much larger army, thought that the force could be used against a permanent member guilty of aggression. Furthermore, the United Kingdom stated that the problem of the veto could be avoided by meeting aggression committed by a permanent member by combining Article 43 and Article 51, not Articles 42 and 43.[115] In other words, aggression could be met by the UN army, minus the aggressor State's troops, in an action in collective self-defence rather than as authorised by the Security Council. Indeed, when we come to examine the handful of UN military operations to date, such a confusion of the right of collective self-defence and the concept of collective security is apparent.[116] Nevertheless, in terms of Charter law it must be true that Articles 42 and 43 are within the exclusive competence of the Security Council, and as such must be utilised by the Security Council voting for such an operation in accordance with the voting rules as laid down by Article 27 and interpreted by subsequent practice.

With no likelihood of consensus between the permanent members, at least during the Cold War, the idea of a standing army was shelved, although the Military Staff Committee continued its formal, and unproductive, meetings. It is generally thought that in the absence of agreements reached under Article 43, the Council is unable to 'decide' on the use of military measures under Article 42.[117] Articles 39 and 42 seem to envisage the Council having the power to make binding, mandatory decisions directed at member States to take military action against a transgressor. Without the agreements under Article 43, it would seem difficult for the Council to impose an obligation on member States to provide armed forces when the Council demands them. A counter-argument would be to point to Article 41 which empowers the Security Council to impose mandatory sanctions against a State, a decision binding on all member States without the requirement for any prior agreements between the member States and the Organization beyond that contained in Article 25. However, the rationale behind Article 43 was the recognition that for the Council to undertake military action requires a much higher degree of coordination and logistical organization. Without that a mandatory demand that States provide military forces would appear vacuous. Furthermore, Article 106 of the Charter permits the permanent members to make transitional arrangements for military action 'pending the coming into force of such special agreements referred to in Article 43 as in the opinion of the Security Council enable it to begin the exercise of its responsibilities under Article 42'. This implies that the agreements in Article 43 are a prerequisite to the utilisation of Article 42 by the Security Council.[118]

However, it is incorrect to state that there is an inextricable link between Articles 42 and 43 in the sense that it would be a misuse of power for the Council to decide on the use of military measures under Articles 39 and 42 without any *a priori* agreements under Article 43. It would appear acceptable for the Council to use the power granted to it in Article 42 without the mechanisms that were designed to make the imposition of military coercion a practical option. If an alternative practical option emerges such as an *ad hoc* coalition prepared to act under UN authority then it would appear to be *prima facie* lawful. During the Cold War the possibility of the Council acting under Article 42 with or without the agreements under Article 43 was such a remote possibility that Article 42 was effectively a dead letter. However, with the ending of the Cold War, there is the possibility of the Security Council utilising Article 42. Furthermore, there have been suggestions of having at least a small UN force ready to take military action. At the special Security Council Summit of Heads of State on 31 January 1992, President Mitterand of France offered to make 1,000 troops available to the UN under the control of the Military Staff Committee.[119]

Although it may be argued that the agreements under Article 43 are not necessary to make the Council's military option under Article 42 a practicality, the Charter does strongly indicate that UN control of such military operations is an essential prerequisite for the legality of military action by the Security Council. This appears to be made clear by Articles 46 and 47(3) which provide that 'plans for the application of armed force shall be made by the Security Council with the assistance of the Military Staff Committee', and 'the Military Staff Committee shall be responsible under the Security Council for the strategic direction of any armed forces placed at the disposal of the Security Council . . .'. Strategic control by the Military Staff Committee and overall political control by the Security Council appear necessary for the achievement of the collective security concept, in that they embody the centralisation of the collective use of force. This argument can be used to criticise the Security Council's practice in the use of the military option, when it has simply delegated authority and control to a State or group of States.

A counter-argument would be to state that if the Security Council simply authorises a State to use force to achieve an objective within the ambit of the UN's security role, despite the fact that it is being performed by one State, it is still a *collective* use of force, in that it is being performed to carry out the collective will of the Security Council on behalf of the United Nations. This is all the more so when the Security Council authorises a group of States to carry out such a function. The question remains whether control by the Security Council and the Military Staff Committee is essential to properly fulfil the collective security function. It could be argued that the provisions of Articles 46 and 47(3) as well as Article 43 are simply formalities which if in operation would facilitate the use of the power contained in Article 42. They can be seen as just one method of allowing the Council to fulfil its collective security role. Following from this it would appear to be unnecessary to make these formalities a prerequisite to the use of military enforcement action by the Security Council.

What is required is a clear indication by the Security Council of the extent and nature of the armed force that it is requesting States to undertake. Problems of lack of continuous control can be overcome by a clear and unambiguous mandate at the outset. If States using force under this authority then wish to use more or less force, they must seek a change in mandate from the Security Council. This seems to be an acceptable compromise between complete delegation to States and unnecessary formalities and bureaucratic control by Committee. It appears unnecessary to place military operations under the complete control of the UN to achieve the centralisation of force necessary to fulfil the concept of collective security, if at the outset the Security Council effectively centralises the *objectives* of the military operation, thereby preventing the use of military action for purposes other than those of the Security Council.

If the Security Council is dominated by a State or group of States and they manage to persuade it to undertake military action that fulfils the objective of that State or group of States, as well as those of the UN, then as long as the Council has defined those purposes clearly, according to this interpretation of Charter law, the Security Council, not the State or group of States, is the initiator of the use of force. Use of centralised power to achieve the ends of a dominant individual or group within any society is not necessarily unlawful, if that power is channelled correctly through the institutional structures. Current dominance by the West in the Security Council does not mean that when it uses that organ to fulfil the collective security purposes of the Organisation as well as its own ends, it is automatically a misuse of power. The result may be an erratic collective security system, stuttering into life only when the interests of the West are affected, but is that not better than none at all? Indeed, arguments of self-interest may embarrass the West into agreeing that the Council can be used to fulfil purposes beyond narrow Western interests, evidenced by the West's reluctant proposal to use limited military measures to bring humanitarian relief to Bosnia embodied in Council resolution 770 adopted on 13 August 1992.

Whether one sees the development of the military option as a power implied from Article 39 or 42, or both, is not of great importance, if the power is used to fulfil the purposes of the UN and is clearly formulated at the outset of the operation. What is clear at the moment is that the Security Council has not yet 'decided' to use military force, it has simply recommended that States, on a voluntary basis, use force in particular situations and for particular purposes. In two instances, the Council has simply recommended that limited force be used to prevent cargoes from reaching the port of Beira in 1966, and from leaving or reaching Iraq in 1990. On both these occasions the recommendations were intended to make a UN embargo more effective.

On 9 April 1966, the Council adopted resolution 221 which, *inter alia*, authorised Britain 'to prevent, by the use of force if necessary, the arrival at Beira of vessels reasonably believed to be carrying oil for Southern Rhodesia', after determining that the arrival of oil at Beira destined for Rhodesia was a threat to the peace. In the absence of any Article 42 agreement between Britain and the United Nations, this resolution can only be regarded as a recommendation to Britain, presumably under Article 39, to take enforcement action. Although under no obligation to carry out the patrol, Britain, as the proposer of the resolution, willingly and effectively carried out the task.

The Beira patrol was maintained successfully by Britain until 1975. Resolution 221 was itself a result of a threatened breach of the voluntary oil embargo imposed against Rhodesia by two Greek registered tankers.[120] The

'Joanna V' was already in Beira, but as a result of resolution 221, which also empowered the United Kingdom to arrest the ship upon her departure if she discharged her oil, it left with a full load. The 'Manuela' was stopped by a British warship before entering the port with the result that the captain changed the tanker's course away from Beira.[121]

Such a limited mandate to use military coercion to enforce an embargo was extended in the Gulf crisis to enforce the mandatory, comprehensive, embargo against Iraq. Resolution 665 of 25 August 1990 called upon 'those Member States cooperating with the Government of Kuwait which are deploying maritime forces to the area to use such measures commensurate to the specific circumstances as may be necessary under the authority of the Security Council to halt all inward and outward maritime shipping in order to inspect and verify their cargoes and destinations and to ensure strict implementation of the provisions related to such shipping laid down in resolution 661'. As with the Beira patrol resolution, this resolution was proposed by those States willing and able to carry out the enforcement action.[122]

The United Kingdom and the United States were already effectively enforcing the embargo using their naval forces in the Gulf, relying on the right of collective self-defence on behalf of, and at the request of, the government of Kuwait.[123] Despite this liberal attitude to Article 51, which as we have seen, *prima facie*, prohibits action in self-defence once the Security Council is dealing with the situation under Articles 41 or 42, the Western States sought and gained the request of the Security Council that they should use force. The two Western States claimed that this gave the naval operation an 'additional' legal basis.[124] This gave the appearance that the Security Council was being used to legitimise the activities of a few States, but one must remember that they were volunteering to enforce an embargo imposed by the Security Council, an action which was necessary to make the embargo effective and as such fulfilled the aims of the Security Council.

However, the Gulf, and to a lesser extent, the Beira, resolutions were unclear in that they did not specify what level of force was to be used, for example firing across the bows or firing at the suspected sanctions busting ship. Indeed the later resolution managed to avoid mentioning force at all. This raises question marks about whether the authorisation to use force was adequately centralised. It may have been for this reason that resolution 665 further requested 'the States concerned to co-ordinate their actions . . . using as appropriate mechanisms of the Military Staff Committee . . .'. The Committee apparently met but did not attempt to interfere or in any way exert control over the US-led Coalition command structure regarding naval and ground operations in the Gulf.

Despite the lack of centralisation in the above operations, there is no evidence to suggest that the States concerned in any way interpreted the language of the enabling resolutions to enable them to pursue national aims beyond those stated by the Security Council. There is of course a far greater danger of this happening when the Security Council authorises the full-scale use of force against an aggressor.

The first instance of this was set in motion when on 25 June 1950, 100,000 North Korean troops crossed the 38th parallel that had divided the country after the Second World War. The communist North Korean aim was to unite the country by force. The United States requested a meeting of the Security Council, and with the Soviet representative absent in protest at the continued presence of Nationalist China in the permanent seat, the Council adopted a US proposal. Resolution 82 of 25 June determined that the 'armed attack' by North Korea constituted a 'breach of the peace', and called for an immediate cessation of hostilities and a withdrawal of North Korean forces to the 38th parallel. North Korea ignored this demand with the result that the United States sent combat forces to South Korea.[125] Although not specified as an action in collective self-defence, the United States' action could only have been justified as such at this early stage in the war.[126]

However, the United States sought to utilise the other exception to the ban on armed force contained in Article 2(4), namely the use of force under the auspices of the Security Council, by proposing what was to become resolution 83 of 27 June 1950. This recommended 'that the Members of the United Nations furnish such assistance to the Republic of Korea as may be necessary to repel the armed attack and to restore international peace and security in the area'. Secretary General Lie wished for some form of central UN control of this force,[127] but the United States rejected this idea. Instead the Council adopted a French and British proposal as resolution 84 on 7 July 1950. This recommended 'that all Members providing military forces . . . make such forces available to a unified command under the United States of America'. The resolution also authorised the use of the UN flag concurrently with the flags of the contributing States, and finally requested the United States to provide the Security Council with regular reports 'on the course of action taken by the unified command'.

The British representative, Sir Gladwyn Jebb, explained the military action in Korea as coming under Article 39 of the Charter on the basis that in the absence of agreements made under Article 43, the Council could not 'decide' on military action within the terms of Article 42, but could call on States to volunteer to help.[128] This appears to be an acceptable implication of power but it cannot involve a total delegation of authority to a single State without adequate safeguards that prevent the obvious national interests motivating the State to volunteer its forces outstripping the collective security interests of the Security Council. Resolution 84 appeared simply to delegate or even abdicate responsibility to the United States, which supplied 90 per cent of the force. The force was not controlled by the UN, instead its commander, General MacArthur, was appointed by the United States and took his orders from the White House.

When Ambassador Malik of the Soviet Union returned to the permanent seat at the end of July 1950, thereby preventing the Security Council from adopting any further substantive resolutions on the war, the United States war effort was well under way and did not require any further enabling resolutions. Resolution 82, mandating the military action, was sufficiently ambiguous that it was not clear whether it simply authorised the pushing back of North Korea, or whether the elliptical phrase 'to restore international peace and security to the area', allowed the US-led army to push into North Korea. In any event the Western dominated General Assembly adopted a resolution on 7 October 1950 calling for stability throughout Korea and for steps to be taken for the establishment of a unified Korea. Furthermore the resolution stated that UN forces should stay in Korea until these objectives were fulfilled, implicitly authorising the crossing of the 38th parallel.[129]

Unfortunately the crossing of the parallel did not restore peace and security to Korea. Instead when the UN forces pushed towards the Chinese frontier, the Peoples Republic of China responded with massive force. The war then swung towards the communists until the UN forces eventually managed to hold them around the 38th parallel by July 1951. Negotiations between the United Nations Command, in fact the United States,[130] and a North Korean and Chinese delegation eventually produced an armistice in July 1953 dividing the country, an agreement which has lasted until the present day.

It can be strongly argued that the UN operation in Korea was an unconstitutional delegation of authority to the United States enabling it to use the Organisation to go beyond the collective objectives of the body to fulfil the national objectives of the United States in its attempts to fight communism. However, such an argument is difficult to prove in that combating aggression is one of the prime aims of the Organisation as embodied in Article 1(1) of the Charter. Doubts about whether the objectives of the operation were sufficiently collective could have been allayed, either by more control of the armed forces by means of a Committee established by the Security Council, or by being much more specific in the war aims of the UN response. Presumably the Security Council can authorise action going beyond simply the defensive. There appears no restriction on the Security Council authorising offensive action if that is what is required to maintain or restore international peace and security.[131] However, if the Council is going to authorise offensive force then the resolution, or subsequent resolutions, should clearly state as such. If there are doubts then the response should be limited to a defensive action. In this respect the UN action is akin to an action in collective self-defence although its legal basis remains distinct, deriving from Article 39 (and possibly 42) rather than Article 51 of the Charter.[132] This argument signifies that the American decision to push into North Korea went too far, putting American war aims above those of the United Nations. However, the United States did gain the somewhat ambiguous support of the General Assembly. The question whether the General Assembly has the power to authorise the use of force will be examined in Part Two.

Limitations on the extent of the use of force under UN authority seem to have influenced the US-led action against Iraq, in that coercion was used in January and February 1991 principally to remove Iraq from Kuwait in a mainly defensive operation.[133] Between the Iraqi invasion of Kuwait on 2 August 1990 and the authorisation to use force on 29 November 1990, the Security Council had used its powers to demand Iraqi withdrawal under Articles 39 and 40, and had imposed comprehensive mandatory sanctions under Articles 39 and 41. In addition the Council adopted numerous other resolutions which were either of a condemnatory quasi-judicial character, for instance the declaration that the Iraqi annexation of Kuwait was 'null and void', and the demand that Iraq release the foreign nationals it was holding in Iraq and Kuwait,[134] or were resolutions aimed at improving the embargo imposed by resolution 661 on 6 August 1990.

On 7 August 1990, the United States and Saudi Arabia agreed that American troops were to be sent to Saudi Arabia to prevent any further Iraqi advance in accordance with Article 51 of the UN Charter.[135] This was the basis of the defensive posture adopted by the United States and various allies that gathered in Saudi Arabia and the Gulf in the months after the Iraqi aggression. The United States and the United Kingdom also stated that they had the option of acting in collective self-defence of Kuwait at the request of the deposed rulers of that country even though the Security Council had imposed sanctions. This contention has been dealt with in chapter two above.

As with Korea, the United States decided that it was politically necessary to have the support of the Security Council in order to make any military operation internationally acceptable. They managed to persuade twelve members of the Security Council to vote for a resolution authorising the use of force, with Cuba and Yemen voting against on the basis that the resolution granted 'authority without accountability', and 'carte blanche' to the United States and its allies to use military force. China abstained on the grounds that it preferred that a peaceful solution be sought to the crisis. Indeed, resolution 678 was very ambiguous in its direction to States in that it appeared first of all to be an ultimatum to the Iraqis and only secondly an authorisation to use force. The time delay was inserted at the insistence of the Soviet Union in the hope that the mere threat of force would compel the Iraqis to withdraw. Operative paragraph 2 of resolution 678 of 29 November 1990, authorised 'Member States co-operating with the Government of Kuwait, unless Iraq on or before 15 January 1991 fully implements . . . the foregoing resolutions [of the Council on the crisis], to use all necessary means to uphold and implement Security Council resolution 660 and all subsequent resolutions and to restore international peace and security in the area'.

The unnecessarily ambiguous language of this resolution can be cleared up in part by statements made by some of the members of the Council and not objected to by others. The representative of Malaysia stated that the resolution did 'not provide a blank cheque for excessive and indiscriminate use of force' and warned against any action 'purportedly taken under this resolution that would lead to the virtual destruction of Iraq'. Mr Hurd, the UK Foreign Secretary, stated that Iraq was required to 'withdraw all its forces unconditionally to the positions on which they stood on 1 August . . . If not, then Member States . . . are authorised to use such force as may be necessary to compel compliance'. Indeed, it could be argued that the phrase 'necessary' implies proportionality within the customary law of self-defence, so that the resolution simply authorised a defensive action.[136] However, the fact was that debate about the extent of the UN's war aims in resolution 678 would not have been necessary if a far more detailed resolution was adopted excluding or at least clarifying the phrase 'to restore international peace and security in the area', which, by itself, suggests the possibility of offensive force to remove the source of the aggression.

A clear enabling resolution would have dispelled doubts about the delegation of control to the United States, which contributed two-thirds of the troops of the 750,000 strong army from twenty-nine States, making the action little different to the Korean War. As with the Korean War, the war against Iraq served American interests, in this case the protection of Western oil supplies. However, this does not mean that the authorisation to use force to expel Iraq was an abuse of power if that authorisation was fulfilling carefully defined UN aims. Prevention of aggression is a legitimate and indeed ultimate aim of a collective security system, but the methods of achieving it need to be clearly stated and approved.

There should have been detailed discussions, either in the Military Staff Committee, or in less formal forums about the extent of the armed force to be applied against Iraq *before* it was used. Security Council approval of the Coalition's war plan should have been sought immediately before the deadline against Iraq ran out. As it was the Security Council did not convene formally after the adoption of resolution 678 until the war had ended in March 1991. The only obligation in this period was to provid regular reports to the Security Council during the campaign which related to events in the war *after* they had occurred and not to the strategy and plans of the Coalition.[137] There was an obvious need not to inform Iraq of the Coalition's every move beforehand, but this should not have prevented overall UN control of the objectives of the action as it was after all meant to be a UN operation.

The need for greater UN control of the operation does not necessarily signify that the operation was contrary to the UN Charter. The use of force needs to be assessed to see if it achieved those aims set out in resolution 678 as restrictively interpreted above. The Coalition of forces operating under the umbrella of the UN, but not on this occasion using its flag, started its air campaign against Iraq on 16 January 1991 soon after the deadline in resolution 678 ran out. The ground offensive for the liberation of Kuwait started on 24 February 1991 and was successful in achieving the liberation of Kuwait within five days. It appears that, individual actions in the campaign apart which must be judged by the laws of war,[138] the Coalition did adopt a reasonable interpretation of resolution 678 limiting the military action to the enforcement of resolution 660 and other resolutions of the Security Council aimed at securing the withdrawal of Iraq from Kuwait. Although the air campaign did penetrate deep into Iraq and was aimed at industrial as well as military targets, and the ground offensive included a large part of southern Iraq, as well as a temporary occupation of part of the south after the war, these actions appeared necessary to achieve the successful liberation of Kuwait without the need for a long drawn out and even more destructive war between Iraq and the Coalition.

The campaign against Iraq was limited to UN objectives, it was not hijacked for Western aims beyond those objectives that coincided with Western purposes, and so did not secure the overthrow of the aggressive regime in Iraq advocated by some in the West.[139] Although it is probable that the Security Council could authorise an offensive war involving the overthrow of a regime, such as that in Iraq, with a record of aggression, such an aim should be clearly spelt out in the enabling resolutions. Nevertheless, the defeat of Iraq enabled the Security Council to impose a temporary cease-fire on Iraq in mandatory resolution 686 of 2 March 1991, which, *inter alia*, forced Iraq to rescind its annexation of Kuwait, accept its liability for damages caused by its aggression, release third State nationals and prisoners of war, return all property seized in Kuwait, and to provide information on all mines and weapons left in Kuwait. Iraq complied and also agreed to the even more stringent mandatory resolution providing for a permanent cessation of hostilities, resolution 687, adopted on 3 April 1991 which has been reviewed above. The Security Council, in effect, decided that it would maintain pressure on the Iraqi regime by the use of sanctions rather than the use of force.

There are undoubted problems with relying on a system of volunteers to uphold collective security ideals, not the least of which is the erratic nature of such a method in that aggression will only be met by force when there are volunteers to be found. States will generally only volunteer when it will serve their purposes as well as those of the UN. Political considerations apart, the legality of these UN authorised operations is still a matter of heated debate, but there are now, within the UN's terms, two precedents for recommendatory military action. Despite manifest deficiencies in the institutional centralisation of armed force either in the form of clear and relatively precise enabling resolution or by means of control of these operations (or even better, both), and despite the feeling that the use of force was perhaps not the best method of dealing with the problem, it is not possible to state that these operations were unlawful, except in the Korean operation when the US-led force tried forcefully to unify the country. This latter problem leads us into the question of the General Assembly's powers.

Notes

1 Cot and Pellet, *La Charte des Nations Unies*, 627 (1985).
2 R. B. Russell and J. E. Muther, *A History of the United Nations Charter*, 657 (1958).
3 L. M. Goodrich, E. Hambro and P. S. Simons, *The Charter of the United Nations*, 258, 2nd ed. (1969).
4 See UN doc. S/14942 (1982).
5 SC 2345 mtg, 37 UN SCOR (1982).
6 SC 2349 mtg, 37 UN SCOR (1982).
7 SC Res. 502, 37 UN SCOR Resolutions 15 (1982).
8 SC Res. 530, 38 UN SCOR Resolutions 10 (1983).
9 UN doc. S/14941 (1982).
10 SC Res. 479, 35 UN SCOR Resolutions 23 (1980).
11 See for example SC Res. 582, 41 UN SCOR Resolutions 13 (1986).
12 Goodrich, Hambro and Simons, *The Charter*, 161. But see A. C. Arend, 'The obligation to pursue peaceful settlement in international disputes during hostilities', 24 *Virginia Journal of International Law* (1983), 97.
13 SC Res. 15, 1 UN SCOR Resolutions 6 (1946).
14 UN doc. S/360/Rev 1 (1947).
15 SC 136 mtg, 2 UN SCOR (1947).
16 SC Res. 289, 25 UN SCOR Resolutions 13 (1970) re Guinea; SC Res. 294, 26 UN SCOR Resolutions 2 (1971) re Senegal. See also SC Res. 568, 40 UN SCOR Resolutions 20 (1985) re South African attacks on Botswana; and SC Res. 57, 40 UN SCOR Resolutions 16 (1985) re South African incursions into Angola.
17 SC Res. 290, 25 UN SCOR Resolutions 13 (1970). But see SC Res. 302, 26 UN SCOR Resolutions 3 (1971) re Senegal.
18 32 UN SCOR Special Supp. (No. 3) (1977).
19 SC Res. 419, 32 UN SCOR Resolutions 18 (1977).
20 See above note 16. See also SC Res. 189, 19 UN SCOR Resolutions 11 (1964) to

investigate alleged aggression against Cambodia; SC Res. 496, 36 UN SCOR Resolutions 11 (1981) to investigate mercenary aggression against the Seychelles.

21 See SC Res. 377, 30 UN SCOR Resolutions 7 (1975) for the investigation which started the Western Saharan peace process; SC Res. 39, 3 UN SCOR Resolutions 2 (1948), for the investigation which led to the cessation of hostilities in Kashmir and the emplacement of an observer force.

22 SC 2802 mtg, 43 UN SCOR (1988).

23 E. Lauterpacht, *Aspects of the Administration of International Justice*, 42 (1991).

24 75 UNTS 31.

25 SC Res. 672, 45 UN SCOR Resolutions 7 (1990).

26 SC Res. 673, 45 UN SCOR Resolutions 7 (1990). See UN doc. S/21219 (1990).

27 SC mtg, 9 November 1990.

28 GA Res. 46/59, 46 UN A/PV (1992).

29 SC mtg, 12 May 1992.

30 UN doc. S/649/Rev 1 (1947).

31 SC Res. 27, 2 UN SCOR Resolutions 6 (1947).

32 SC Res. 30, 2 UN SCOR Resolutions 6 (1947).

33 SC Res. 36, 2 UN SCOR Resolutions 9 (1947).

34 UN doc. S/537 (1947).

35 SC Res. 593, 41 UN SCOR Resolutions 16 (1986).

36 SC Res. 186, 19 UN SCOR Resolutions (1964).

37 SC 2823 mtg, 43 UN SCOR (1988)

38 UN doc. S/21803 (1990).

39 R. Higgins, 'The place of international law in the settlement of disputes by the UN Security Council', 63 *A.J.I.L.* (1970), 1, at 4.

40 *Ibid.* See also O. Schachter, 'The quasi-judicial role of the Security Council and the General Assembly', 58 *A.J.I.L.* (1964), 960.

41 UN docs S/20093, S/20242, S/20442 (1988).

42 UN doc. S/23273 (1991).

43 G. Perry, 'Security Council Resolution 242: the withdrawal clause', 31 *Middle East Journal* (1977), 413, at 432.

44 See for example SC mtg, 9 June 1989.

45 For example SC Res. 641, 44 UN SCOR Resolutions (1989).

46 For example SC Res. 726, 47 UN S/PV (1992).

47 SC 417 mtg, 4 UN SCOR (1949).

48 UN doc. S/1274 (1949).

49 SC Res. 269, 24 UN SCOR Resolutions 2 (1969).

50 UN doc. S/12857 (1978).

51 The stopping of new investments, the prohibition on the sale of krugerands, and sporting and cultural restrictions; SC Res. 6, 40 UN SCOR Resolutions 11 (1985).

52 UN doc. S/17633 (1985).

53 UN doc. S/12636 (1978).

54 SC Res. 757, 47 UN S/PV (1992).

55 485 UNTS 321.

56 UN docs S/22465, S/22480 (1991).

57 UN doc. 23 May 91. 28(3) *UN Chronicle* (1991), 15.

58 See SC Res. 773, 47 UN S/PV (1992).

59 UN doc. S/22661 (1991).
60 See also SC Res. 712, 46 UN SCOR Resolutions (1991).
61 UN doc. S/23514 (1991).
62 UN docs S/23268, S/23295 (1991).
63 UN doc. S/23514 (1992).
64 UN docs S/22871/Rev 1, S/22872/Rev. 1 (1991).
65 *Reparation for Injuries Suffered in the Service of the United Nations*, I.C.J. *Rep.* 1949, 174, at 198.
66 See the dissenting opinion of Judge Alvarez, *Competence of the General Assembly for the Admission of a State to the United Nations*, I.C.J. *Rep.* 1950, 4, at 15–19.
67 F. Seyersted, *United Nations Forces: In the Law of Peace and War*, 154–5 (1966).
68 SC Res. 22, 2 UN SCOR Resolutions 3 (1947).
69 *Corfu Channel Case*, I.C.J. *Rep.* 1949, 15, at 31–2.
70 UN doc. S/12167 (1978).
71 See *The Aegean Sea Continental Shelf* case, I.C.J. *Rep.* 1978, 3.
72 *Lockerbie* case (provisional measures), I.C.J. *Rep.* 1992, 114.
73 Cot and Pellet, *La Charte*, 616–17.
74 UN doc. S/7906 (1967).
75 See SC 1341–1346 mtgs, 22 UN SCOR (1967).
76 SC Res. 233, 22 UN SCOR Resolutions 2 (1967).
77 SC Res. 235, 22 UN SCOR Resolutions 3 (1967).
78 SC Res. 242, 22 UN SCOR Resolutions 8 (1967).
79 SC Res. 164, 16 UN SCOR Resolutions 9 (1961).
80 For example SC Res. 588, 41 UN SCOR Resolutions 13 (1986).
81 SC Res. 353, 29 UN SCOR Resolutions 7 (1974).
82 SC Res. 354, 29 UN SCOR Resolutions 7 (1974).
83 SC Res. 355, 29 UN SCOR Resolutions 8 (1974).
84 SC Res. 502, 505, 37 UN SCOR Resolutions 15–17 (1982).
85 SC Res. 82, 5 UN SCOR Resolutions 4 (1950).
86 SC Res. 660, 45 UN SCOR Resolutions (1990).
87 SC Res. 217, 20 UN SCOR Resolutions 8 (1965).
88 SC 1265 mtg, 20 UN SCOR 15 (US) 16 (UK) 6 (Ivory Coast) (1965).
89 SC Res. 232, 21 UN SCOR Resolutions 7 (1966); SC Res. 253, 23 UN SCOR Resolutions 8 (1968).
90 SC Res. 181, 18 UN SCOR Resolutions 7 (1963).
91 SC Res. 418, 32 UN SCOR Resolutions 5 (1977).
92 SC Res. 733, 47 UN S/PV (1992).
93 See UN doc. S/12265 (1975).
94 J. A. Sigmon, 'Dispute Resolution in the United Nations: an inefficient forum?', 10 *Brooklyn Journal of International Law* (1984), 437, at 450.
95 J. Pokalas, 'Economic sanctions: an effective alternative to military coercion?', 4 *Brooklyn Journal of International Law* (1980), 289, at 312.
96 See GA Res. 1747, 17 UN GAOR Supp. (No. 17A) 3 (1962).
97 Pokalas, 4 *Brooklyn Journal of International Law* (1980), 312.
98 SC Res. 333, 28 UN SCOR Resolutions 14 (1973).
99 J. C. Nkala, *The United Nations, International Law, and the Rhodesian Indepen-*

dence Crisis, 81 (1985).

100 H. R. Strack, *Sanctions: The Case of Rhodesia*, 162–4 (1978).

101 SC Res. 320, 27 UN SCOR Resolutions 9 (1972).

102 Pokalas, 4 *Brooklyn Journal of International Law* (1980), 314.

103 SC Res. 460, 34 UN SCOR Resolutions 15 (1979).

104 Pokalas, 4 *Brooklyn Journal of International Law* (1980), 306.

105 D. Bethlehem (ed.), *The Kuwait Crisis: Sanctions and their Economic Consequences*, xxxiv-xxxvi (1991). UN doc. S/21585 (1990).

106 *Ibid.*, xliii.

107 SC Res. 666, 669, 670, 45 UN SCOR Resolutions (1990).

108 UN doc. 11 July 1992.

109 Provisional record of the 5th meeting of the Sanctions Committee, 31 August 1991, USSR, Bethlehem, *The Kuwait Crisis: Sanctions*, 797.

110 See for example argument between Cuba and the United States over a cargo of powdered milk, *ibid.*, 809–10.

111 UN doc. S/22799 (1991); *Keesing's* (1991), 38597–8, 38696; (1992), 38743, 38788.

112 See also the attempt to deal with negative effect of sanctions regime on other States economies, SC Res. 669, 45 UN SCOR Resolutions (1990).

113 SC 105 mtg, 2 UN SCOR (1947).

114 Special Supp. (No. 1), 2 UN SCOR (1947).

115 Goodrich, Hambro and Simons, *The Charter*, 323.

116 See O. Schachter, 'United Nations law in the Gulf conflict', 85 *A.J.I.L.* (1991), 452 at 459–60.

117 Cot and Pellet, *La Charte*, 709–11.

118 But see J. Quigley, 'The United States and the United Nations in the Persian Gulf War: new order or disorder?', 25 *Cornell International Law Journal* (1992), 1, at 33–7.

119 SC 3046 mtg, 47 UN S/PV 18 (1992).

120 SC 1276 mtg, 21 UN SCOR 5 (1966), UK.

121 UN doc. S/7249 (1966).

122 UN doc. S/21460 (1990).

123 SC 2938 mtg, 45 UN SCOR (1990), UK.

124 *Ibid.*, US.

125 See statement by President Truman, 27 June 1950, *United States Policy in the Korean Crisis*, 18 (1950).

126 But see the Secretary General's view, T. Lie, *In the Cause of Peace*, 332 (1954).

127 *Ibid.*, 334.

128 SC 477 mtg, 5 UN SCOR (1950).

129 GA Res. 376, 5 UN GAOR (1950).

130 L. Goodrich, 'Korea: collective measures against aggression', 494 *International Conciliation* (1953), 157, at 178.

131 J. N. Singh, *Use of Force under International Law*, 82 (1984).

132 But see J. Stone, *Legal Control of International Conflict*, 234–7 (1954).

133 But see Quigley, 25 *Cornell International Law Journal* (1992), 17–19.

134 SC Res. 662, 664, 45 UN SCOR Resolutions (1990).

135 UN doc. S/21492 (1990).

136 SC 2963 mtg, 45 UN SCOR (1990).
137 Quigley, 25 *Cornell International Law Journal* (1992), 15–17.
138 N. D. White and H. McCoubrey, 'International law and the use of force in the Gulf', 10 *International Relations* (1991), 347, at 359–73.
139 But see the imposition of air exclusion zones by Western States over northern Iraq in March 1991, and over southern Iraq in August 1992. There appears to be no explicit Council authority for these measures, although they were justified by Western leaders as coming under UN cease-fire terms, and under resolution 688, respectively. See *Keesing's* (1991), 38081.

PART TWO
The General Assembly

CHAPTER FOUR

The political context

Whereas the Security Council's position as the primary body responsible for the maintenance of international peace and security is reasonably well established and defined, the General Assembly's role in this context is nebulous and ill-defined. The drafting of the provisions of the UN Charter relating to the General Assembly's functions and powers was a source of contention between the smaller States represented at San Francisco and the sponsoring powers. The latter group's Dumbarton Oaks proposals gave the Assembly no real power. At San Francisco, the smaller States insisted that all the power should not be in the hands of the Council, or more specifically in the hands of the veto-wielding members. As a result Chapter IV, which contains the powers of the General Assembly, became a compromise between the provisions granting generous powers to the Assembly to placate the smaller nations, namely Articles 10 and 14, and provisions attempting to restrict the powers and competence of the Assembly, that is Articles 11 and 12.

The result is an example of political compromise, an ambiguous set of provisions which have been interpreted advantageously by and for the benefit of whichever group or groups of States is dominating the Assembly at a particular time. In the early years of the Organisation the body was Western dominated. With the advent of rapid decolonisation in the late 1950s and during the 1960s the whole complexion of the Organisation changed with the Non-Aligned movement seizing virtual control of the Assembly. Unlike the Security Council, where the Cold War was a relatively constant factor in limiting the use and development of the Council's powers, there were two distinct phases in the Cold War influences on the General Assembly.

The Cold War era

During the early years the Soviet Union protected its interests by the use of the veto in the Security Council and was fiercely critical of any attempt to give the Western dominated Assembly more than subsidiary powers in the field of international peace, basing their objections on a narrow interpretation of the relevant Charter provisions. Nevertheless, the West used its dominant position to introduce procedures and bodies to circumvent the paralysis in the Council brought on by the Soviet veto, using a liberal interpretation of the Charter.

An example of this wide interpretation of the Charter was the adoption by the Western dominated Assembly in 1950 of the so-called Uniting for Peace resolution, a Western initiative which purported to allow the Assembly to recommend the use of military action to combat breaches of the peace when the Council was unable to act because of the veto. The aim was to allow the General Assembly to take over the role of the Council in the maintenance of peace and it was made even more poignant in that it was adopted against the background of the Korean War, the first UN authorised military operation. The United States, realising that Security Council authorisation of military action was unlikely to reoccur as long as the Cold War continued, wanted to allow the Assembly to authorise Korean-type operations in the future. The legality of this resolution and other Western ploys adopted during the Assembly's first decade will be discussed in chapter five. It is worth emphasising at this point that the clear Cold War motivations behind such initiatives do not *ipso facto* render them unlawful. Many laws or interpretations of laws are politically motivated. Furthermore, a politically motivated interpretation of the Charter, if constitutional, can be used by subsequent political groupings to the detriment of the original sponsors of the interpretation.

This happened to a certain extent in the next phase of the General Assembly's life during the Cold War, in that after the end of the period of Western domination, 1945–55, the new majority in the Assembly used Western-type interpretations of the Charter to further their political goals, though in the absence of military or economic might in this group, the achievements were more rhetorical than coercive. In 1945 the membership of the United Nations numbered 51 whereas by the end of the Cold War this had increased to 159. The bulk of this increase consisted of the 100 or so members of the Non-Aligned (sometimes called the Group of 77) new States emerging from the decolonisation process, dramatically altering the balance of power in the Assembly. During this period, the then Socialist States cleverly adopted similar stances to the Non-Aligned on such issues as colonialism and self-determination, which understandably were and still are of considerable concern to the Non-Aligned. Paradoxically, the West, which one would expect to dominate questions of freedom and self-determination (though not in colonial contexts), was not able to align itself on these issues with the newly independent States. Thus it was the erstwhile colonial powers and their allies (namely the 'West') which were, in the majority of discussions and votes, in the minority in the Assembly. Consequently, the West withdrew its liberal interpretation of the Charter which it used so successfully in the early years, and argued instead on a narrow constitutional basis that the Security Council was the primary body, where, predictably, the number of Western vetoes in protection of Western interests increased dramatically, and further that the General Assembly had a limited discursive, and moreover, subsidiary, role.

Relatively, the number of Western and Socialist bloc countries remained constant during this period; the variable factor was the group of newly independent States without a permanent member, from within its ranks, on the Security Council protecting its interests. Consequently, there was an increasing divergence on similar issues between the views of the Assembly where a majority of two-thirds could adopt a resolution on 'important questions' such as those concerning international peace,[1] and those of the Council where the overriding consideration was one of compromise in order to avoid the veto. In the early years the West dominated both bodies and so used the Assembly as a means of dealing with issues on which the Soviet Union was sensitive. Nevertheless, there was still a link between the Assembly and the Council during the Cold War period. The Cold War indeed continued during the 1950s and 1960s, but the introduction of a third factor, the newly independent States, meant that the link between the Assembly and the Council became increasingly tenuous. The Assembly began to take initiatives and became antagonistic towards the Council.

The new majority viewed the Council as a private club protecting the interests of the superpowers and their allies,[2] a view highlighted by the decreasing representation in the Security Council of the membership of the Organisation. In 1945 the ratio of members of the Security Council to members of the Organisation was 11:51 (21.6 per cent). In 1985 this percentage had decreased to 9.4 (15:159). It would have taken a Security Council of thirty-three members to reproduce the original ratio in 1985, and a non-permanent member could hope for election to the club once every sixteen years.[3] As we shall see in the next section, the membership of the Organisation has increased even further so that the Security Council has become even less representative. These figures emphasise the decreasing ties between the Council and the Assembly with the latter acting with increasing independence in the field of international peace and security in this period, with a subsequent expansion in the *de facto* competence of the Assembly. Whether this expansion breached the *de jure* restrictions in the Charter will be examined in the next chapter, but one must bear in mind the flexible nature of the Charter, a fact particularly apparent in Chapter IV concerning the General Assembly.

Luard accurately summarises the implications and importance to the

Non-Aligned of its political power in the General Assembly.

If the West had been tempted to use its votes to force through its own views with little thought of negotiations to impose the tyranny of the majority, how much more would the third world when it came to power, be tempted to do so? The West at least had possessed alternative means of securing the ends it cherished, overwhelming military power, widespread diplomatic opportunities, huge economic strength, unrivalled political leverage. The third world had none of these assets. It had no military power, little diplomatic experience, negligible economic strength, and insignificant political leverage. For these countries, it appeared, the one weapon at their disposal was the UN, which not long after [the period of Western domination] they knew to be permanently at their disposal. It is scarcely surprising that, armed with this weapon, and inspired by the example presented by their predecessors, they proceeded, over the coming decades, to exploit, to the best of their ability, the one asset at their disposal.[4]

It will be illustrated that the Non-Aligned and Socialist majority used its voting power to adopt resolutions on a wide range of situations and issues concerning international relations. However, this was not a revolutionary development, for at San Francisco the smaller States had made proposals for wide-ranging competence, to authorise the Assembly to consider, for example, 'any matter within the sphere of international relations' or 'affecting international relations'.[5] However, at the time, such provisions were not specifically included, although the compromise that was achieved left sufficient loopholes for the Assembly to develop its powers in a direction similar to that envisaged by the smaller States in 1945.

It is important to note, however, that it was neither envisaged at the time, nor has it emerged since, that the Assembly has any formal mandatory powers along the lines of those possessed by the Security Council under Chapter VII. Although the Assembly has been assertive, 'demanding' and 'deciding', as well as 'recommending' and 'calling', there is no real suggestion that the Assembly can adopt anything more, in Charter terms, than a recommendation on matters of international peace and security. One issue that will emerge in chapter five is that the Assembly, while not having a mandatory power conferred upon it by the Charter, can adopt resolutions that are binding in the sense that they are based on established principles of international law. However, the Assembly is in this instance simply acting as a focal point for States' views on international law, an important function, but not one that can be said to create a mandatory power, and certainly not one that grants the Assembly a coercive power to *order* economic or military enforcement measures.

After the Cold War

The decolonisation process can be seen to have continued in an altered form to span the divide between the world order before and after the end of the Cold War. New States have emerged and are emerging out of the collapse of the Soviet Union and the Socialist bloc in general. In 1989 the membership of the United Nations was 159 and had been relatively stable for a number of years following the rapid expansion in the 1950s and 1960s with the admittance of newly independent African and Asian States. By 31 July 1992 the membership of the Organisation had increased to 179.

One can see nearly all the new member States as part of the 'fall-out' from the end of the Cold War. The former Soviet Republics of Armenia, Azerbaijan, Georgia, Kazakhstan, Kyrgyzstan, Moldova, Tajikikstan, Turkmenistan and Uzbekistan,[6] as well as the more recent acquisitions to the former Soviet empire, the Baltic States of Latvia, Lithuania, and Estonia, are clear examples. The same can be said about those new States emerging from the collapse of the communist regime in Yugoslavia, namely, Bosnia and Herzegovina, Croatia, and Slovenia, with some more still to be admitted under Article 4 of the UN Charter upon recommendation by the Security Council and decision of the General Assembly, in addition to the new member States of Namibia, the Democratic People's Republic of Korea, and the Republic of Korea. The remainder of the new membership, namely the Federated States of Micronesia, Liechtenstein, the Marshall Islands, and San Marino, are all so-called 'micro-States'.

The West's victory in the Cold War, is confirmed in part by the fact that many of the new States, particularly the Baltic States, the former Yugoslav republics and some of the former Soviet republics, have Western aspirations, alongside those States in Eastern Europe which once formed part of the communist bloc but are now taking faltering steps towards Western-style governments and economies. These States have not continued to take an anti-Western stance in the General Assembly with the result that the Assembly's condemnations of South Africa and Israel, which during the Cold War, were overwhelming, are either not so strongly supported, or are not so vehement in their condemnatory tones.

The voting patterns are changing in the General Assembly. Although the Non-Aligned group of developing States do still command a sufficient majority for such resolutions to be adopted, the force of these resolutions is less impressive with a significant minority now abstaining or voting against. In addition, with many of the Non-Aligned in effect dependent on economic aid from the West, there appears to be less possibility of the General Assembly challenging the Security Council in any way as the organ dealing with a situation or dispute that endangers or threatens international peace and security. Whereas during the Cold War the Assembly did usurp the primary responsibility of the Security Council on quite a number of occasions, it now appears to be clearly a subsidiary organ. In addition, given the resurgence in the Security Council's activities, the Assembly has often little choice but to take a secondary or silent role. The overwhelming, and more importantly, unchallenged economic, military and political strength of the West in the post Cold War era has led to a resurgent Security Council and a curtailed General Assembly. It has not resulted, however, in a return to the situation that existed in the first decade when both organs were dominated by the West. The Non- Aligned States still form the majority in the General Assembly.

Indeed, given the collapse of the bipolar world, it seems a little incongruous to talk about Non-Alignment, which essentially was a position somewhere between the Western and Eastern blocs. Instead we have a rough division of the world along North-South lines, with the richer nations of the northern hemisphere being pressured in international forums for a more equitable distribution of wealth and technology. This conflict is reflected in the debates and resolutions adopted by the General Assembly as a result of recommendations by the membership in the Second Committee of the General Assembly relating to Economic and Financial matters, but does not fully impinge on the Assembly's role in the maintenance of international peace and security. Indeed, the attitude of the majority appears at the moment to be one of leaving the Security Council to deal with situations concerning peace and security even though the Council may be pursuing Western policy. Furthermore there is evidence of a developing trend in which the General Assembly adopts resolutions tentatively supporting the Security Council's efforts to resolve a dispute or deal with a situation that threatens the peace or has actually breached it. This phenomenon will be more fully examined elsewhere, though one or two examples will be pertinent here.

Even though Iraq invaded Kuwait shortly before the General Assembly opened its 45th annual session in September 1990, the General Assembly essentially took a back seat during the Gulf Crisis of 1990–91. It did provide some limited support for the Security Council when it adopted a resolution on 28 November 1990, condemning the acts of violence against diplomatic and consular commissions.[7] This was obviously directed at Iraq and indeed that country cast the sole vote against the resolution, but it failed to mention Iraq by name although it recalled those Security Council resolutions that had condemned Iraq's violations of diplomatic law. It must be noted also that the resolution was adopted the day before the Security Council adopted resolution 678 which authorised the Coalition to use force against Iraq to remove it from Kuwait. One can see that the General Assembly has maintained its independence in that the same resolution also called upon States 'to make use of the means for the peaceful settlement of disputes'. This was obviously not deemed to be a tacit condemnation of the proposed use of force against Iraq for Western States were able to support the resolution as well, but it cannot be construed as amounting to anything more than limited support for the Security Council's approach to Iraq. In a later resolution at its 45th session, the General Assembly did condemn Iraq for its human rights violations in Kuwait and against third State nationals.[8] During its 46th session on 17 December 1991, it adopted a resolution supporting the Security Council's condemnation of the Iraqi suppression of sections of its own people in Council resolution 688 of 5 April 1991.[9]

There is also limited evidence that the Assembly may be starting to support Western ideals more in its resolutions. Following the overthrow of the government of Haiti on 29 September 1991 which had been elected under UN observation on 16 December 1990, the General Assembly adopted a resolution without a vote on 11 October 1991 condemning the coup and expressing its support for 'the development of democracy in Haiti'.[10] This may be seen as support for the Western concept of democracy as well as concerning the situation in Haiti, although it did follow the refusal of the Security Council to deal with the dispute despite the protestations of the deposed President of Haiti on 3 October 1991 before the Council.[11] Furthermore, it had been the General Assembly that had supported Haiti's original request for observation in the December 1990 elections. The Assembly had authorised the observers on 10 October 1990,[12] although the Secretary General ensured that the Security Council approved of the General Assembly's action first in an exchange of letters with the President of the Security Council in September and October 1990.[13] This episode illustrates that the Assembly is still acting independently of the Council but is not as directly antagonistic towards it as it was during the Cold War period.

Before turning to the question of whether the Assembly has the legal competence to adopt such resolutions, it must be noted that the division outlined above, where the Assembly consisted of three blocs during the Cold War – Western, Non-Aligned and Socialist – and two divisions since, North and South, is too simplistic a view. The General Assembly consists of many sub-divisions based loosely on regions such as the Group of Western States, League of Arab States, Group of African States, Group of Asian States, and the Group of Latin American States. Sometimes these become more definitive and take the form of regional organisations from which one member is chosen from each to represent its views in the Assembly. The European Community, the Organisation of African Unity, the Organisation of American States, the Organisation of the Islamic Conference, the Association of Southeast Asian States are examples of regional bodies which are represented in the General Assembly, each with a different degree of cohesiveness.

However, the Assembly is not like a political party system as found in a democratic society.[14] Nevertheless, in the course of examining and voting upon problems involving the use of force in international relations during the Cold War, the Assembly very regularly divided into the three blocs

discussed above. East-West relations were of great significance in the maintenance of peace through the United Nations, and the Non-Aligned united
on this issue on so many occasions because its militarily weak members were
so often the victims of the use of force in which a superpower was involved.
Whether the Non-Aligned Movement can maintain itself as a significant
coalition and as a united advocate of the non use of force in international
relations remains to be seen now the Cold War has ended, and the General
Assembly is once again redefining its 'subsidiary' role in the maintenance of
international peace and security. The indications are that it will continue to
adopt resolutions condemning the illegal use of force by the United States,
evidenced by its condemnation of the American military intervention in
Panama in 1989,[15] but it is significant that it failed to adopt a resolution
directly condemning the Iraqi invasion of Kuwait in 1990. This contrast is
perhaps illustrative of the North-South divide creeping into the actions of
the General Assembly, in that it was prepared to condemn an unlawful use
of force by a developed State, but was not so prepared when that act was
committed by a developing State. Such an approach, if it continues, will
undermine the considerable credibility the General Assembly has in its
consistent condemnations of unlawful acts of aggression.

Notes

1 See Article 18(2) of the Charter.
2 GA Res. 1991, 18 UN GAOR Supp. (No. 15) 21 (1963), established the composition of the Council as follows: 5 permanent members, 5 from Afro-Asian States, 1
   from Eastern Europe, 2 from Latin America, 2 from Western European and
   other States.
3 D. Nicol, *The United Nations Security Council: Towards Greater Effectiveness*, 4
   (1982).
4 E. Luard, *A History of the United Nations: Vol.1 The Years of Western Domination (1945–1955)*, 383 (1982).
5 See for example the delegates from New Zealand and Australia, UNCIO, vol. 9,
   272, 266.
6 Belarus, formerly Byelorussia, and the Ukraine have been members since 1945
   originally at the insistence of the Soviet Union, in order to provide some balance
   in the Organisation between the two power blocs.
7 GA Res. 45/39, 45 UN GAOR Supp. (No. 49) 360 (1990).
8 GA Res. 45/170, 45 UN GAOR Supp. (No. 49) 283 (1990).
9 GA Res. 46/134, 46 UN GAOR (1991).
10 GA Res. 46/7, 46 UN GAOR (1991).
11 SC 3011 mtg, 46 S/PV (1991).
12 GA Res. 45/2, 45 UN GAOR Supp. (No. 49) 12 (1990).
13 UN docs S/21845, 21847 (1990).
14 S. D. Bailey, *The General Assembly*, 23 (1960).
15 GA Res. 44/240, 44 UN GAOR (1989).

CHAPTER FIVE

The subsidiary powers of the General Assembly

The idea that Articles 10, 11, 12, and 14 of the UN Charter, containing the source of the General Assembly's powers, can be subject to varying interpretations has already been raised in the introductory section to this Part when it was stated that the Western governments have changed their position from that of favouring a wide interpretation of these provisions giving the Assembly wide powers in the field of international peace, to a more narrow constitutional position in later years. The West still maintains this position despite the ending of the Cold War and its current dominance of the Security Council due to the fact that it is still in the minority in the subsidiary body.

General powers

Proponents of a wide view of the competence of the General Assembly would point to Articles 10 and 14 of the Charter. According to Article 10:

The General Assembly may discuss any questions or any matters within the scope of the present Charter or relating to the powers or functions of any organs provided for in the present Charter, and, except as provided in Article 12, may make recommendations to the Members of the United Nations or to the Security Council or to both on any such questions or matters.

Article 10 establishes a general competence for the Assembly to discuss any matter within the jurisdiction of the United Nations as determined by the Charter.[1] This power indeed makes the Assembly the 'town meeting place of the world', and 'the open conscience of humanity', as intended.[2] Its power to make recommendations on any such matter must also cover the same area as the more concrete recommendatory powers of the Security Council under Chapters VI and VII as regards the maintenance of international peace and security. Hence Article 10 is subject to Article 12 which attempts to delineate between the functions of the Assembly and those of the Security Council.

Once it is established that Article 10 creates the widest possible sphere of competence for the Assembly subject to Article 12, then the other provisions defining the powers of the Assembly are to some extent unnecessary unless they detract from the powers contained in Article 10. Article 11 deals more specifically and in a more limited fashion with the Assembly's role in the maintenance of international peace, but is subject to paragraph 4 which states that 'the powers of the General Assembly set forth in this Article shall not limit the general scope of Article 10'.

If Article 10 is insufficient to grant the Assembly the full range of recommendatory powers, Article 14 re-emphasises its potentially wide jurisdiction with specific reference to international security by providing that:

Subject to the provisions of Article 12, the General Assembly may recommend measures for the peaceful adjustment of any situation, regardless of origin, which it deems likely to impair the general welfare or friendly relations among nations, including situations resulting from a violation of the present Charter setting forth the Purposes and Principles of the United Nations.

Article 14 with its jurisdictional threshold of a situation deemed 'likely to impair the general welfare or friendly relations among nations' appears to give the Assembly access to a much wider range of situations in the field of international peace and security than the Security Council which technically requires a danger to international peace, a threat to or breach of the peace or an act of aggression to act under Chapter VI or VII.[3] The test under Article 14 covers the whole spectrum of situations which might impair peace, whereas the provisions contained in Articles 34 and 39 deal with the more important, global and potentially explosive situations. The Assembly can, under Articles 10 and 14, discuss situations contained in Articles 34 and 39, but to prevent any clash between the work of the Security Council, which is primarily concerned with such situations, and the General Assembly, Article 14, as well as Article 10, is subject to the limitation contained in Article 12.

Despite the fact that Article 14 is rarely cited or quoted in Assembly resolutions,[4] it, along with Article 10, forms the basis of most resolutions directed towards the maintenance of international peace and security, enabling the Assembly to suggest measures or sanctions against States and enabling it to bypass the domestic jurisdiction limitation contained in Article 2(7).[5]

Goodrich, Hambro and Simons agree that Article 14 has formed the basis of Assembly resolutions dealing with fundamental human rights and self-determination 'in the face of arguments that the questions being dealt with are matters of domestic jurisdiction'.[6] The above authors cite the report of the Special Commission set up by the Assembly in 1953 to study the apartheid policies of South Africa. The Commission interpreted the scope of

Article 14 as covering cases which 'were likely to bring interests into conflict with one another'.[7] This epitomises a rather more relaxed approach to Article 2(7) in the General Assembly compared to the Security Council, where the situation must usually be a threat to the peace or of international concern before intervention, in the form of a resolution, takes place.

The reference in Article 14 to the purposes and principles of the United Nations indicates that perhaps one of the major roles of the General Assembly is to deal with the right to self-determination contained in Article 1(2). Also Articles 1(3) and 13(1)(b) contain references to 'human rights and fundamental freedoms'. These provisions combined with the Assembly's role as regards the maintenance of international peace and security contained in Articles 10, 14 and indeed Article 11, suggest that the General Assembly has a major, if not primary role in situations concerning either human rights or the question of self-determination, or both, even when the situation also concerns the maintenance of international peace.

Whether one could say that the proper division of functions between the Security Council and the General Assembly as regards the maintenance of international peace and security depends on whether the situation is predominantly one of human rights and self-determination (in which case the General Assembly is perhaps the organ jurisdictionally competent to deal with it) will be examined later. For the moment it is sufficient to say that this view is practice based.[8]

Division of competence between the Security Council and the General Assembly according to the Charter

Articles 10 and 14 empower the General Assembly to discuss and make recommendations on matters which may be a danger to international peace within the meaning of Article 34, Chapter VI, or which constitute a threat to or breach of the peace within the meaning of Article 39, Chapter VII. Since these are the jurisdictional thresholds to the Security Council's competence in the field of international peace and security clearly there is a large area of overlap between the two organs. It is clear from Article 24(1) that the Security Council has 'primary responsibility' for peace and security, a position which Articles 11 and 12 of the UN Charter attempt to elaborate upon.

Article 11 in paragraphs 2 and 3 attempts to clarify the relationship between the Assembly and the Security Council as regards questions which come within Chapter VII or situations under Chapter VI. Nevertheless, these provisions of limitation must be read subject to paragraph 4 of Article 11, whereby Article 10 is stated not to be subject to the restrictions contained in Article 11, which suggests that Article 11 has no effect on the division of competence at all. This confusing situation may be explained by the compromise between the smaller States advocating wide powers and the sponsoring States attempting to limit these powers that produced these provisions.

Article 11(2) and (3) attempts to refine the wide area of overlap between the two organs created by Articles 10 and 14. Article 11(3) deals specifically with a situation which comes within Chapter VI, as defined by Article 34. 'The General Assembly may call the attention of the Security Council to situations which are likely to endanger international peace'. Article 11(3) seems to envisage the possibility of concurrent jurisdiction between the two organs in that it does not place an obligation on the Assembly to refer any such situation to the Council.

Article 24(2) refers to Chapter VI as containing 'specific powers granted to the Security Council' for the discharge of its primary responsibility, and all the Articles, except Article 35, seem to envisage exclusivity of operation to the Security Council. Nevertheless, Articles 10 and 14 empower the Assembly to make recommendations for pacific settlement similar to those contained in Chapter VI. Article 11(3) operates as a safety valve in that the Security Council is the body designed to deal with such situations. Article 11(3) does perform this function to a certain extent as evidenced by the fact that it is one of the rare Charter provisions actually cited in Assembly resolutions, for example as regards the situation in South Africa,[9] but it cannot be said to operate to oblige the General Assembly to refer such matters to the Security Council; it simply appears to be a rule of guidance which the Assembly can ignore if it wishes.

Article 24(2) also states that Chapter VII contains the specific powers of the Security Council, and, indeed, its power conferring provisions (Articles 39–42) do not mention the Assembly nor seem to envisage the Assembly entering into Chapter VII. Article 11(2) provides an answer to the conundrum of whether the Assembly can utilise Chapter VII by providing,

The General Assembly may discuss any questions relating to the maintenance of international peace and security brought before it by any Member of the United Nations, or by the Security Council, or by a state which is not a Member of the United Nations in accordance with Article 35, paragraph 2, and, except as provided in Article 12, may make recommendations with regard to any such questions to the state or states concerned or to the Security Council or to both. Any such question on which action is necessary shall be referred to the Security Council by the General Assembly either before or after discussion.

Article 11(2) enables the General Assembly to find a 'threat to the peace', a 'breach of the peace' or an 'act of aggression' and to make recommendations thereon to restore international peace, a power concurrent with that of the Security Council under Article 39. It is a recommendatory power only, any coercive measures under Chapter VII requiring a mandatory decision can only be adopted by the Security Council.[10]

This interpretation of Article 11(2) is supported by the International

Court in the *Expenses* case, when the Court stated,

The Court considers that the kind of action referred to in Article 11, paragraph 2, is coercive or enforcement action . . . The word 'action' must mean such action as is solely within the province of the Security Council. It cannot refer to recommendations which the Security Council might make, as for instance under Article 38, because the General Assembly under Article 11 has a comparable power . . . If the word 'action' in Article 11, paragraph 2, were interpreted to mean that the General Assembly could make recommendations only of a general character affecting peace and security in the abstract, and not in relation to specific cases, the paragraph would not have provided that the General Assembly may make recommendations on questions brought before it by States or by the Security Council.[11]

Although ambiguous, in that this does not make clear whether coercive or enforcement 'action' within the meaning of Article 11(2) is of a mandatory character or not, the tenor of this section of the judgement suggests that the General Assembly has a similar recommendatory power to the Security Council. Indeed, earlier in the judgement the Court makes it clear that the Security Council has a monopoly only on *mandatory* coercive action, not voluntary or recommendatory measures, when it states that 'only the Security Council . . . can *require* enforcement by coercive action' and further that 'it is the Security Council which, exclusively, may *order* coercive action'.[12] It follows from this that the Assembly can go so far as to recommend action by the Security Council, or to suggest voluntary sanctions, or further to recommend military measures.

Kelsen thought that the limitation in Article 11(2) precluded the recommendation of enforcement action, but considered that in any case Article 10 could be used.[13] Indeed on the assumption that Article 10 contains the *lex generalis* and Article 11 and, to a certain extent, Article 14, contain the *lex specialis*, the provisions of Article 11 are to a certain extent unnecessary under the principle that the extent of the Assembly's powers are defined by the general and in this case wider, rather than the specific, and in this case narrower, provisions. Nevertheless, the power of the Assembly to recommend economic or military action is controversial in that in the original Charter scheme the only way in which the United Nations could undertake economic or military action was by a mandatory decision of the *Security Council* under Articles 41 or 42. The express provisions of the Charter did not permit the Council to take recommendatory action and therefore the Assembly was similarly precluded. It is only by the development, or by implication, of a recommendatory power to the Security Council, which is not without controversy itself, that one can argue that the Assembly is similarly possessed.

Nevertheless, it is submitted that the General Assembly is not limited by Article 11(2) except that it confirms the Assembly's lack of power to undertake coercive action on more than a recommendatory basis. The only other provision which purports to delimit the functions of the Council and the Assembly is Article 12. We have already noted that Article 10 and 14 as well as 11(2) are subject to the limitation contained in Article 12(1) which states that:

While the Security Council is exercising in respect of any dispute or situation the functions assigned to it in the present Charter, the General Assembly shall not make any recommendations with regard to that dispute or situation unless the Security Council so requests.

Article 12 is probably the most difficult provision, in constitutional terms, to reconcile with the practice of the General Assembly. As we have seen, the other provisions can be interpreted to enable the Assembly to pass resolutions on any matter concerning the maintenance of peace as long as they do not purport to be mandatory. However, as shall be illustrated when we look at the division of competence in practice, the Assembly often adopts resolutions on a matter at the same time at which the Security Council is considering the question. Two arguments to escape Article 12 could be employed in this situation – that the Security Council, although considering the question and perhaps even adopting resolutions on it, is not actually performing the 'functions assigned to it in the Charter', or that the resolution adopted by the General Assembly is not actually a recommendation.[14]

It seems to have been established at an early stage that when an item is placed on the Security Council's agenda it is deemed to be exercising its functions in accordance with Article 12(1). The theory behind the list of matters which the Secretary General submits to the General Assembly is that it tells the Assembly which issues it is not allowed to discuss because they are receiving attention in the Security Council.[15] In effect, this amounts to defining 'functions' in Article 12(1) with reference to Article 12(2) which states,

The Secretary General, with the consent of the Security Council, shall notify the General Assembly at each session of any matters relative to the maintenance of international peace and security which are being dealt with by the Security Council and shall similarly notify the General Assembly, or the Members of the United Nations if the General Assembly is not in session, immediately the Security Council ceases to deal with such matters.

Professor Bowett subscribes to the view that Article 12(2) defines whether the Council is functioning or not. However, he recognises the artificiality of the process and concedes that, in practice, the Assembly is not limited by the list nor would it be reasonable to expect it to be. Even when the Council adopts a resolution the Assembly will sometimes adopt its own on the same question, the justification, according to this approach, being not one of legal interpretation 'but of necessity for the Assembly to promote the aims of the Charter when the Security Council cannot or will not do so'.[16]

The question of whether a recommendation adopted in the face of Article 12 with the requisite two-thirds majority with or without minority objections is *ultra vires* will be examined later. Suffice to say for the moment that the procedure in which the list of matters seized by the Security Council is also deemed to contain those matters in relation to which it is exercising the functions assigned to it may still be formally accepted, but in practice it has all but been disregarded.

Nevertheless, in the early years, this procedural rule was applied with some regularity. One of these cases was the Greek question (1947–48) which is worth examining in some detail because it is illustrative of how Western domination of the Organisation enabled it to manipulate the procedure to its own advantage.

The United States had committed itself by the Truman Doctrine to the economic and military support of Greece and Turkey. It was therefore interested in the prevention of a communist take-over in Greece. In the Security Council it managed to establish a Commission to examine the situation.[17] In May 1947 the majority of the Commission reported that Yugoslavia, Bulgaria and Albania had supported guerrilla warfare in Greece.[18] The United States proposed that the Council endorse the Commission's recommendation to send a permanent body to Greece to observe her borders.[19] This was seen by the communist countries as a Cold War move by a Council and a Commission dominated by Western countries. The proposal was vetoed by the Soviet Union.[20]

The United States simply waited for the regular session of the General Assembly in the autumn of 1947 to propose a similar resolution condemning Albania, Bulgaria and Yugoslavia and establishing a permanent Committee, UNSCOB, to help observe the borders.[21] Thus the United States had successfully used its overwhelming support in the United Nations to pass resolutions to reinforce its sphere of influence in the Balkans and to prevent the encroachment of communism.

Technically, however, the United States and its supporters managed to keep within the provisions of the Charter, in that after the Soviets had vetoed its last draft resolution in the Council, it proposed that the item be removed from the agenda to signify to the Assembly that it had ceased to deal with the matter allowing the Assembly to make recommendations thereon.[22] It was simply because the West dominated both organs that it could switch from Council to Assembly within the accepted constitutional procedure. It could easily win a procedural vote in the Council.

Whereas the Western States could use this method of transferring issues from the Council to the Assembly during the early Cold War period, the Non-Aligned group, once it became an established force in the 1960s, was not assured even with Socialist support, of winning a procedural vote in the Council and so in practice it tended to ignore legal technicalities. In view of the importance of the United Nations to the Non-Aligned, it was not surprising that they took the attitude that their disregard of a technical procedure adopted during a period of Western domination was no more reprehensible than the cynical manipulation by the West of the same procedure during the earlier period. This attitude to Article 12 seems set to continue despite the ending of the Cold War, although there is evidence that with the Security Council now 'functioning' more or less continuously and dealing positively with most issues brought before it, the Assembly has considerably less opportunity to assert its authority.

To restrict the General Assembly to matters which are not still formally on the Council's agenda is revealed to be unduly limiting if one examines the list of matters formally seized by the Security Council, in that it still contains matters first considered over forty years ago. For example the Palestine question was first put on the Council agenda in 1947, the India-Pakistan question in 1948, South Africa in 1960, and Western Sahara in 1975.[23] If a comparison is made between these and the examples of Assembly resolutions contained in the sections below, it is clear that the restrictive, procedural construction of Article 12 has been breached on many occasions.

An examination of the meaning of the term 'recommendation' in Article 12 has important implications because the provisions granting powers to the General Assembly as regards international peace (Articles 10, 11 and 14) only envisage Assembly resolutions in the form of recommendations. The question remains whether the Assembly can pass resolutions which are not technically recommendations and so escape the limitation contained in Article 12. The International Court answered this question in the affirmative in the *Expenses* case.

Thus while it is the Security Council which, exclusively, may order coercive action, the functions and powers conferred on the General Assembly are not confined to discussion, consideration, the initiation of studies and the making of recommendations, they are not merely hortatory. Article 18 deals with '*decisions*' of the General Assembly on 'important questions'. These 'decisions' do indeed include certain recommendations, but others have dispositive force and effect. Among these latter decisions, Article 18 includes suspension of rights and privileges of membership, expulsion of Members, 'and budgetary questions'.[24]

The Court's judgement confers recognition on non-recommendatory-type resolutions, which on a literal interpretation would not be subject to the limitation contained in Article 12. Chapter six which contains an examination of the concrete forms that General Assembly resolutions take will illustrate that the Assembly often condemns, decides (in a hortatory, non-mandatory sense), demands, or declares, thus leading to an argument that these types of resolution are not covered by Article 12.

Nevertheless, it is very difficult to maintain that all but a few General Assembly resolutions are compatible with this analysis. Often the resolution may demand or decide in one part and recommend in another, particularly with the increased length of resolutions passed regularly on subjects such as the Middle East and South Africa. Also those resolutions which appear to confirm Security Council resolutions, and so could be said to be confirmatory rather than recommendatory, do often go beyond them and contain further recommendations than their Council counterparts.

The domestic jurisdiction limitation

Article 2(7) prohibits the *United Nations* from intervening 'essentially within the domestic jurisdiction of any State'. This provision has already been examined in relation to the Security Council, when it was stated that the domestic jurisdiction limitation is inapplicable not only in those cases requiring enforcement measures under Chapter VII, as catered for by Article 2(7) itself, but also in cases of a threat to the peace without such measures, or, indeed, in situations deemed to be of international concern requiring only pacification under Chapter VI.

The General Assembly, however, has not developed a similar jurisprudence, or, indeed, any discernable principles governing the applicability of Article 2(7).[25] It is submitted that an agreed interpretation is not possible because the equilibrium between national and international interests sought by the drafters of Article 2(7) is not constant.[26]

As will be shown below, the denial of the right to self-determination was originally within the domestic jurisdiction of a State and so outside the purview of the United Nations, but now it is of international concern and so subject to review. In the Security Council it only takes one permanent member to use Article 2(7) as a basis for its veto and so that body has a more substantial jurisprudence on the meaning of the domestic jurisdiction limitation. Nevertheless, it is possible to chart the involvement of the General Assembly in what might superficially appear to be internal matters as developed in over forty years of practice.

The first clear interference in domestic internal affairs involved the Assembly examining the regime of a State. In December 1946, the Assembly passed a resolution which recommended the banning of Spain from the United Nations and its specialised agencies and requested that all Member States should recall their ambassadors from Spain. It also stated that if a democratic Spanish government was not established within a reasonable time, the Security Council should consider adequate measures to remedy the situation.[27]

The next area developed by General Assembly practice which effectively puts it outside the limitation contained in Article 2(7), concerned Non-Self-Governing Territories. Rajan cites many cases which will be discussed elsewhere, Tunisia, Algeria, the Portuguese Territories, Namibia and

Southern Rhodesia – to conclude that 'after all these actions' 'there is no shred of evidence to sustain the view that non self-governing territories fall under the domestic jurisdiction of their respective metropolitan powers',[28] despite objections by the colonial powers.[29] These objections are apt to be ephemeral, for example the United Kingdom initially relied on Article 2(7) to deny vehemently the United Nations' jurisdiction as regards Southern Rhodesia,[30] but after UDI it was Britain which requested the Organisation's involvement.[31]

The Assembly's disregard of Article 2(7) on issues of human rights and fundamental freedoms can be traced back to the era of Western domination when that body was used to criticise the Eastern bloc. At its third annual session in 1949, the Assembly adopted a resolution expressing concern at the 'grave accusations made against the governments of Bulgaria and Hungary regarding the suppression of human rights and fundamental freedoms'.[32] At the same session the Assembly criticised the Soviet Union declaring that the measures preventing the wives of foreign nationals from leaving their own country to join their husbands were 'not in conformity with the Charter, and that if the wives were persons belonging to foreign diplomatic missions, such measures were contrary to diplomatic practice and likely to impair friendly relations between States'. The resolution therefore called on the Soviet Union to withdraw the measures.[33]

The use of Article 14 language in the latter case is illustrative of how that provision was used to empower the Assembly to discuss relatively trivial matters for the practice criticised was hardly likely even remotely to endanger peace. It is not surprising therefore, that with such a relatively minor matter escaping the provisions of Article 2(7), the Non-Aligned majority established since the 1950s has not paid much heed to its limitations.

The United Nations' involvement in the South African problem cannot be classified as a trivial concern, but it is a good illustration of how the Assembly has now elevated the denial of human rights and fundamental freedoms to one of international concern. Only the South African government has persistently based its objections on Article 2(7).[34] Although it was initially supported by some Western States,[35] it now stands alone and indeed the 1990s has seen a slow process of change away from the iniquitous apartheid system.

A natural extension from the Assembly's concern for non-self-governing territories and cases concerning human rights and fundamental freedoms, is that of cases concerning the denial of the right to self-determination, an issue also raised by the South African situation. It will be a constant theme throughout this Part that one of the Assembly's major purposes is the furtherance of the right to self-determination. It has virtually established that the denial of that right is a matter of international concern and so no longer within the sovereign domain of a State.[36] This trend has been reinforced in the post Cold War era exemplified when the removal of the elected government in Haiti in 1991 by an internal military coup provoked a quick response from the General Assembly demanding, in a resolution supported by all Members, 'the immediate restoration of the legitimate government' and 'the full observance of human rights in Haiti'.[37]

The above instances all involve primary consideration of matters such as human rights and self-determination which may have consequences for international peace. It must be noted, however, that in cases primarily concerned with international peace and security, arguments based on domestic jurisdiction are used. Cases such as the Lebanon and Jordan (1958), Bangladesh (1971), Kampuchea (1979), and Afghanistan (1980), all involved arguments that the situation was internal and so covered by Article 2(7), but only usually by one party or power bloc involved in the dispute. Unlike the Security Council, however, these subjective arguments did not prevent the General Assembly from adopting resolutions.

Arguments of ultra vires

States objecting to the General Assembly adopting resolutions sometimes argue that the resolution is *ultra vires*. The argument is founded on Article 12 or Article 2(7). The Assembly's continued consideration of the apartheid policies of the South African government has produced many objections based on Article 2(7). Until the reform process started in the 1990s, the South African ambassador had consistently asserted that his government must regard 'any resolution emanating from a discussion on or the consideration of the present item as *ultra vires* and, therefore, null and void'.[38] One can find many examples of objections based on Article 2(7).[39] However, if they are in the minority they do not appear to have any effect on the jurisdiction of the Assembly. On these occasions, it sometimes appears, to the observer, that the Assembly's jurisdiction is determined by that body and not necessarily by the Charter.

An example of a resolution being introduced despite objections based on Article 12 is the Uniting for Peace resolution of 1950.[40] The resolution proposed to give competence to the Assembly, including the power to recommend enforcement measures, when the Security Council was paralysed by the veto. The Soviet Union and other Socialist States, being in the minority bloc at the time, objected to the resolution on the grounds that it was unconstitutional in that the 'functions' of the Security Council within the meaning of Article 12 included cases where the veto was used, since the veto was an integral part of the constitution of the Security Council. On this basis the Soviet representative thus asserted that the proposed procedure would amend the Charter without going through the amendment procedure envisaged by Article 109.[41] Nevertheless, the majority proceeded to adopt the resolution, the *procedure* of which has become established in Assembly practice, although the substantive powers embodied in the Resolution have not. In other words, although the Uniting for Peace Resolution has been used to transfer a matter from the Council to the Assembly, it has not been used as a basis for recommendatory military action by the Assembly, apart from peacekeeping operations.

From a legal point of view the Charter of the United Nations 'is the primary source of its jurisdiction'.[42] Admittedly, as far as the provisions conferring powers on the General Assembly are concerned, there is considerable confusion as to the limits of its jurisdiction. Nevertheless, Articles 12 and 2(7) represent relatively defined limitations on its competence, and it can be argued that clear breaches of these provisions are unconstitutional and therefore *ultra vires*. Even the doctrine of implied powers would not appear to save such resolutions. According to the World Court in the *Reparation* case, 'under international law, the Organisation must be deemed to have those powers which though not expressly provided in the Charter are conferred upon it by necessary implication as being essential to the performance of its duties'.[43] The Court does not allow the Organisation to imply powers which go against its Charter. Indeed, Ciobanu ties implied powers very securely to express provisions when he states that 'powers not expressed cannot freely be implied; implied powers flow from the grant of express powers, and are limited to those that are necessary to the exercise of powers expressly granted'.[44]

Even if one takes a much more liberal approach to implied or inherent powers than this, there is little possibility of accommodating a clear breach of an express provision within their framework. Inherent powers have been defined very widely to allow international organisations to 'perform in principle every sovereign activity or take every action under international law, if they are really in a position to accomplish such purposes, provided their constitutions do not preclude such an activity'.[45] This approach to the question of powers seems to go beyond the *dictum* of the International Court in the *Reparation* case in that it gives the Assembly virtual *carte blanche* to determine its own competence as long as it does not do so in contradiction to the express terms.

However, there are many factors preventing what appears to be a clear breach of the Charter from being null and void. First there is a World Court judgement which, as part of a teleological approach to treaty interpretation, favoured a presumption against *ultra vires* where the action taken 'was appropriate for the fulfilment of one of the stated purposes of the United Nations'.[46] The presumption against *ultra vires* is a practical approach to the problem recognising that a resolution adopted according to the voting provisions of the Charter has to be presumed to be valid otherwise the

Assembly's resolutions would remain in a state of limbo until the unlikely event of their challenge before the International Court. It is the lack of procedure for the challenge of resolutions that leads to this presumption. Judge Morelli made this clear in a separate judgement when he stated that 'the failure of an organ to conform to the rules concerning competence has no influence on the validity of the act, which amounts to saying that each organ of the United Nations is the judge of its own competence'.[47]

The same arguments apply to decisions of the Security Council except that the Council is less likely than the Assembly to pass resolutions which are apparently in contravention to the Charter. One of the permanent members would probably prevent this by using its veto to protect its interests. To this extent, the veto operates as a safeguard against the adoption of *ultra vires* resolutions, although the end of the political limitations on the Council in the post Cold War era has, as we have seen in chapter two, also resulted in the Council pushing its powers to the limit and perhaps beyond its constitution in the strict sense. However, the Council has a much greater competence in the field of international peace than the Assembly which is much more likely to contravene the provisions of the Charter such as Article 12 which attempt to limit its competence and keep it as the subsidiary body.

The approach that recognises the theory of 'la compétence de la compétence', simply that the Council and Assembly act as judges of their own competence,[48] was not without recognition at San Francisco where the relevant Committee stated that 'it is inevitable that each organ will interpret such parts of the Charter as are applicable to its particular functions. This process is inherent in the functioning of any body which operates under an instrument defining its functions and powers'.[49] In addition to the legal recognition of the Assembly's (and Council's) ability to act as its own judge, one must not forget the inherent difficulty in making an *ultra vires* objection count, a problem made worse by the practice of the Assembly of not citing the source of its authority in its resolutions. If there is no clear basis as to the resolution it is indeed difficult to challenge it for the challenge itself must be based on an interpretation of the provision.

The principle of subsequent practice

A related question to that discussed in the above section is whether the Assembly has reinterpreted the Charter by its subsequent practice. The principle of subsequent practice as regards treaty interpretation is reasonably clear and accepted as affording legitimate evidence as to its correct interpretation. A common, consistent practice by the vast majority of parties to a multilateral treaty such as the Charter of the United Nations 'must come near to being conclusive on how the treaty should be interpreted'. Indeed, this amounts to 'not so much the meaning of an existing text, as a revision of it, but a revision brought about by practice or conduct, rather than affected by and recorded in writing'. Further, 'conduct usually forms a more reliable guide to intention or purpose than anything to be found for instance in the preparatory work of the treaty simply because it has taken concrete and active, and not merely paper or verbal, form'.[50]

So if the Assembly has consistently adopted resolutions on matters subject to Article 2(7) and Article 12 by a sufficiently large majority throughout its forty years of practice it might be possible to state that this amounts to a revision of those provisions. On the presumption that a consistent two-thirds majority, present and voting (which is required for important questions), is sufficient, it is submitted that such a revision has taken place. The revision amounts to a severe restriction on the domestic jurisdiction limitation contained in Article 2(7); a virtual disregard of the division of competence between the Assembly and the Council contained in Article 12; and, in effect, an interpretation of the vague powers contained in Articles 10, 11 and 14 to give the Assembly competence and powers with regard to any matter in international relations with the exception of the ability to take mandatory measures.

The following section and chapter six will attempt to rationalise and categorise the practice of the Assembly first in the matter of competence, particularly as regards the Security Council, and, secondly, as regards the concrete forms which the powers of the Assembly, derived from its competence, take.

The division of competence between the General Assembly and the Security Council in practice

Given that it has been established in this chapter that Article 11(2) only operated to prohibit the Assembly from taking mandatory, coercive action and that Article 12 had been revised by Assembly practice, it remains to be seen as to what form this revision has taken. A loose categorisation is made in the following section into situations in which the Assembly has acted in the following ways towards the Security Council: in a parallel manner; in a complementary way; in a manner which pre-empts or pre-judges any potential decision or resolution of the Security Council; in a manner that concentrates on self-determination and human rights as opposed to security matters; and finally in a manner that amounts to performing the role of the Security Council.

Parallel resolutions
On a number of occasions the Assembly has acted in a parallel manner to the Security Council by simply repeating the resolutions of the Council. Good examples of this can be found in the Assembly's resolutions on the Gulf War

between Iran and Iraq, on Cyprus after the Turkish invasion of 1974, and in the recent peace efforts in Cambodia in 1990–91.

During the Gulf War of 1980–88, the General Assembly did little more than to parallel the Security Council. The Assembly adopted a resolution in 1982 on the conflict which was to all intents and purposes a reaffirmation of previous Council resolutions.[51] The only value of the resolution was that of repetition for it even recognised, when calling for a cease-fire, that 'the Security Council has already called for an immediate cease fire and end to all military operations'. It reflected the Council's jurisdictional findings when it deemed that the conflict endangered international peace and security. It did not seek to pre-judge the Council by determining that the conflict was a breach of the peace, although some members thought that the Assembly should have made such a determination.[52] It was not until 1987 that the Council finally reached such a conclusion.

Although the Iraq-Iran war was on the Council's agenda and was the subject of frequent resolutions calling for a cease-fire, the Members of the Assembly apparently did not see the resolution as treading on the toes of the Council. The representative of Jamaica made it plain that nothing in the resolution 'proposes the removal of the issue from the purview' of the Council and was not 'an attempt to circumvent the fundamental role of the Security Council'.[53]

Sometimes, in the case of disputes which are never off the Security Council's agenda, it appears as if the General Assembly, in its annual session of three to four months, is taking part of the burden off the Council by adopting resolutions on the conflict. In some cases the Assembly seizes this opportunity either to complement the Council's resolutions or to pre-empt them. In the case of Cyprus, however, the Assembly has added little to the work of the Council except perhaps an increased weight of international opinion.

After the Greek-backed coup against Makarios and the Turkish invasion of the northern part of Cyprus in 1974, the General Assembly virtually repeated earlier Council resolutions in its own resolution passed at its 29th session in 1974 which expressed grave concern 'about the continuation of the Cyprus crisis, which constitutes a threat to international peace and security', urged the withdrawal of foreign forces and the cessation of all 'foreign interference in its affairs'.[54]

By the time the Assembly passed this resolution the Turkish intervention had become a *fait accompli*. This partly explains why the Assembly and the Council share the responsibility of dealing with the Cyprus situation, for once the Council had acted promptly in accordance with Article 28(1) of the Charter during the initial crisis in 1974 and the situation had become ongoing, there was no practical reason why both organs should not share the burden even though the situation is primarily one of international peace and in theory Article 12 should apply.

Parallel resolutions by the General Assembly during the Cold War were less apparent than resolutions antagonistic towards the Security Council. The Gulf and Cyprus are examples of where neither superpower had the upper hand. As we shall see the Assembly tended to be the primary organ when it came to UN resolutions on superpower interventions, or situations in which one superpower was predominant. One of these instances followed the Vietnamese intervention in Kampuchea (Cambodia) in 1978, an action which was not condemned by the Security Council because of the Soviet veto, but which was consistently condemned by the General Assembly. However, since the end of the Cold War, the collapse of the Soviet Union, and the withdrawal of Vietnam from Cambodia, the warring factions in Cambodia have moved towards a peaceful settlement, guided by both the Security Council and the General Assembly with the latter acting more as the subsidiary body lending support to the Council by means of simple reiteration.

In addition, whereas the resolutions condemning the Vietnamese military intervention in Kampuchea were adopted by a majority, the resolutions supporting a Security Council-backed peace plan were adopted without a vote. This adds significantly to their weight. At its 45th and 46th sessions, the Assembly adopted resolutions supporting significant agreements between the warring factions, at Jakarta on 10 September 1990 and at Paris on 23 October 1991.[55] These agreements were effectively brokered by the permanent five of the Security Council and had received endorsement in that body. The General Assembly was simply adding its weight to the process and also to the mandate of the Secretary General who was responsible for the implementation of the peace plan under the Security Council's resolutions.

One can strongly argue that when the Assembly acts in a parallel fashion, simply repeating the work of the Security Council, it is actually complementing the role of the primary organ by maintaining the focus of world attention on the dispute or situation. On other occasions the Assembly complements the Council in additional ways, without prejudice to the Council position.

Complementary resolutions

As regards the Indonesian invasion of East Timor in 1975, although the General Assembly produced a resolution which was remarkably similar to its Council counterpart,[56] it could not be accused of merely repeating or paralleling the Council for it seized the issue and adopted its resolution *before* the Council. Indonesia had moved its troops into East Timor on 7 December, the General Assembly adopted its resolution on the 12th, whereas the Council could only virtually repeat the Assembly's call on the

22nd. The Assembly did not really pre-empt the Council for the resolution contained no findings under Article 39 but did contain a request to the Council 'in conformity with' Article 11(3) to consider the situation. The Assembly was not performing the Council's role, for the Council did act eventually, only more slowly. It was a case of the Assembly aiding the Council, the machinery of which, on this occasion, lacked the necessary alacrity.

After the Security Council had failed to adopt a resolution which dealt more than temporarily with the Tunisian conflict,[57] the General Assembly held its Third Special Session in August 1961 under Article 20 of the Charter.

The representative of Tunisia stated that the General Assembly should act because of the inability of the Council to end French aggression and to secure the withdrawal of French troops who were in Tunisia 'against the will of the people'.[58] Nevertheless, the Assembly did not adopt a resolution condemning French aggression; instead it adopted one calling for negotiations and French withdrawal. The resolution classified the situation as a 'source of international friction' and a danger to international peace and security.[59]

Although the resolution did not favour the French, it built upon rather than detracted from the work of the Council. The Council was able to act with some immediacy and call for a cease-fire but as on so many occasions was unable to go that step further and recommend a basis for settlement. Instead, the Assembly performed this task making explicit what was implicit in the Council resolution, that the situation was of a kind that should be subject to pacific settlement. The Assembly did not upset the work of the Council by finding a 'breach of the peace' or 'act of aggression' which would not have induced any settlement.

Pre-emptive resolutions

Nevertheless, with the change in composition of the Assembly during the 1960s, the new majority often found itself at loggerheads with the Security Council. The chief instance of this is when the Assembly pre-judged or pre-empted the work of the Council by making a determination of a threat to or breach of the peace within the meaning of Article 39. This was particularly so as regards colonial and neo-colonial situations.

As early as 1962 the General Assembly found 'that the policy and acts of the Portuguese Government with regard to the territories under its administration have constituted a serious threat to international peace and security'. This determination within the terms of Article 39 suggests that the situation required 'action' by the Security Council which should have had the question referred to it under Article 11(2). The resolution appeared to recognise this in that it requested the Security Council to take steps to 'secure the compliance of Portugal with its obligations as a Member State'.[60] Nevertheless, the Council did not enter into Chapter VII. Furthermore, was not until 1972 that it found that the situation in the Portuguese Territories was a 'danger' to international peace.[61]

In the case of Southern Rhodesia the Assembly found the situation constituted a threat to the peace in 1963 several years before the Security Council.[62] A finding of a threat to the peace is mainly a political decision and so one might expect a difference in the timing of such a finding in the two organs. Nevertheless, once the situation came to a head with UDI in 1965 one might have expected the Security Council to take the lead. Not so, for the General Assembly was first to condemn UDI and referred the matter to the Security Council.[63] It even urged the Security Council to adopt enforcement measures under Chapter VII before the Council had even agreed to condemn UDI.[64]

The Assembly, throughout the problems in Southern Rhodesia, seemed to be pushing the Council, reaching decisions which the Council often reluctantly followed, and above all acting as the conscience of the Security Council. There were objections. The Dutch representative pointed out that the Security Council had been seized of the problem since 1963 and so by virtue of Article 12 the Assembly could not make recommendations unless the Council so requested.[65] He also stated that the situation was not a threat to the peace with the consequence that no enforcement measures could be taken. His and other objections were ignored as the Council adopted mandatory economic measures against the minority Smith regime. Nevertheless, the Assembly did not stop pushing to have the embargo made more effective. It called on the Council to take the next logical and legal step within the meaning of Articles 2(5), 4 and 5 of the Charter of taking mandatory sanctions against the sanction breakers, principally South Africa and Portugal.[66] This call was repeated (but never followed) in 1973 in a resolution which contained an appeal to those vetoing permanent members (the United States, Britain and France) to stop preventing the Council from performing its duty.[67] It may have been stepping on the toes of the Council, but the Assembly took it upon itself to act as the conscience of the Council, particularly the permanent members.

During the early years of its consideration of the South African problem the Assembly was contented with finding that the continuance of the policies of the South African government 'seriously endangers international peace and security' while calling on the Security Council to consider the question under Article 11(3).[68]

However, four years later in 1965 the Socialist/Non-Aligned majority's patience ran out when it adopted a resolution which drew the Council's attention to the fact that the 'situation in South Africa constitutes a threat to international peace and security; that action under Chapter VII of the

Charter is essential to solve the problem of apartheid and that universally applied economic sanctions are the only means of achieving a peaceful solution'.[69]

The General Assembly had pre-empted the Security Council's prerogative of making a determination under Article 39. The majority ignored the problem of division of powers. The representative of Norway, however, expressed the minority view that it was 'the Security Council and the Security Council alone, which has the authority to stipulate if a situation or crisis is of such a nature that sanctions should be imposed'. He stated that although the 'General Assembly can and should exert its influence on the Security Council', in his opinion, the resolution went too far in finding a threat to the peace.[70] Nevertheless, the Assembly maintained this attitude until its 46th session in 1991. Up until then it reiterated that the situation in South Africa constituted a threat to the peace,[71] and urged the imposition of mandatory economic sanctions by the Security Council under Chapter VII of the Charter.[72] However, the reforms started in the 1990s by the South African government, although not leading as yet to majority rule, have resulted in a toning down of the Assembly's resolutions. Whereas the 1989 resolution reaffirmed that 'apartheid is a crime against humanity and a threat to international peace and security', the 1991 resolution simply reaffirmed the Assembly's 'support for the legitimate struggle of the South African people for the total eradication of apartheid through peaceful means'. It did not contain any call for the Security Council to impose mandatory sanctions.[73]

There appeared less antagonism between the Council and the Assembly over the illegal South African occupation of South West Africa/Namibia. In 1966 the General Assembly terminated South Africa's mandate over Namibia and called 'the attention of the Security Council to the present resolution'.[74] This represented quite a good example of the dovetailing of the Assembly and the Council; a fact recognised by the International Court in the *Namibia* case when it stated:

By resolution 2145 the General Assembly terminated the Mandate. However, lacking the necessary powers to ensure the withdrawal of South Africa from the Territory, it enlisted the help of the Security Council by calling the latter's attention to the resolution, thus acting in accordance with Article 11, paragraph 2 of the Charter.[75]

The Council went on to adopt resolutions for this purpose. However, this brief period of harmony was sandwiched between Assembly resolutions which went far beyond the rather tentative approach of the Council. The Assembly had first addressed the issue of South West Africa in 1946,[76] but it did not reach a jurisdictional finding until 1960 when it considered 'with grave concern that the present situation in South West Africa constitutes a serious threat to international peace and security'.[77] Nevertheless, it did not request, under Article 11(2) or (3), that the Security Council meet even though by finding of a 'threat to the peace' it brought the situation within the ambit of the Council's primary responsibility.

After the termination of South Africa's mandate, the Assembly became increasingly exasperated with the Council's inability to end South Africa's presence in Namibia. For instance in 1981, the Assembly named France, the United States and the United Kingdom as being 'in collusion with the South African racists as manifested in their triple vetoes in the Security Council where the majority of the world body demonstrated its determination to adopt concrete political and economic measures aimed at isolating terrorist South Africa in order to compel it to vacate Namibia'.[78] It maintained this approach up until the independence of Namibia in 1990, condemning the linkage of South African withdrawal from Namibia with Cuban withdrawal from Angola contained in the 1988 peace plan agreed between Angola, Cuba and South Africa.[79]

Western States objected to many of these resolutions, and used Articles 11(2) and 12 as a legal basis.[80] However, the attitude of Western States was summed up by the representative of Canada who in explaining his negative vote on a 1981 resolution stated that 'the authority of the General Assembly is recommendatory in character; moreover, the General Assembly cannot arrogate to itself powers it does not have by using language appropriate only to the Security Council. Nothing in this text, therefore, gives rise to a legal obligation'.[81] This is illustrative of the Western States, realising that they could not stop the resolutions from being adopted, simply refusing to accept that they imposed any obligation on Members. Since the resolutions were validly adopted according to the voting rules, arguments based on Articles 11 and 12 would have been futile, so the thrust of the West's arguments, when it bothered to state one, was that the resolutions of the Assembly were of paper value only, mere recommendations, the real power of decision making lay with the Security Council. The Western States attempted to confine the Assembly to a forum where the majority of Members let off steam.

The Assembly's actions over Palestine also reflect the fact that in the early years, when there was a Western majority in both organs, the Assembly acted as a complement to the Council, whereas after the mid-1950s, with the increase in newly independent, Non-Aligned countries, the Assembly's resolutions became increasingly extreme and divorced from those of the Council.

After the failure of its partition plan for Palestine, reviewed in chapter six, the Assembly set about complementing the Council in its efforts to restore peace and stability to the region. For example it passed a resolution in 1948 which strongly affirmed the General Assembly's 'support for the efforts of the Security Council to secure a truce in Palestine'. To further the Council's efforts, the Assembly appointed a mediator to 'promote a peaceful adjustment of the future situation in Palestine' and to 'co-operate with the Truce Commission for Palestine appointed by the Security Council on 23 April 1948'.[82]

From this relatively harmonious position the Assembly and Council have become increasingly divorced in their dealings with the Palestinian problem. Annual resolutions on the Palestine situation have been adopted since the mid-1970s, based on the reports of the Committee on the Exercise of the Inalienable Rights of the Palestinian people, a heavily biased Committee on which the West refuses to serve.

In its resolutions on the Middle East question the Assembly has shown the same propensity for entering the Council's area of competence while isolating the generally pro-Israeli Western countries even though it may appear as if the Assembly is supporting the relevant Council resolution. For example, in 1971 the Assembly adopted a resolution which appeared to accord with the Council's actions in that it stated 'that the Security Council resolution 242 (1967) should be implemented in all its parts in order to achieve a just and lasting peace in the Middle East'. However, the resolution went further and found a 'threat to the peace' which the Council had not and suggested the Council take steps for the implementation of 242. The West's main objections, however, were with the alterations of the balance of the Council's resolution such as the Assembly's expression of grave concern at Israel's 'continued occupation' rather than with the introduction of the term 'threat to the peace' which in Assembly terms, unlike those of the Council, cannot make the resolution mandatory.[83] The Dutch also felt 'as a conscientious Member of the United Nations, that Article 12 of the Charter should be scrupulously observed'.[84]

Nevertheless, more than two-thirds of the Assembly were not so 'conscientious' and in 1975 it adopted a resolution which in addition to a finding of a threat to the peace provided an example of a comprehensive, pre-emptive request to the Council to take measures 'to ensure complete Israeli withdrawal from all the occupied Arab territories as well as a full recognition of the inalienable national rights of the Palestinian people and the attainment of those rights'.[85]

The resolutions have become increasingly antagonistic; condemning the United States for aiding Israeli 'aggression' against the Palestinian people;[86] calling for voluntary measures against Israel and demanding that it comply with Article 25 as regards Council resolutions;[87] condemning Israel's links with South Africa; and criticising the United States for vetoing a draft resolution in the Security Council which prevented that body from taking Chapter VII action against Israel for its invasion of the Lebanon.[88] In effect, the Assembly abrogated to itself a virtually limitless competence as far as recommendatory resolutions were concerned.

Even with the superpower sponsored Middle East peace process starting after the Gulf Crisis with a Peace Conference in Madrid in October 1991, the General Assembly adopted a resolution on Palestine two months later at its 46th session, calling for a full International Peace Conference on the Middle East under the auspices of the United Nations, with all the parties to the conflict participating including the PLO. This in effect was a criticism of the peace process under way which was not under UN auspices and did not include the PLO. In addition the resolution, while purporting to be furthering Security Council resolution 242 (1967), in effect went further by explicitly mentioning Jerusalem in the list of those territories from which Israel should withdraw, and stating that Israel should dismantle the settlements it has built in the Occupied Territories since 1967. Although the resolution attempted a balanced approach by stating that the guarantee of the security of all States in the area in addition to freedom of access to holy places were also principles for the achievement of a comprehensive peace, it effectively was an attempt to undermine a legitimate peace process by listing those principles which the Assembly, not the parties, thought should form the basis for peace.[89]

Focus on self-determination and human rights

Many of the above instances can be seen as cases in which the General Assembly has acted within its own area of competence even though they also concern international peace and security. If a conflict is dominated by questions of fundamental human rights or the problem of self-determination then, arguably, the General Assembly has the primary role as the body responsible for the protection of those rights, even though the situation also involves the maintenance of international peace.

It has been suggested earlier in this chapter that the expansive jurisdiction of the General Assembly can be explained partly by its desire to further and protect the right of self-determination and human rights. These principles are enshrined in the Charter but no specific organ is entrusted with their protection. It is therefore natural that the Assembly, embodying the United Nations, should put itself forward as the defender of these principles. Often issues of self-determination and human rights involve questions of peace and security and thus we frequently have both the Security Council and the General Assembly involved. Strictly, on this basis, the Assembly should only concentrate on the aspects of self-determination and human rights, without considering the security situation, but, as shall be illustrated below, this is often impossible in situations where the denial of self-determination is in itself seen as a threat to the peace.

The Assembly's resolutions on the Middle East and Southern Africa can be grouped together under this heading for they are illustrative of how, in long-running situations, the Assembly will stray from its true sphere of competence. This is usually due to a majority of Members equating a denial of self-determination with a threat to the peace. The General Assembly then sees its function as trying to bring the Security Council into line with this finding and urging it to take the appropriate measures. These areas have been discussed above in the section on the pre-emption of the Council. This section is an alternative way of looking at the problem. The section on pre-judging can perhaps be seen as an example of how by ritualising the topics the Assembly loses sight of its purpose, namely the protection of fundamental human rights and the right of self-determination, and concentrates on the question of peace based on its finding of a threat, which, generally speaking, should be dealt with by the Security Council.

In the Southern Rhodesian situation the Assembly was primarily concerned with the implementation of the 1960 Declaration on the Granting of Independence to Colonial Countries and Peoples and not with problems of international peace and security as such.[90] However, this culminated in the merging of the two areas in 1963 when the Assembly decided that the failure to accord 'basic political rights' to the 'vast majority of the African population' and the 'entrenchment of the minority regime in power' created an 'explosive situation' which constituted a 'threat to international peace and security'.[91] The equation of a denial of human rights and self-determination with a threat to the peace shifted the emphasis towards the Council.[92] One could argue that after the Council had made a similar finding in 1966 the Assembly should have left the situation to the Council. Nevertheless, the Assembly kept pre-judging the work of the Council until the settlement of the situation in 1980.

The situation in the Portuguese territories parallels that of Southern Rhodesia. For example in 1962, the Assembly found 'that the continued refusal of Portugal to recognise the legitimate aspirations of the Angolan people to self-determination' constituted a threat to international peace and security.[93]

The Socialist and Non-Aligned majority in the Assembly seemed to favour the view that a denial of self-determination constituted a threat to the peace.[94] Thus the Assembly was often in disagreement with the Council where the Western vetoes denied such findings. Thus with the Assembly and Council out of step, the Assembly found itself constantly urging the Council to align itself with the majority resulting in resolutions which pre-empt and pre-judge the work of the Council.

Again in the case of South Africa, the Assembly began by concentrating on the denial of self-determination and of human rights. In 1952 the Assembly established a Commission of Three to examine the question of race conflict in South Africa.[95] The Commission's report concluded that the racial policies of the government of South Africa were contrary to the

Charter and the Universal Declaration of Human Rights and that the continuance of these policies would endanger friendly relations among States.[96] The Assembly established the basis of its examination of the South Africa problem in 1953 when it found that:

enduring peace will not be secured solely by collective arrangements against breaches of international peace, but that a genuine and lasting peace depends upon the observance of all the Purposes and Principles established in the Charter intended to achieve the maintenance of international peace and security, and especially upon respect for and observance of human rights and fundamental freedoms for all.[97]

This inevitably led the Assembly to find a threat to the peace and then to urge the Council to step in line. The problem is that with Western States believing that there is no question of finding a threat to the peace based solely on a denial of human rights, there is bound to be antagonism between the Council and the Assembly. The Western States believe that findings of a threat to the peace must be made by the Council alone which suggests that there must be something more than a denial of human rights.[98]

As long as the West takes this view the two organs will not be in accord. The Assembly will continue to attack the problem from the angle of a denial of human rights and self-determination, whereas a minority in the Council will continue to look for some sign of a danger to international peace arising from something more than the internal situation. These conflicting perspectives are unlikely to change with the demise of the Socialist bloc, although the slow process of change in South Africa has resulted in the Assembly not making a determination that the situation in South Africa is a threat to the peace at its 46th session in 1991, although it still continues to support the 'legitimate struggle' of the South African people.[99]

As we have seen, the General Assembly's consideration of the Palestinian problem has been expanded into a consideration of the whole Middle Eastern question which is essentially one of international peace. Nevertheless, the basis of the Assembly's involvement is centred around the self-determination of the Palestinian people. Its resolution of 1974 is a typical example containing an expression of deep concern 'that the problem of Palestine continues to endanger international peace and security'. Article 11(3) would tend to suggest that the Security Council should be called on to deal with the situation. However, the rest of the resolution is concerned with a reaffirmation of the Palestinians' right to self-determination, independence and sovereignty and recognises the 'right of the Palestinian people to regain its rights by all means in accordance with the purposes and principles of the Charter of the United Nations'.[100] For the Assembly the issues of self-determination and the maintenance of peace are inextricably linked.

The difficulty is that since the resolutions are pro-Palestinian and thus anti-Israeli, Israel's supporters on the Security Council are unlikely to take up the Assembly's resolutions. This leads the majority of the Assembly to adopt resolutions which increasingly impinge on the area of competence of the Security Council. As we have seen in the section on pre-judging resolutions, this trend has not discontinued with the end of the Cold War though it has become more focused on the current peace process.

The General Assembly as primary organ

This section is concerned with instances when the Assembly has performed the functions of the Security Council. In other words it has taken over the role of the Council which has failed to fulfil its primary responsibility for the maintenance of international peace and security under Article 24.

There are three methods by which the General Assembly has become the primary organ as regards a situation concerning international peace: by means of the Interim Committee or Little Assembly, by the Uniting for Peace procedure in Emergency Special Session, or by Special Session under Article 20. Only the last of these is specifically authorised by the Charter. The former two methods were both created in the period of Western domination (1945–55) in an attempt to give the Assembly power when the Security Council was paralysed by the Soviet veto.

The first method the pro-Western majority employed in an attempt to give more primacy in affairs of peace and security to the Assembly concentrated on increasing the effective length of the Assembly's session beyond its four-monthly regular session. The Assembly adopted a proposal by the United States creating a Little Assembly consisting of all the Members which could be convened all year round.[101] What was intended was to give the Assembly competence in the area of international peace when not in regular session, in other words an 'all year' Assembly.

Its responsibilities included the study of problems relating to international peace and reporting to the Assembly at its regular session. Thus the power of recommendation still remained with the Assembly proper and so the Little Assembly did not represent a serious revision of the Charter to extend the Assembly's period of competence. In practice it represented even less of a threat to the Council's primacy for although it did submit reports to the General Assembly during the first decade, it was severely paralysed by the Soviet boycott and was eclipsed by another Western sponsored idea, the Uniting for Peace resolution.

The creators of the Interim Committee saw it as a subsidiary organ of the General Assembly under Article 22. Prandler argues that it was created unconstitutionally, for theoretically its powers in the field of international peace undermined those of the Security Council and it is doubtful whether subsidiary bodies can have an independent scope of duties.[102] One would have thought that the Little Assembly's powers came under the Assembly's umbrella of powers, either Articles 10, 11 or 14, and so it had no duties independent of the Assembly, and only undermined the Security Council's competence in that it attempted to extend the Assembly's period of session.

The immediate reason for the adoption of the Uniting for Peace resolution,[103] was the return, in August 1950, of the Soviet Union to the Security Council leading to the discontinuation of the Council as the body dealing with Korea. In fact the Assembly adopted a resolution on Korea after the Soviets had returned to the Security Council but before the Uniting for Peace resolution was adopted.[104] However, the reasons for Uniting for Peace went beyond Korea, in that the Western influenced majority in the General Assembly was also of the view that the frequent use of the Soviet veto during the period 1946–50 was an abuse of that right and that the ideal of Great Power unanimity at San Francisco was no longer attainable. The Western States wanted an alternative form of collective security, based not on permanent member agreement in the Security Council, but on the basis of the will of the majority in the Assembly. Such a concept of collective security, whilst opening up the potential for economic and military actions against transgressors, also had the potential for allowing the General Assembly to authorise military action against one of the permanent members if the majority so wished, and if between them they had sufficient military might. It may be because this system of collective security was potentially dangerous that the resolution restricted the Assembly's power to recommend military measures to the most flagrant violations of international peace, namely breaches of the peace or acts of aggression, and did not expressly permit the Assembly to take such measures as a response to threats to the peace.

The method proposed by the United States, Canada, France, the Philippines, the United Kingdom, Turkey and Uruguay, by which paralysis of the Security Council would be circumvented was the Uniting for Peace resolution, the salient part of which resolved:

that if the Security Council, because of lack of unanimity of the permanent members, fails to exercise its primary responsibility for the maintenance of international peace and security in any case where there appears to be a threat to the peace, breach of the peace, or act of aggression, the General Assembly shall consider the matter immediately with a view to making the appropriate recommendations to Members for collective measures, including in the case of a breach of the peace or act of aggression the use of armed force when necessary, to maintain or restore international peace and security. If not in session at the time, the General Assembly may meet in emergency special session within 24 hours of the request therefor. Such emergency special session shall be called if requested by the Security Council on a vote of any seven [now nine] members, or by a majority of the Members of the United Nations.[105]

The resolution was introduced at the height of the Cold War and predictably led to an East-West dichotomy in the discussions leading up to it. Since it was the time of Western domination, the Socialist countries argued against its adoption on the basis that Articles 10 to 14 of the Charter indicated that the Security Council and the General Assembly 'cannot be substituted for one another, they merely complement each other'.[106] The pro-Western States argued, *inter alia*, that the resolution was valid on a wide interpretation of Article 12, for when the Council was paralysed by the veto it was not 'functioning' in the sense of that provision.[107] To this the representative of the Soviet Union replied that the operation of the veto was an integral function of the Security Council. He also objected on the ground that the proposed resolution would only require a procedural vote to transfer the matter from the Security Council to the Assembly, whilst Special Sessions called for under Article 20 needed a substantive vote. Finally the Soviet Union argued that the proposed resolution was unconstitutional because by Article 11(2) coercive action was within the sole ambit of the Council.[108]

The World Court in the *Expenses* case stated that 'action' in Article 11(2) refers to coercive action but it failed to state whether this excluded the Assembly from recommending coercive measures. At some points the Court suggested that 'action' is restricted to mandatory, coercive action 'ordered' by the Security Council. In other words the Assembly may not be barred from recommending enforcement action as part of its significant responsibility for the maintenance of peace as recognised by the Court.[109] If one accepts this line of argument, and it is by no means settled, then the Assembly can recommend that members take economic and military measures when there is a breach of the peace or act of aggression. Furthermore, there appears to be no cogent objection to allowing the Assembly to recommend military measures to combat a threat to the peace.

It is this writer's opinion that the ambiguous statements of the Court, in addition to the presumption against *ultra vires*, signify that the Uniting for Peace resolution is not unconstitutional. It represents an interpretation of Articles 11(2) and 12 that has been accepted and acted upon by the members of the United Nations, including the Soviet Union and other Members originally opposed to the resolution,[110] although not to the extent of recommending military action. To cast doubts on the legal validity of the resolution would mean that any action taken under the resolution would be suspect until the World Court is asked to decide on the issue. This would jeopardise a not insignificant segment of Assembly resolutions.

However, if one looks at the issue from the perspective of the ban on the use of armed force, a rule of *jus cogens* from which no derogation is allowed, contained in Article 2(4) of the Charter, doubts may be cast on the legality of the Uniting for Peace resolution and the power of the Assembly to recommend military measures. The exceptions to Article 2(4) are explicitly stated in the UN Charter to include only action in self-defence under Article 51 of the UN Charter and military action by the Security Council within Article

42. To state that the General Assembly can authorise military action creates a third exception which would be contrary to the *jus cogens* in Article 2(4). However, the Security Council is authorising military action on behalf of the *United Nations* and so a counter-argument is that the exceptions to the ban on force are those undertaken in legitimate self-defence and those authorised by the *United Nations*. The question of which organ within the UN authorises them is an internal issue and does not effect the legitimacy of UN action *vis-à-vis* a transgressing State. The internal issue can be resolved in favour of both organs having the ability to authorise military action, given that the Assembly effectively has all those recommendatory powers the Council possesses. The Council has an implied power to recommend military action, and so it follows that the Assembly also has such a power. It is submitted that it is only if the Council does not have the implied power to recommend military action under Article 39 in the absence of a power of decision under Article 42, that one can cast doubts on the Assembly's power to recommend military action. We concluded in Part One that, subject to certain conditions, the Council has the power to recommend military action.

Despite the complex legal issues surrounding Uniting for Peace and the power it contains, in over forty years of practice there have been only nine emergency special sessions called using the procedure contained in the resolution for transferring a matter from the Council to the Assembly.[111] This cannot be regarded as making the procedure a major factor in the extension of the competence of the General Assembly. As has been pointed out, at the time of the resolution's adoption there was a significant link between both organs in that they were dominated by a Western majority. The West tried to strengthen the link in terms of the transfer of problems from one organ to the other by means of the Uniting for Peace resolution. With the new majority in the Assembly the Uniting for Peace procedure has no such use, for the Security Council is not controlled by that majority but by the permanent members. Thus the procedure has become a vehicle, either for condemnation of aggressions not subject to Council disapproval because of the veto, or for the reinforcement of the Assembly's previous recommendations on a particular topic.

Before the adoption of the Uniting for Peace resolution, President Truman spoke before the General Assembly and indicated that he envisaged the procedure being used in situations such as Korea.[112] In fact the Assembly had already made a substantial contribution to UN action in Korea by passing a resolution which allowed the UN force to continue its operations to establish 'a unified, independent and democratic government of Korea' after the Security Council had been deadlocked by the return of the Soviet representative.[113] This resolution implied that General MacArthur had been given the authority to cross the 38th parallel and so could be classified as authorising enforcement action. President Truman probably had this in mind when he and Secretary of State Acheson introduced the Uniting for Peace resolution.

The early successes of the procedure lay in the development of the peacekeeping function – the establishment of UNEF in the Middle East in 1956, and the facility to take over the running of ONUC in the Congo in 1960 when the Security Council was paralysed by the Soviet veto. However, the peacekeeping function has gradually gravitated towards the Security Council, evidenced by the failure of the General Assembly to produce any constructive resolution on the Middle East in its Fifth Emergency Special Session after the Six Day War in 1967. The resolution adopted merely passed the records of the session to the Security Council because after four weeks of discussion the Assembly itself could not agree on a compromise.[114]

Without a role in the peacekeeping function and with situations like Korea being unlikely to arise again it was becoming clear that the Uniting for Peace resolution was not going to result in the primacy of the General Assembly in matters of international peace. Gradually its function was to evolve into one where the Assembly was used to condemn cases of direct superpower intervention which obviously resulted in a paralysed Security Council. The signs were there as early as the Second Emergency Special Session on Hungary in 1956 in which the Assembly adopted a resolution which virtually paralleled the draft resolution vetoed in the Security Council, in that it condemned the Soviet attack without classifying it as a breach of the peace or act of aggression as would seem to be required by the terms of the Uniting for Peace resolution itself.[115] Again in 1958, when American and British troops were invited into Lebanon and Jordan respectively, the Assembly could merely adopt a nondescript resolution which called for non-interference in Arab countries.[116]

However, on one occasion the General Assembly managed to act in a manner which suggested that it could take on the role of the Council. During the Bangladesh crisis in 1971 the Security Council was hopelessly deadlocked and so sought the help of the Assembly which was in its 26th session at the time. The Council resolution cited the Uniting for Peace procedure although the Assembly did not meet in emergency special session.[117] The Assembly responded with commendable alacrity by adopting a resolution which found that the 'hostilities between India and Pakistan constitute an immediate threat to international peace and security' and called for a cease-fire and withdrawal.[118] Admittedly there was no recommendation of enforcement action (which was highly unlikely anyway); nevertheless, the Assembly made a finding of a threat and made the recommendations which the Council, at the minimum, should have made much earlier in the conflict. The Assembly was in fact performing the role of the Council.

Since Bangladesh, the Uniting for Peace procedure has become indistinguishable in its impact from Assembly actions taken in ordinary or special sessions. The Sixth Emergency Special Session on Afghanistan adopted a resolution which was a mirror image of the draft resolution defeated in the Security Council by the Soviet veto. It deplored the 'recent armed intervention' after expressing grave concern 'at the recent developments in Afghanistan and their implications for international peace and security'.[119] Its call for withdrawal was repeated annually until 1988. The Assembly's repeated condemnation may have contributed to the Soviet withdrawal in 1989 by adding to the weight of world opinion against its intervention, an argument that can be used to support most Assembly resolutions on a particular conflict. The advent of the Geneva Accords on Afghanistan in April 1988 led to the Assembly, at its 43rd session, supporting the implementation of the Accords but also urging a comprehensive internal settlement, a call repeated at subsequent sessions.[120]

As well as using the resolution as a means of expressing condemnation of military aggressions, Uniting for Peace has become an additional tool in the hands of the majority of the Members, who, for example, in 1981 called the Eighth Emergency Special Session of the Assembly to discuss the Namibian situation. The resolution produced added nothing to the plethora of Assembly resolutions passed at its annual sessions. It blamed the three Western permanent members for vetoing drafts aimed at introducing mandatory economic sanctions and called on the Council to respond to the 'overwhelming demand of the international community' to impose mandatory sanctions in the 'light of the serious threat to the peace'.[121]

In this respect they are little different from the special sessions which can be called by a majority of Members under Article 20 of the Charter which provides that 'the General Assembly shall meet in regular annual sessions and in such special session as occasion may require. Special sessions shall be convoked by the Secretary General at the request of the Security Council or of a majority of the Members of the United Nations'.

The procedure envisaged by the Charter for convoking a special session does not appear significantly different from that established under the Uniting for Peace resolution, except that a simple procedural vote is required for the Security Council to call for an emergency special session under the resolution, whereas a substantive vote, including positive votes or abstentions from all the permanent members, is required for the Security Council to invoke a special session. In addition, the Uniting for Peace resolution specifically grants the Assembly the power to recommend collective measures and establishes the machinery to enable it to carry out these measures. We have already seen that Article 10 in itself grants the power to the Assembly to recommend voluntary measures, so that whether in normal or special session it has the same powers as those purportedly granted by the

Uniting for Peace resolution. Subsequent practice also has shown that the Assembly has the power to recommend voluntary measures, which means in effect that Article 20 and the Uniting for Peace resolution are conterminous, their only impact is to extend the Assembly's powers of consideration and recommendation beyond the annual regular session. What seems to have confused the sponsors of the Uniting for Peace resolution is doubts over whether the Assembly could recommend enforcement measures. They failed to take account of the perfectly valid argument in favour of the Assembly having this power, a power it had already utilised in the Korean situation. The Uniting for Peace resolution thus remains an unnecessary monument to the era of Western domination of the Assembly.

Up until 1991 there were eighteen Special Sessions of the General Assembly, which, disarmament and economic matters apart, differed little from the Emergency Special Sessions of that body.[122] For example, the Eighth Emergency Special Session on Namibia discussed in the section above was a parallel of the Ninth Special Session which again produced nothing of difference from the annual Namibian debate.[123] Both procedures are used by the majority in an attempt to assert the independence of the Assembly from the Security Council on matters relating to international peace.

Notes

1 H. Kelsen, *The Law of the United Nations*, 198 (1951).
2 See the *Yearbook of the United Nations* (1946–47), 51.
3 But see Article 35(1).
4 See for example GA Res. 721, 8 UN GAOR Supp. (No. 17) 6 (1953).
5 J. P. Cot and A. Pellet, *La Charte des Nations Unies*, 337–40 (1985).
6 L. M. Goodrich, E. Hambro and P. S. Simons, *The Charter of the United Nations*, 143, 2nd ed. (1969).
7 8 UN GAOR Supp. (No. 16) para. 114.
8 *Repertory of the United Nations Practice*, Supp. (No. 1) 173, at para. 16.
9 See for example GA Res. 1663, 16 UN GAOR Supp. (No. 17) 10 (1961).
10 Cot and Pellet, *La Charte*, 288–9.
11 *Certain Expenses of the United Nations*, I.C.J. *Rep.* 1962, 151, at 164–5.
12 *Ibid.*, at 163. Emphasis added.
13 Kelsen, *Law of the UN*, 205.
14 See the opinions given by the UN Legal Counsel, *U.N. Juridical Yearbook* (1964) 228, (1968) 185.
15 For example UN doc. S/23370 (1992).
16 D. W. Bowett, *The Law of International Institutions*, 48–9, 4th ed. (1982).
17 SC Res. 15, 1 UN SCOR Resolutions 6 (1946).
18 UN doc. S/360/Rev 1 (1947).
19 UN doc. S/391 (1947).
20 SC 170 mtg, 2 UN SCOR (1947).

21 GA Res. 109, 2 UN GAOR Resolutions 12 (1947).
22 SC 170 mtg, 2 UN SCOR (1947).
23 UN doc. S/23370 (1992).
24 I.C.J. *Rep*. 1962, 163.
25 Cot and Pellet, *La Charte*, 159.
26 *Nationality Decrees in Tunis and Morocco* case, [1923] *P.C.I.J.* ser. B, No. 4, at 24.
27 GA Res. 39. 1 UN GAOR Resolutions 12 (1946).
28 M. S.Rajan, *The Expanding Jurisdiction of the United Nations*, 84 (1982).
29 For French objections see for example GA 996 plen. mtg, 3 UN GAOR SS (1961), re Tunisia; GA 956 plen. mtg, 15 UN GAOR (1960), re Algeria. For Portuguese objections see for example GA 1099 plen. mtg, 17 UN GAOR (1962).
30 GA 1163 plen. mtg, 17 UN GAOR 656 (1962).
31 SC 276 mtg, 21 UN SCOR 5 (1966).
32 GA Res. 272, 3 UN GAOR Resolutions 17 (1949).
33 GA Res. 285, 3 UN GAOR Resolutions
34 (1949). 34 GA 401 plen. mtg, 7 UN GAOR 332 (1952).
35 *Ibid.*, 334–5 (UK and France).
36 D. Ciobanu, *Preliminary Objections Related to the Jurisdiction of the United Nations Political Organs*, 40–2 (1975).
37 GA Res. 46/7, 46 UN GAOR (1991).
38 GA 401 plen. mtg, 17 UN GAOR 336 (1962).
39 On Afghanistan see GA 1 plen. mtg, 6 UN GAOR ESS para. 112 (1980), Poland. On Kampuchea see GA 64 plen. mtg, 34 UN GAOR 60–1, 120 (1979), GDR, Bulgaria and Czechoslovakia.
40 GA Res. 377, 5 UN GAOR Supp. (No. 20) 10 (1950).
41 GA 301 plen. mtg, 5 UN GAOR para. 138 (1950).
42 Ciobanu, *Preliminary Objections*, 67.
43 *Reparation for Injuries Suffered in the Service of the United Nations* case, I.C.J. *Rep*. 1949, 174, at 182.
44 Ciobanu, *Preliminary Objections*, 68.
45 A. Prandler, 'Competence of the Security Council and the General Assembly', *Questions of International Law* (1977), 153, at 167.
46 *Expenses* case, I.C.J. *Rep*. 1962, at 168.
47 *Ibid.*, 223–4.
48 Ciobanu, *Preliminary Objections*, 162–73.
49 UNCIO, vol. 13, 709.
50 G. Fitzmaurice, 'The law and procedure of the International Court of Justice', 33 *B.Y.I.L.* (1957), 223–5. See also McNair, *Law of Treaties*, 424–31 (1961), G. Haraszti, *Some Fundamental Problems of the Law of Treaties*, 138–45 (1973), and I. Sinclair, *The Vienna Convention on the Law of Treaties*, 136–8, 2nd ed. (1984).
51 GA Res. 37/3, 37 UN GAOR Supp. (No. 51) 14 (1982).
52 GA 41 plen. mtg, 37 UN GAOR (1982), Mexico and Bhutan.
53 *Ibid*.
54 GA Res. 3312, 29 UN GAOR Supp. (No. 31) 3 (1974).
55 GA Res. 45/3, 45 UN GAOR Supp. (No. 49) 12 (1990); GA Res. 46/18, 46 UN GAOR (1991).

56 GA Res. 3485, 30 UN GAOR Supp. (No. 34) 118 (1975). Compare SC Res. 384, 30 UN SCOR Resolutions 10 (1975).

57 SC Res. 164, 16 UN SCOR Resolutions 9 (1961).

58 GA 966 plen. mtg, 3 UN GAOR SS 3 (1961).

59 GA Res. 1622, 3 UN GAOR SS Resolutions 2 (1961).

60 GA Res. 1807, 17 UN GAOR Supp. (No. 17) 39 (1962).

61 SC Res. 312, 27 UN SCOR Resolutions 10 (1972).

62 GA Res. 1889, 18 UN GAOR Supp. (No. 15) 46 (1963).

63 GA Res. 2024, 20 UN GAOR Supp. (No. 14) 55 (1965).

64 GA Res. 2151, 20 UN GAOR Supp. (No. 16) 68 (1966).

65 GA 1468 plen. mtg, 21 UN GAOR 4 (1966).

66 GA Res. 2652, 25 UN GAOR Supp. (No. 28) 89 (1970).

67 GA Res. 3116, 28 UN GAOR Supp. (No. 30) 99 (1973).

68 GA Res. 1663, 16 UN GAOR Supp. (No. 17) 10 (1961).

69 GA Res. 2054, 20 UN GAOR Supp. (No. 14) 52 (1965).

70 GA 1395 plen. mtg, 20 UN GAOR 12 (1965).

71 See the report of the Special Committee Against Apartheid, UN doc. A/34/22 (1979).

72 GA Res. 44/27, 44 UN GAOR (1989). Also GA Res. 45/176, 45 UN GAOR Supp. (No. 49) 42 (1990).

73 GA Res. 46/79, 46 UN GAOR (1991).

74 GA Res. 2145, 21 UN GAOR Supp. (No. 16) 2 (1966).

75 *Namibia* case, I.C.J. *Rep.* 1971, 16, at para.106.

76 GA Res. 65, 1 UN GAOR Resolutions 123 (1946).

77 GA Res. 1568, 15 UN GAOR Supp. (No. 16) 33 (1960).

78 GA Res. 36/121, 36 UN GAOR Supp. (No. 51) 29 (1981).

79 GA Res. 43/26, 43 UN GAOR (1988).

80 See for example GA 1671 plen. mtg, 22 UN GAOR 2 (1968), Netherlands.

81 GA 8 plen. mtg, 8 UN GAOR ESS 197 (1981).

82 GA Res. 186, 2 UN GAOR SS Resolutions 5 (1948).

83 GA 2016 plen. mtg, 26 UN GAOR 25 (1971), US.

84 GA 2009 plen. mtg, 26 UN GAOR 8 (1971).

85 GA Res. 3414, 30 UN GAOR Supp. (No. 34) 6 (1975).

86 GA Res. 36/226, 36 UN GAOR Supp. (No. 51) 47 (1981).

87 GA Res. 37/123, 37 UN GAOR Supp. (No. 51) 36 (1982).

88 GA Res. 40/168, 40 UN GAOR Supp. (No. 53) 57 (1985).

89 GA Res. 46/75, 46 UN GAOR (1991).

90 See GA Res. 1747, 16 UN GAOR Supp. (No. 17A) 3 (1962).

91 GA Res. 1889, 18 UN GAOR Supp. (No. 15) 46 (1963).

92 See GA 1367 plen. mtg, 20 UN GAOR 11 (1965), where the Soviet Union makes this equation; contrast US and UK at 8 and 14.

93 GA Res. 1742, 16 UN GAOR Supp. (No. 17) 67 (1962).

94 GA 1099 plen. mtg, 16 UN GAOR 1304 (1962), Yugoslavia re Portuguese Territories.

95 GA Res. 616, 7 UN GAOR Supp. (No. 20) 8 (1952).

96 UN doc. A/2505 (1953).

97 GA Res. 721, 8 UN GAOR Supp. (No. 17) 6 (1953).

98 GA 98 plen. mtg, 35 UN GAOR 1716 (1980), UK.
99 GA Res. 46/79, 46 UN GAOR (1991). Contrast with GA Res. 45/176, 45 UN GAOR Supp. (No. 49) 39 (1990).
100 GA Res. 3236, 29 UN GAOR Supp. (No. 31) 4 (1974).
101 GA Res. 111, 2 UN GAOR Resolutions 15 (1947).
102 Prandler, *Questions of International Law* (1977), 154.
103 GA Res. 377, 5 UN GAOR Resolutions 10 (1950).
104 GA Res. 376, 5 UN GAOR Resolutions 9 (1950).
105 The resolution also established a Peace Observation Commission and a Collective Measures Committee.
106 GA 299 plen. mtg, 5 UN GAOR 305 (1950), Poland.
107 *Ibid.*, at 314, Bolivia.
108 GA 301 plen. mtg, 5 UN GAOR 332 (1950).
109 *Expenses* case, I.C.J. *Rep.* 1962, 162–5.
110 Blaine Sloane, *United Nations General Assembly Resolutions in Our Changing World*, 25 (1991).
111 1st 1956 UNEF; 2nd 1956 Hungary; 3rd 1958 Lebanon and Jordan; 4th 1960 Congo; 5th 1967 Middle East; 6th 1980 Afghanistan; 7th 1980 and 1982 Palestine; 8th 1981 Namibia; 9th 1982 Israeli Occupied Territories.
112 GA 295 plen. mtg, 5 UN GAOR (1950).
113 GA Res. 376 (1950).
114 GA Res. 2256, 5 UN GAOR ESS Supp. (No. 1) 1 (1967).
115 GA Res. 1004, 2 UN GAOR ESS Supp. (No. 1) 2 (1956). Compare UN doc. S/3760/Rev 1 (1956).
116 GA Res. 1237, 3 UN GAOR ESS Supp. (No. 1) 1 (1958).
117 SC Res. 303, 26 UN SCOR Resolutions 10 (1971).
118 GA Res. 2793, 26 UN GAOR Supp. (No. 29) 3 (1971).
119 GA Res. ES-6/2, 6 UN GAOR ESS Supp. (No. 1) 2 (1980). Compare UN doc. S/13729 (1980).
120 GA Res. 43/20, 43 UN GAOR (1988).
121 GA Res. ES-8/2, 8 UN GAOR ESS (1981).
122 1st 1947 Palestine; 2nd 1948 Palestine; 3rd 1961 Tunisia; 5th 1967 S.W. Africa; 9th 1978 Namibia; 14th 1986 Namibia, 16th 1989, Apartheid.
123 See GA Res. S-9/2, 9 UN GAOR SS Supp. (No. 2) 3 (1978).

CHAPTER SIX

The powers of the General Assembly in practice

Due to the poor drafting of Articles 10–14 of the UN Charter it has been possible to argue that these provisions can be interpreted to give the Assembly a wide range of recommendatory powers, equivalent to the Security Council's powers of recommendation within Chapters VI and VII. This chapter will contain an examination of how the practice of the Assembly has followed this path to such an extent that in certain areas of recommendation, for example on disarmament and on general principles of international peace, the General Assembly is undoubtedly the primary organ. Theoretically the Assembly's resolutions are non-mandatory, and in practice this remains so although in certain instances the language of the resolutions reflect the present day majority's desire that perhaps they should be binding.

Disarmament

Article 11(1) of the Charter states that:

The General Assembly may consider the general principles of co-operation in the maintenance of international peace and security, including the principles governing disarmament and the regulation of armaments, and may make recommendations with regard to such principles to the Members or to the Security Council or to both.

It is generally recognised that this is the basis of disarmament resolutions adopted by the General Assembly while resolutions concerning general principles, reviewed in the next section, come under Article 13(1)(a).[1] In fact the General Assembly has taken on the responsibilities of the United Nations as regards disarmament for the Security Council has abstained in general from exercising its competence as regards disarmament given it under Article 26, although it has made a recent specific exception for Iraq in 1991–92.

In practice the Assembly has elevated disarmament from the relatively low-key treatment given to it under the Charter, to it being one of the most important areas of UN work. The work on disarmament is not only done in the regular and special sessions of the Assembly, but also by bodies set up or brought under the auspices of the United Nations, for example the Disarmament Commission and the Conference on Disarmament.

The Assembly has interpreted its powers under Article 11(1) widely to go beyond the recommendation of mere principles to resolutions establishing bodies to study the problem and to provide the machinery for the negotiation of disarmament. Indeed, it was remarkable that during the period of over forty years of superpower arms build-up in the Cold War, the discussions and agreements on disarmament, either inside or outside the United Nations, continued. To this extent the General Assembly proved an effective organ, not for achieving disarmament, but for maintaining a dialogue over levels and the regulation of armament. To this end, a major success was achieved during the period of *détente* in the 1970s, resulting in the adoption by consensus in 1978 of a resolution at the Tenth Special Session. The resolution embodied the goals, principles, objectives and priorities for disarmament and new machinery for putting them into effect.[2]

The Committee on Disarmament which has been meeting in Geneva since 1962, having a membership of 31 States under the co-chairmanship of the Soviet Union and the United States, was brought under UN auspices by the 1978 resolution. The resolution opened the Committee up to all nuclear weapon States and 32–35 others to be chosen in consultation with the President of the General Assembly, with a personal representative of the Secretary General serving as Secretary to the Committee. It was also agreed to establish a Disarmament Commission made up of the entire UN membership to follow up the work of the special session, make recommendations on various disarmament problems, and consider the elements of a comprehensive disarmament programme.

The resolution begins with a statement that 'States for a long time have sought to maintain their security through possession of arms yet the accumulation of weapons today constitutes much more a threat than a protection for the future of mankind'. 'The time has come', it says, 'to abandon the use of force in international relations and to seek security in disarmament through a gradual but effective process beginning with a reduction in the present level of armaments'. The document expands on these principles by emphasising the importance of refraining from threats against the sovereignty and territorial integrity of any State or against peoples under a colonial or foreign domination. Non-intervention in internal affairs, the inviolability of frontiers, and the peaceful settlement of disputes are also stressed. From these premises, the resolution states that all nations have the right to participate in disarmament negotiations, that disarmament measures should be equitable and balanced to ensure security to each State, and that they should be accompanied by adequate verification.

From general principles the resolution moves on to a more practical approach by establishing a programme of action which sets forth objectives and priorities, immediate and short-term measures to halt and reverse the arms race. Special importance is given to efforts to curb nuclear and other mass destruction weapons. Negotiations for the reduction of conventional arms and armed forces are also called for. Emphasising the need to work towards the complete elimination of nuclear weapons, the programme favours such measures as an agreement on a comprehensive nuclear test ban, further Soviet-United States negotiations on strategic arms limitations and reductions, nuclear weapon free zones, and expanded non-proliferation agreements. Suggested as especially desirable measures are steps by the Security Council to 'prevent the frustration' of the objective of a denuclearised Africa, and consideration of steps to give effect to the proposal for a nuclear weapon free zone in the Middle East. Other provisions call for an expert study of the relationship between disarmament and development, and continuation of a study of the interrelationship between disarmament and international security.

The 1978 Special Session resolution has been analysed in some detail because it represents possibly the most important achievement of the United Nations as regards disarmament. Its adoption by consensus represented the crossing of ideological and political frontiers. It may appear, in some respects, naive, for example in expressing the hope that the Security Council would become involved in disarmament. However, it must be remembered that the period of *détente* had raised hopes of a Council less divided by East-West ideology. Undoubtedly, the resolution put the UN at the centre of the disarmament stage.

However, the next decade saw the return of the Cold War, which meant that disarmament talks, once again, were dominated by the spirit of confrontation.[3] The Twelfth and Fifteenth Special Sessions on disarmament in 1982 and 1988 produced no new concrete proposals or recommendations. Again we saw the schism in the Assembly which so often put the Western States in the minority, a trend that seems to have continued even with the end of the Cold War in the late 1980s, although the division is now more between those nuclear States unwilling to make concessions on the one hand, and those that say they are and the vast majority of non-nuclear States on the other.

The Assembly has certainly expressed support for the several bilateral agreements between the superpowers for nuclear weapons reduction, for instance the Treaty on the Elimination of Intermediate Range and Shorter Range Missiles of 1987,[4] but it has continued a policy of isolation of nuclear weapon States, particularly the United States. For instance, the Assembly has consistently called for a convention prohibiting all nuclear test explosions to replace the Partial Test Ban Treaty of 1963. At its 44th session the Assembly adopted this resolution with two votes against, France and the United States.[5] At its 46th session in 1991, France and the United States were still the only votes against.[6] The number of abstentions was 6 and 4 respectively, including China, the United Kingdom and Israel. One can contrast this with resolutions adopted during the Cold War, for instance at its 35th session in 1980, the Assembly adopted a similar resolution with two votes against, this time the United Kingdom and the United States, the difference being that 31 States abstained, including most other Western countries and the former Socialist States.[7] In disarmament matters at least, the former Socialist States and many non-nuclear Western States have now joined the majority, so isolating France, the United Kingdom, the United States, and China.

Nevertheless, the States in isolation on disarmament matters are fewer than during the Cold War, and in some non-nuclear areas there has been consensus. Indeed, the number of rhetorical and confrontational resolutions coming from the First Committee has been reduced,[8] and the overall picture is of a future in which the General Assembly can become centre stage on disarmament matters if the Member States voting for resolutions actually do carry out the content therein. Two small step were taken at the Assembly's 46th session in 1991. Its resolution on the topic of general and complete disarmament was inspired by the realisation that the end of the Cold War was not going to lead to a reduction in local or regional conflicts. The resolution invited Member States to provide the Secretary General with annual reports from 1 January 1992, on their conventional arms inventories and the export or import of battle tanks, armoured combat vehicles, large calibre artillery systems, combat aircraft, attack helicopters, warships and missiles, as well as calling on States to take steps to eradicate the illicit trade in all kinds of weapons. In an earlier resolution on the subject of chemical and biological weapons, the General Assembly noted the progress the Conference on Disarmament was making on a draft convention prohibiting the development, production, stockpiling and use of chemical weapons.[9] The Conference agreed on a final draft in June 1992 which should be approved by the Assembly at its 47th session in 1992. The Convention will set up an International Organisation for the Prohibition of Chemical Weapons, with powers to inspect State parties without giving much notice.[10]

From these recent developments, one can see the Assembly, whilst not moving entirely away from rhetorical confrontation between non-nuclear and nuclear States in the area of nuclear weapons, is moving positively towards arms control in conventional weapons, although the voluntary register is only a small step, and is moving even further in the area of chemical weapons, not only by sponsoring a Convention, but also by insisting on enforcement mechanisms within a treaty system.[11]

General principles

Article 13(1)(a) of the Charter allows the Assembly to initiate studies and make recommendations for the purpose of 'promoting international cooperation in the political field and encouraging the progressive development of international law and its codification', while sub-paragraph (b) gives the same power, *inter alia*, for 'assisting in the realisation of human rights and fundamental freedoms'.

It is out of sub-paragraph (a) that the power to adopt resolutions enunciating general principles has developed. Nevertheless, sub-paragraph (b) is significant in that the general principles usually represent a compromise between the human rights lobby (and more recently the national liberation or self-determination lobby) and those States who want to emphasise the (greater) importance of sovereignty and territorial integrity. This aspect will be concentrated on for it is illustrative of the influence of the various factions of the General Assembly, an influence which tends to result in an unsatisfactory compromise.

In 1949, a majority of States were still committed to the principle of the inviolability of the sovereignty of States which in 1945 was embodied in Article 2(7) of the Charter. The Draft Declaration on Rights and Duties of States was adopted unanimously in 1949 in accordance with Article 13.[12] It represented an affirmation and clarification of the sovereignty principle. The Declaration stated that every State had: complete jurisdiction in its own territory; the right of independence including freedom to choose its own government; the duty not to intervene in another State or to foment civil strife therein; and the duty to treat all persons under its jurisdiction with respect for their human rights and fundamental freedoms.

Although the balance of the resolution is clearly in favour of affirming the doctrine of absolute sovereignty, there are suggestions that perhaps this concept is subject to the principle of self-determination (right to choose a government) and respect for human rights. In 1949, it was the United States and its allies who supported these nascent principles, even advocating that all the contents of the draft resolution embodied international law, reflecting the Western majority's criticism of the form of government and abuse of rights in Eastern Europe. The Eastern bloc doubted that the principles contained in the declaration embodied international law.[13]

However, by 1960 the tables had turned, and it was the Soviet Union and the newly independent countries advocating firm anti-colonial and hence pro self-determination resolutions.[14] The Declaration on the Granting of Independence to Colonial Countries and Peoples recognised the 'increasingly powerful trend towards freedom' in dependent territories and emphasised that colonialism was not only a denial of self-determination but also of fundamental human rights and therefore was contrary to the

Charter.[15] This represented a move away from the sovereignty principle at least in so far as metropolitan powers and their dominions were concerned.

The resolution was adopted by 89 votes to nil. However, 9 Western and pro-Western States abstained,[16] the United States abandoning their previous principled approach for more practical reasoning. The all or nothing approach (no stage between a colony and an independent State) of the resolution was criticised by the representative of the United States because it would lead to the political fragmentation of some States and would 'fly in the face of political and economic realities in many areas of the world'.[17] The United States' preference for an approach based on economic realities has increasingly alienated it from the majority of Assembly Members who prefer a more abstract, principled approach.

The impact of the decolonised majority became increasingly apparent in 1965 with the unanimous adoption of the Declaration on the Inadmissibility of Intervention in the Domestic Affairs of States.[18] Although compromise was necessary to achieve unanimity, the influence of the national liberation lobby eroded even further the Western support for non-intervention and sovereignty, and to this extent correlated with the demise of Article 2(7).

The resolution declared that no State had the right to intervene in the affairs of another. This included indirect intervention which was defined as helping or financing subversive activities against a State. So far the Declaration entirely supported the Western view. However, the resolution then contradicted itself. After reaffirming the principles of self-determination and respect for human rights and fundamental freedoms, it stated that 'all States shall contribute to the complete elimination of racial discrimination and colonialism'. This suggested that indirect intervention was permissible if it aided self-determination in colonial or racial situations. The Western States voted for the resolution on the understanding that the word 'contribute' did not allow intervention in favour of self-determination.[19] Inevitably, the Soviets favoured the view that it did, and increased the Cold War rhetoric against the United States by accusing it of denying self-determination in Vietnam and the Dominican Republic,[20] whereas the United States accused the Soviet Union of intervention in violation of the sovereignty of Vietnam.[21]

Similarly in 1970, the Declaration on Principles Concerning Friendly Relations and Cooperation among States in accordance with the United Nations' Charter represented a compromise.[22] Indirect intervention was declared illegal but, at the same time, the Declaration expressed the right of peoples to take 'forcible action in pursuit of their right to self-determination' and stated that they were 'entitled to seek and receive support in accordance with the purposes and principles of the Charter'. Support for forcible action suggested that the support could be forcible as well. However, the reference to the Charter tended to suggest that it was support short of the use or threat of force, which after all would be contrary to Article 2(4), and as the representative of Australia pointed out, a mere recommendatory Assembly resolution could not amend the Charter.[23] Most Western States explicitly granted their vote on the understanding that the Declaration did not diminish the principle of the non-use of force.[24] The Socialist and Non-Aligned nations did not express a view, probably in order not to provoke any negative Western votes, but it is interesting that they saw the Declaration as a crystallisation of international law.[25]

The unhappy compromise between Western powers and the national liberation lobby was continued when, in 1974, the Assembly finally adopted by consensus the Definition of Aggression which has been discussed in chapter two. The Definition purportedly outlawed indirect as well as direct aggression, but made this subject to the right of peoples striving to achieve self-determination 'to struggle to that end and to seek and receive support'. Indeed, despite the World Court's judgement in the *Nicaragua* case, which seized on those parts of the Definition which strengthened the principle of the non-use of force whilst ignoring those parts detrimental to it, the Assembly adopted a further resolution in 1987 which, while purporting to ban intervention and aggression, still declared that peoples, 'particularly those under colonial and racist regimes', had the right 'to achieve self-determination and have the right to seek and receive support'.[26]

Due to the inherent defect in each of the above resolutions it can be strongly argued that the power of the General Assembly to adopt resolutions on general principles has not led to 'the progressive development of international law' in the area of the non-use of force. Instead, the principle contained in Article 2(4) has been seriously weakened by these recommendations which suggest that the principle is subject to the use of allowable force in the pursuit of the right to self-determination or national liberation. This represents a serious undermining of the fundamental provision of the Charter.[27]

However, such a contention must be tempered in the light of the Court's judgement in the *Nicaragua* case when it relied on the 1965 Declaration on Non Intervention, the 1970 Declaration on Friendly Relations, and the 1974 Definition of Aggression as evidence of *opinio juris* on the illegality of intervention in the form of funding of an armed opposition group within a State, arming and advising such a group, and virtually controlling such a group. It found that the United States' support for the Contra rebels in Nicaragua constituted an unlawful intervention and an unlawful use of force against Nicaragua. It also said that if clear evidence could be adduced to show that Nicaragua was supplying arms to the rebels in El Salvador this would be a breach of the principles of non-intervention and the non-use of force. The Court did not find sufficient evidence of this, but stated that even if there was adequate proof, the supply of arms did not constitute an intervention amounting to an 'armed attack' within the meaning of Article 51 of the UN Charter, which would justify the United States' sponsored operation as an exercise of the right of self-defence on behalf of El Salvador.[28]

The Court did not directly address the issue of self-determination since it was not raised in the case before it, although there were passages in the judgement which not only made clear that intervention to preserve or impose some form of ideology was unlawful, but also that human rights (and presumably self-determination) could not be enforced or protected by out-side States by military means.[29] The judgement could be said to constitute a pro-Western interpretation of General Assembly resolutions, despite the fact that on the substantive issues the Court found against the major Western power involved. Furthermore, the judgement provided support for the fact that many aspects of the General Assembly's resolutions have passed into customary international law, whilst those parts which are too ambiguous to embody any legal obligation are effectively left behind as monuments to the Cold War.

With that confrontation now behind it the Assembly has the opportunity to produce resolutions that have greater clarity and so have a greater impact on customary international law. There is some evidence that such resolutions are emerging via the Sixth (Legal) Committee of the Assembly, not only on enhancing the ban on the use of armed force within the meaning of Article 2(4),[30] but also on the provision of humanitarian assistance,[31] the prevention of terrorism,[32] and on methods of making the UN machinery more effective.[33] Although not binding as such, General Assembly resolutions can eventually become so if they pass into customary international law as a result of States consistently referring to them as part of their legal arguments in disputes or in discussions in international settings.

Cease-fire and withdrawal

Whereas Assembly recommendations on disarmament and those enunciating general principles on the use of force are directly adopted under Articles 11(1) and 13(1) respectively, resolutions which call for a cease-fire, withdrawal, or for voluntary measures or recommend a settlement cannot be attributed to any particular Charter provision, but, instead, are concrete manifestations of the general powers of Articles 10, 11(2) and 14. As has already been stated in chapter five, Article 10 can be interpreted to give the Assembly similar recommendatory powers to those granted to the Council in Chapters VI and VII. To a large extent the powers examined below are similar to those recommendatory powers employed by the Security Council.

The Assembly makes relatively few cease-fire and withdrawal calls. The Security Council usually responds first and makes the necessary call. However, if the General Assembly is in its regular session it may be able to make the call more quickly than the Council. The Assembly has made such calls in the case of the Indonesian invasion of East Timor in 1975,[34] and in the case of the Turkish invasion of Cyprus in 1974.[35]

If the Council is deadlocked by a conflict of interests of the permanent members, the General Assembly sometimes takes up the role of the organ making the preliminary call for a cease-fire and withdrawal. This is done either immediately, under the Uniting for Peace procedure, or the Assembly waits until its regular session. If done in emergency special session the call has greater immediacy than if the regular session is awaited. However, the Council is likely to be paralysed because of permanent member involvement and so any cease-fire call is seen as a gesture. In this respect it does not matter if the regular session is waited for.

In the case of the Soviet intervention in Hungary in 1956,[36] the Assembly met in emergency special session and called for a cease-fire and a withdrawal of Soviet troops.[37] The call was seen as a gesture by some members or more optimistically as a warning or holding measure to prevent further Soviet interventions by others.[38] In the case of the Vietnamese intervention in Kampuchea (Cambodia) in 1978, the Assembly waited eleven months before calling for a cease-fire.[39] This wait could hardly justify some of the members hailing the resolution as a valiant effort to save the 'dying' Kampuchean people.[40] Often the Assembly passes a resolution in order to save the Organisation's face when the primary body is racked by arguments and vetoes. For example, the Assembly's resolution calling for a cease-fire in the Bangladesh situation was seen as essential in rescuing the UN from its 'darkest hour'.[41] In terms of effectiveness, therefore, the Assembly's calls have not directly brought about an immediate cease-fire or withdrawal, instead they add to the weight of opinion against belligerents which eventually may lead to a cease-fire and more importantly a withdrawal.

In terms of withdrawal calls, the Assembly's most important ones were in the cases of Hungary, Bangladesh, Cyprus, East Timor, Kampuchea, Afghanistan, Grenada and Panama.[42] In the cases of Bangladesh, Grenada and Panama, withdrawal was achieved only after the intervening forces had achieved their objectives. However, in the case of Afghanistan, Soviet withdrawal in 1989 occurred without the political objectives behind the intervention being achieved. This was mainly due to the fact that the Soviet Union found that it could not achieve its goals after nearly a decade of fighting. However, it may be that the weight of world opinion represented by the Assembly in its annual resolutions was a factor influencing the decision to withdraw. Similarly, the withdrawal of Vietnamese troops from Cambodia in 1989 was due to a combination of factors, political and economic, including the consistent Assembly calls for Vietnamese withdrawal. Indeed, now that the foreign forces have withdrawn from the combat zones of Afghanistan and Cambodia, the Assembly, as part of the wider UN peace effort, has called on the parties to the internal conflicts within those countries to cease hostilities so that the peace plans may succeed.[43] The Assembly acts to focus world attention and pressure on warring parties, and while its resolutions *per se* can only be said to have peripheral impact, they do serve to indicate the wider economic and political pressure that may be brought to bear on the conflict.

Voluntary measures

The most radical interpretation of the Assembly's powers involves its use of voluntary measures. We have seen in chapter three, in the case of the Security Council, that it can recommend military measures under Article 39 and has adopted the practice of suggesting economic measures under Article 41. Both these recommendatory powers used by the Security Council were not envisaged by the drafters of the Charter and so represent an extension by subsequent practice. It has been argued that the General Assembly has similar recommendatory powers to the Council, and by extension, it has the power to recommend military action and to recommend voluntary sanctions. The former power has been expressly granted by the Uniting for Peace resolution, although it can be argued that the Assembly has had such powers from the time that the Security Council claimed similar powers.

Nevertheless, the Assembly has very rarely used its power to recommend military action. The only clear instance, which occurred marginally before the Uniting for Peace resolution was adopted, was in the case of Korea when the Assembly recommended a 'unified, independent and democratic' Korea be established and that UN forces remain in Korea for that purpose.[44] This implied that General MacArthur had been authorised to cross the 38th parallel into North Korea. Paradoxically, although the Uniting for Peace resolution was adopted only a few days later there has been no further clear instance of the Assembly recommending coercive measures in the form of military action.

Korea also involved one of the first instances of the Assembly recommending voluntary sanctions.[45] These were not only directed against North Korea, but also communist China which had entered the war when General MacArthur's forces threatened the Chinese border, and involved an embargo on military supplies and equipment.[46] The Soviet Union declared these sanctions invalid on the grounds that they constituted 'action' within the meaning of Article 11(2).[47]

Since Korea, the Assembly has, in practice, firmly established the power to recommend voluntary sanctions. However, in contrast with the Korean precedent such sanctions have mainly been adopted on the instigation and affirmative votes of the Non-Aligned and Socialist majority. Voluntary sanctions have been called for in the cases of South Africa, the Portuguese territories, and Southern Rhodesia.[48] The Assembly's power to recommend voluntary measures has been confined, in practice, to colonial or racist situations (and then mainly in Africa), although by tying zionism to racism in 1975,[49] it was able to justify recommending voluntary measures against Israel.[50]

A US-instigated campaign in 1991 led to the repeal of the equation of zionism with racism at the Assembly's 46th session by a majority of 113 to 13 with 25 abstentions.[51] It is also interesting to note that at its 46th session, the Assembly did not explicitly repeat its call for voluntary measures in any of its numerous resolutions on the subject, although it continued to express support for the *intifadah* (uprising) of the Palestinian people in the Occupied Territories which had started in 1987.[52] American pressure and the continuing Middle East peace process started in 1991 probably explain this change of direction. Similarly, the latest resolutions on South Africa, whilst not wholeheartedly endorsing the slow internal process of reform, recommend a lifting of the sports boycott and further called on States 'to review existing restrictive measures as warranted by developments', whilst calling for the maintenance of the mandatory arms embargo by the Security Council and repeating its recommendation for an oil embargo.[53]

Although question marks must be raised against the effectiveness of voluntary measures themselves, the easing off of Assembly calls for sanctions in the past few years is indicative of the changed climate at the UN and the fact that the established international pariahs, South Africa and Israel, have started to negotiate with those that oppose them. Of the new international pariahs, Iraq, Libya and Yugoslavia (Serbia and Montenegro), Iraq and Libya have not yet been singled out by the Assembly. However, on 22 September 1992, the General Assembly, by a large majority of 127 votes to 6, denied the Federal Republic of Yugoslavia (Serbia and Montenegro) automatic membership of the General Assembly as successor State to the former, and much bigger, Socialist Federal Republic of Yugoslavia.

Political settlement

Political settlement of a dispute or problem requires some degree of consent or a (greater) degree of coercion of the parties to the dispute. Whereas the Council has the option of using mandatory coercion, the Assembly only has the power of recommendation and therefore, in general (apart from the recommendation of measures), if it is to succeed it must try to attain some degree of cooperation from the parties. However, throughout its history the Assembly has shown a greater concern for votes than for concrete successes.

The partition of Palestine is a good example of a case where the Assembly sought to impose a solution on the area and the parties through the inadequate means of a non-binding recommendation. Palestine was the subject of the First Special Session of the Assembly in May 1947. The session was requested by the mandatory power, Britain, because it was dissatisfied with its position due to increasing antagonism between Jews and Arabs and the conflicting purposes of achieving a homeland for the Jews and independence for an Arab dominated Palestine. The session established a Special Committee on Palestine,[54] which submitted a report to the Second Annual Session of the Assembly. The report of the majority recommended partition of Palestine as a means of reconciling the above conflicting principles, whereas the minority believed a federated State could achieve this.[55]

The Assembly established an *ad hoc* committee consisting of every member to consider the report. The *ad hoc* committee did not use the report as a basis for negotiation between the parties; instead it supported the majority's proposals and recommended partition with economic union,[56] a proposal which favoured the Jews and which was supported by both the Soviet Union and the United States.[57] The solution recommended was an ideal one aimed at solving the problem of the mandate and the age old problem of a Jewish homeland all at one stroke. It was bound to fail because at no stage were the parties involved in the plan, a plan which was particularly unfavourable to one of the parties to the dispute, namely the Palestinians.

Only the representative of Colombia questioned the recommendation for partition in any great detail. First he criticised the theory behind the majority report stating that 'the legal competence of the General Assembly to set up two independent States in Palestine, without regard to the principle of self-determination has not been established to our satisfaction'.[58] He then proposed a resolution to improve the practical chances of the Assembly successfully helping to end the Palestinian problem,[59] by authorising the *ad hoc* committee to 'take all steps necessary to try to bring about an agreement between the representatives of the Arab and Jewish populations of Palestine as to the future government and political constitution of that country'.

Instead the majority continued on its course which was bound to alienate one of the parties and its supporters, namely the Arabs represented by the Arab Higher Committee. The United States proposed that two sub-committees be set up, one to examine the majority report of the Special Committee, and one to consider the minority report. States supporting the Jewish cause polarised around the first sub-committee while mainly Arab States were represented in the second sub-committee. The result was modified versions of both reports which were more extreme, for example the minority report abandoned the federated State ideal and recommended independence for Palestine based on self-determination.[60] The Assembly was, in effect, driving the two parties further apart. The *ad hoc* committee voted for the partition plan contained in the first sub-committee's report,[61] and finally the Assembly adopted the partition plan.[62] The resolution took the form of a recommendation but was obviously based on the premise that the Council would enforce it if it was ignored. This too was unrealistic, but at the time the relative impotence of the Council was not clear.

Fighting between the two communities despite truce calls by the Council led to the Second Special Session of the Assembly in April and May 1948 one month before the end of the mandate. The idealistic approach of the First Session was replaced by disillusionment and the whole session was without effect. The Assembly failed to adopt a resolution on the state of its rapidly disintegrating partition plan. The United States reversed its support for partition and suggested UN trusteeship.[63] The Assembly did not take up this option. In effect, the Assembly abandoned Palestine to a military solution with the first Arab-Israeli war breaking out on 14 May as the mandate ended. The Assembly was guilty of attempting to decide the fate of Palestine by a majority of only vaguely interested States. It was concerned with voting victories rather than with any practical attempt at reconciliation and negotiation between the parties mainly concerned.

The modern Assembly is overwhelmingly pro-Palestinian in its approach to the Middle East crisis. Thus although its stance on the Middle East has altered, its basic approach has not changed. Its resolutions are pro-Arab and so are not conducive for encouraging Israel to negotiate.

Security Council resolution 242, adopted in 1967 and designed to induce all the parties to negotiate, is a good example of how the requirements of compromise necessary in the Council produce a more balanced approach. The Assembly, however, imposes the will of the majority and in so doing has undermined the Council's work which necessarily has to accommodate the views of the minority pro-Israeli members. The Assembly has consistently adopted resolutions which, while purportedly supporting Council resolution 242, destroys its balance in a variety of ways. Although the post Cold War Assembly has reduced its antagonism towards Israel, it still has not regained its neutrality in the dispute. For example a 1991 Assembly resolution purports to lay down the principles that would govern the negotiation of a solution to the problem at a proposed International Conference on the Middle East under UN auspices,[64] in effect undermining the Middle East peace process started at Madrid in October 1991 under United States and Soviet Union (now Russian) patronage outside the UN framework but operating within the terms of Council resolution 242.[65]

The dispute over South West Africa (Namibia) was slightly different in that South Africa had breached international law by continuing to administer the territory. Thus the UN was in a difficult position, for it would have reflected badly on the Organisation's prestige to negotiate with an illegal occupier of a trusteeship territory. In effect, until the independence of

Namibia in 1990, the United Nations was a party to a dispute with South Africa over Namibia. This is symptomatic of its attitude towards colonial, neo-colonial or racist situations in which the Assembly has a vision of itself as the representative of colonial or repressed peoples, hence its one-sided resolutions.

In 1950 the International Court opined that South West Africa was still under a mandate which could only be modified by South Africa with the 'consent' of the United Nations.[66] The word 'consent' is important here for it is not only required of the UN to achieve a solution but also by South Africa. Without South Africa's consent, and in the absence of effective mandatory measures by the Council, the problem of Namibia was unlikely to be resolved by the UN. However, the Assembly ignored this fact and embarked on a unilateral approach to the problem by adopting resolutions on Namibia which although ideally and legally desirable were, nevertheless, unattainable. Although the Assembly's consistent pressure on South Africa may have contributed in a small way to its withdrawal from Namibia, it took an accord of 1988 negotiated outside the UN and sponsored by the super-powers to solve the problem. The accord, as we shall see in chapter nine, linked South African withdrawal from Namibia with Cuban withdrawal from Angola. The Assembly had consistently rejected the notion of link-age,[67] and so was effectively undermining a legitimate peace process which resulted in an independent Namibia and the prospect of a peaceful Angola.

Ignoring for a moment the problem of self-determination, where the Assembly often loses any pretence at neutrality and objectivity, in other instances the Assembly does attempt to create a viable framework for the settlement of disputes. For example, in 1980, it passed a resolution on the Kampuchean problem,[68] which called for an International Conference on Kampuchea (Cambodia) and laid out the principles to be the basis of discussion: the negotiation of an agreement for Vietnamese withdrawal, observance of human rights, free elections, and non-interference. It did not purport to isolate Vietnam; its purpose was to give it a way out. Over a decade later the peace process is well advanced and, as we shall see in chapter nine, involves a huge peacekeeping and peacemaking operation under the authority of the Security Council. Although the permanent five were involved in the Paris International Conference on Cambodia since it first met in July 1989, and it was the Security Council that converted an Australian peace proposal into a comprehensive peace plan in August 1990, it is the General Assembly that must take a great deal of credit for providing the initial framework for Vietnamese withdrawal and for the International Conference. Unlike the Conference on the Middle East held in Madrid in 1991, the Assembly encouraged and *fully* supported the International Con-ference on Cambodia and the agreements coming out of the conference in October 1991.[69]

In the same vein, the Assembly expressed its unanimous support for the Central American peace plan agreed upon in Guatemala on 7 August 1987.[70] This plan has, as we shall see in Part Three, resulted in the end of civil war in Nicaragua and a promising peace process in El Salvador. Although the details of the peace plans were negotiated by the Secretary General and finally authorised by the Security Council, the Security Council did not fully become involved until 1989. Similarly, it was the General Assembly's encouragement of the Secretary General in his 'good offices' role,[71] that eventually helped to produce the Geneva Accords of 1988 containing an agreement on Afghanistan, which while not settling the internal conflict, did lead to a Soviet withdrawal. It is the General Assembly, not the Security Council which persists in trying to encourage a peaceful settlement in the Afghan conflict.[72] Cambodia, Central America and Afghanistan are good examples of the Assembly providing neutral modalities for belligerents to settle their differences in a diplomatic manner.

The Assembly's non-recommendatory powers

Articles 10–14 seem to create only recommendatory powers for the Assembly, but as we have seen in chapter four, theoretically the Assembly can adopt non-recommendatory resolutions. However, there is no power to enable the Assembly to adopt mandatory resolutions, so, although the resolutions may 'demand', 'decide' or 'declare', they are not mandatory decisions in the sense of Article 25 and Chapter VII. The Assembly uses its declaratory or condemnatory power to strongly emphasise the United Nations' position as regards a particular dispute. In effect it is acting in a quasi-judicial capacity similar to that of the Security Council. Although it does not possess mandatory powers either to oblige Members to comply or to enforce its judgements in the case of non-compliance, it does possess the power to suggest voluntary measures, and if its judgement is based on international law, then it is binding in a more fundamental sense than that found in Article 25.

In 1956, the Assembly declared 'that by using its armed force against the Hungarian people, the government of [the Soviet Union] is violating the political independence of Hungary',[73] as a follow-up to the emergency special session on Hungary calling for withdrawal. The resolution contained an 'objective', 'historical judgement' that the Soviet Union had breached Article 2(4).[74] In this respect the Assembly was acting like an international court in judging the Soviet Union guilty of a breach of the Charter. Although it has no power to make a binding judgement, the verdict is important if the principle contained in Article 2(4) is not to be destroyed by constant breach. In 1986, the Assembly condemned the United States air raids on targets within Libya as 'a violation of the Charter and of International Law',[75] and in 1989 it deplored 'the intervention in Panama by the armed forces of the United States of America, which constitutes a flagrant violation of international law'.[76] Such resolutions, which are just a sample, offer evidence by way of State practice as to the status of Article 2(4) as a peremptory norm of international law, and in fact according to the World Court in the *Nicaragua* case they have helped to strengthen Article 2(4) despite its seemingly frequent breach.[77]

Although the Assembly's declarations are often based on legal concepts it could be argued that they are unlikely to aid a peaceful settlement of the dispute simply because they put one of the parties in the wrong and therefore make it unlikely that it will comply. The Assembly's declarations on South Africa are a case in point. In 1952 the Assembly declared:

that in a multi-racial society harmony and respect for human rights and freedoms and the peaceful development of a unified community are best assured when patterns of legislation and practice are directed towards ensuring equality before the law of all persons regardless of race, creed, or colour, and when economic, social and cultural and political participation of all racial groups is on the basis of equality.[78]

Even a pre-eminent Non-Aligned State was compelled to abstain on the resolution because, 'it expressed general sentiments which are fine and with which we are in complete agreement, but it does not adequately provide a solution for the problem with which the world is faced with today'.[79] The General Assembly has been forced to call on the Security Council to adopt mandatory measures, to force South Africa to give up apartheid, a message which, apart from a mandatory arms embargo, has not been heeded, and will not be heeded with Western dominance of the Council and a slow process of change in South Africa. There is a great deal to be said for the view that the Assembly should reflect the feelings of the international community and to leave South Africa in 'no doubt' as to these sentiments,[80] but the Assembly should not become, as it has towards South Africa, so vitriolic that it cannot then offer neutral assistance to aid the reform process. Without effective enforcement action to reinforce its calls, the Assembly can ill afford to antagonise States such as South Africa, when eventually they look for a method of escaping from their clearly untenable positions.

The Assembly clearly has developed a useful quasi-judicial capacity, in the sense that it passes numerous judgements on disputes, conflicts or situations. If these judgements are based on an objective determination of international law, as many are, they focus world attention on the problem and reinforce the provisions of international law. However, in certain cases, South Africa being a good example, the initial objective determinations have given way to partisan determinations which add little to the judgement and in fact compromise the UN's neutrality. One can detect this abuse of its quasi-judicial power in its 1989 resolution which reaffirmed the Assembly's support for the African National Congress and other national liberation movements in South Africa 'which pursue their noble objective to eliminate apartheid through political, armed and other forms of struggle'.[81] With a move towards reform by the racist government in the 1990s, starting with the release of Nelson Mandela in February 1990, there arose a greater degree of violence as the various factions in South Africa began to fight against each other. After encouraging violence in the 1970s and 1980s the Assembly at its 46th session in 1991 called 'for an immediate end to violence' in South Africa and urged 'the South Africa authorities to take immediate further action to end the recurring violence and acts of terrorism'.[82]

Notes

1 J. P. Cot and A. Pellet, *La Charte des Nations Unies*, 267 (1985); L. M. Goodrich, E. Hambro and P. S. Simons, *The Charter of the United Nations*, 117, 2nd ed. (1969).
2 GA Res. S-10/2, 10 UN GAOR SS Supp. (No. 4) 3 (1978).
3 Cot and Pellet, *La Charte*, 272.
4 *United Nations Disarmament Yearbook*, vol. 12 (1987), appendix VII.
5 GA Res. 44/107, 44 UN GAOR (1989).
6 GA Res. 46/29, 46 UN GAOR (1991).
7 GA Res. 35/145A, 35 UN GAOR (1980).
8 *UN Chronicle*, vol. 29 (1992), 76.
9 GA Res. 46/36H,L., 46 UN GAOR (1991) on general and complete disarmament, see 31 *I.L.M.* (1992) 482. Part L dealing with the arms register was adopted by 150 votes to 0 with 2 absentions (Cuba and Iraq). Part H dealing with international arms transfers was adopted without a vote. GA Res. 46/25C, 46 UN GAOR (1991) on chemical weapons was adopted without a vote.
10 *The Independent*, 23 June 1992.
11 Contrast the UN sponsored 1972 Convention on the Prohibition of the Development, Production and Stockpiling of Bacteriological (Biological) and Toxin Weapons and their Destruction, 1015 UNTS 187.
12 GA Res. 375, 4 UN GAOR Resolutions 66 (1949).
13 4 UN GAOR Supp. (No. 2) Agenda Item 49 (1949).
14 GA 947 plen. mtg, 15 UN GAOR 1278–9 (1960).
15 GA Res. 1514, 15 UN GAOR Supp. (No. 16) 66 (1960).
16 Portugal, Spain, South Africa, United Kingdom, United States, Australia, Dominican Republic, France.
17 GA 947 plen. mtg, 15 UN GAOR 1283 (1960).
18 GA Res. 2131, 20 UN GAOR Supp. (No. 14) 10 (1965).
19 GA 1st Committee 1406 mtg, 19 UN GAOR para. 17 (1965).
20 *Ibid.*, 1404 mtg, 306.
21 *Ibid.*, 1406 mtg, para.17.
22 GA Res. 2625, 25 UN GAOR Supp. (No. 28) 121 (1970).
23 GA, 6th Committee 1178 mtg, 25 UN GAOR 9 (1970).
24 GA, 6th Committee 1181 mtg, 25 UN GAOR 21 (1970), New Zealand; 1182 mtg,

27, Portugal.
25 *Ibid.*, 1178 mtg, 7, Poland; 1180 mtg 17, Senegal.
26 Declaration on the Enhancement of the Effectiveness of the Principle of Refraining from the Threat or Use of Force in International Relations, GA Res. 42/22, 42 UN GAOR (1987).
27 J. Stone, *Conflict Through Consensus*, ch. 6 (1977).
28 *Case Concerning Military and Paramilitary Activities in and Against Nicaragua (Nicaragua v. United States of America*, I.C.J. *Rep.*, 14, at 97–117.
29 *Ibid,.* 130–5.
30 GA Res. 43/51, 43 UN GAOR (1988).
31 GA Res. 46/182, 46 UN GAOR (1991).
32 GA Res. 44/29, 44 UN GAOR (1989).
33 GA Res. 46/59, 46 UN GAOR (1992).
34 GA Res. 3485, 30 UN GAOR Supp. (No. 34) 118 (1975).
35 GA Res. 3212, 29 UN GAOR Supp. (No. 31) 3 (1974).
36 See also the Assembly's cease-fire and withdrawal call regarding Suez in 1956, as a pre-condition of the imposition of its peacekeeping force.
37 GA Res. 1004, 2 UN GAOR ESS Supp. (No. 1) 2 (1956).
38 GA 564 plen. mtg, 2 UN GAOR ESS para. 187, 209 (1956), UK and New Zealand.
39 GA Res. 34/22, 34 UN GAOR Supp. (No. 46) 16 (1979).
40 GA 67 plen. mtg, 34 UN GAOR para. 127 (1979), France.
41 GA Res. 2793, 26 UN GAOR Supp. (No. 29) 3 (1971). GA 2003 plen. mtg, 26 UN GAOR paras. 37, 194, 245 (1971), Ceylon, Nicaragua and Tanzania.
42 GA Res. 1004 (1956); 2793 (1971); 3212 (1974); 3485 (1974); 34/22 (1979); GA Res. ES-6/2, 6 UN GAOR ESS Supp. (No. 1) 2 (1980); GA Res. 38/7, 38 UN GAOR Supp. (No. 47) 19 (1983); GA Res. 44/240, 44 UN GAOR (1989), respectively.
43 See for example, GA Res. 46/18, 46/23, 46 UN GAOR (1991).
44 GA Res. 367, 5 UN GAOR Resolutions 9 (1950). See GA 293 plen. mtg, 5 UN GAOR paras. 37, 70 (1950), France, USSR.
45 See also GA Res. 39, 1 UN GAOR Resolutions 63 (1946), re Spain.
46 GA Res. 500, 5 UN GAOR Supp. (No. 20A) 2 (1951).
47 GA 330 plen. mtg, 5 UN GAOR 739–40 (1951).
48 GA Res. 1663, 16 UN GAOR Supp. (No. 17) 10 (1961); GA Res. 2107, 20 UN GAOR Supp. (No. 14) 62 (1965); GA Res. 2151, 21 UN GAOR Supp. (No. 16) 68 (1966).
49 GA Res. 3379, 30 UN GAOR (1975).
50 See for example GA Res. 39/146, 39 UN GAOR Supp. (No. 51) 50 (1984).
51 GA Res. 46/86, 46 UN GAOR (1991).
52 GA Res. 46/74, 46/76, 46/82, 46/166, 46 UN GAOR (1991).
53 GA Res. 46/79, 46 UN GAOR (1991).
54 GA Res. 106, 1 UN GAOR SS Resolutions 6 (1947).
55 2 UN GAOR Supp. (No. 11) (1947).
56 UN doc. A/364 (1947).
57 GA 124, 125 plen. mtgs, 2 UN GAOR 1324, 1359 (1947), US and USSR.
58 GA 127 plen. mtg, 2 UN GAOR 1398 (1947).

59 UN doc. A/518 (1947).
60 See GA 126 plen. mtg, 2 UN GAOR 1376 (1947).
61 See GA *Ad Hoc* Committee 32 mtg, 2 UN GAOR (1947).
62 GA Res. 181, 2 UN GAOR Resolutions 131 (1947).
63 UN doc. A/C.1/277–8 (1948).
64 GA Res. 46/75, 46 UN GAOR (1991).
65 See UN doc. A/46/652 (1991). GA plen. mtg, 46 UN A/PV (1991).
66 *International Status of South West Africa* case, I.C.J. *Rep*. 1950, 128.
67 GA Res. 43/26, 43 GAOR (1988).
68 GA Res. 35/6, 35 UN GAOR Supp. (No. 48) 13 (1980).
69 GA Res. 46/18, 46 UN GAOR (1991).
70 See GA Res. 42/1, 42 UN GAOR (1987).
71 GA Res. 42/15, 42 UN GAOR (1987).
72 GA Res. 46/23, 46 UN GAOR (1991). UN doc. A/46/577 (1991).
73 GA Res. 1131, 11 UN GAOR Supp. (No. 17) 64 (1956).
74 GA 618 plen. mtg, 11 UN GAOR para. 10 (1956), Peru.
75 GA Res. 41/38, 41 UN GAOR Supp. (No. 53) 34 (1986).
76 GA Res. 44/240, 44 UN GAOR (1989).
77 *Nicaragua* case, I.C.J. *Rep*. 1986, 14, at 98.
78 GA Res. 616, 7 UN GAOR Supp. (No. 20) 8 (1952).
79 GA 401 plen. mtg, 7 UN GAOR para. 120 (1952), India.
80 GA 56 plen. mtg, 38 UN GAOR 8, 18, 23 (1983), Sierra Leone, India, China.
81 GA Res. 44/27, 44 UN GAOR (1989).
82 GA Res. 46/79, 46 UN GAOR (1991).

PART THREE
Peacekeeping

CHAPTER SEVEN

Historical and political background

Introduction

An accurate definition of peacekeeping is to be found in the *Review of United Nations Peacekeeping*, published by the United Nations:

As the United Nations practice has evolved over the years, a peacekeeping operation has come to be defined as an operation involving military personnel, but without enforcement powers, undertaken by the United Nations to help maintain or restore international peace and security in areas of conflict. These operations are voluntary and are based on consent and cooperation. While they involve the use of military personnel, they achieve their objectives not by force of arms, thus contrasting them with the 'enforcement action' of the United Nations under Article 42.[1]

The development of a peacekeeping function is one of the most significant achievements of the United Nations in its attempt to maintain international peace and security. To the layman peacekeeping forces or the 'blue helmets' are concrete manifestations of the United Nations which offset the common view that the Organisation only produces rhetoric and ideologically motivated resolutions. To the political scientist peacekeeping probably represents the most concerted effort the international community makes in regulating conflict, with the exception of military enforcement action. Other peaceful mechanisms are generally unsuccessful as explained by Wiseman:

The tension and struggle between the forces for change and the forces for the maintenance of the *status quo* are constant and dynamic features of the international system. This struggle is manifested in the frequent occurrence of ferocious and intractable conflict. By contrast, but by no means as persistent and powerful as the systematic propensity to conflict, are the creation and utilisation of international structures, instruments, and procedures for the containment and resolution of these conflicts by political means. The attempts to superimpose peaceful regulatory systems upon the disordered world are extremely hazardous and difficult. The national political propensities to make war are far more powerful than the international processes to make peace. Nonetheless, the will, determination and imagination of peoples and States persist in the quest to make order out of chaos and prescribe peaceful measures for progressive social change.[2]

Peacekeeping is such a 'peaceful regulatory system'. Its success lies in the fact that it usually only has limited objectives, for example, in separating two protagonists, not by coercion as with military enforcement, but with their consent and hopefully with their cooperation. Other peaceful measures, such as resolving the conflict by negotiation, are not as successful for they involve far more ambitious objectives. The division between peacekeeping and peacemaking, and peacekeeping and enforcement will be examined in chapter eight.

To the international lawyer peacekeeping represents an intriguing puzzle, raising in particular such questions as the constitutional basis for such operations; whether nations hosting peacekeeping operations are surrendering their sovereignty; whether such forces can use force beyond that required for self-defence; and which political organ of the United Nations can authorise such forces? Consistent answers to such questions have proved difficult to arrive at given the *ad hoc* creation of such forces resulting in various mandates and sizes of forces.

In this respect peacekeeping reflects the crisis management approach of the Organisation's work concerning international peace and security. Despite the establishment, in 1965, by the General Assembly, of a Special Committee on Peacekeeping to try to formulate a more institutionalised basis for peacekeeping, forces are, in the main, only envisaged, created and assembled after a conflict has started, and then only if there is sufficient political consensus in the Security Council or the General Assembly. However, the 1990s has seen some hint of reform. At its 46th session the General Assembly welcomed the progress made by the Special Committee in 1990–91, 'in particular, the agreement reached on a number of conclusions and recommendations'.[3]

Furthermore, the Secretary General in a report entitled 'Agenda for Peace', prepared at the request of the Security Council following the summit meeting of heads of government of 31 January 1992, put forward the following proposal to enhance preventive diplomacy:

United Nations operations in areas of crisis have generally been established after the conflict has occurred. The time has come to plan for circumstances warranting preventive deployment, which could take place in a variety of instances and ways. For example, in conditions of national crisis there could be preventive deployment at the request of the Government or all parties concerned, or with their consent; in inter-State disputes such deployment could take place when two countries feel that a United Nations presence on both sides of their border can discourage hostilities; furthermore, preventive deployment could take place when a country feels threatened and requests the deployment of an appropriate United Nations presence along its side of the border alone. In each situation, the mandate and composition of the United Nations presence would need to be carefully devised and be clear to all.[4]

This proposal would enhance the Organisation's ability to prevent hostilities from breaking out but it must be made clear, as the Secretary General suggests, whether the particular force is a consensual, lightly armed peacekeeping force, or is of an enforcement type armed with both mandate and equipment to repel aggression.

Historical overview

The following peacekeeping and observer forces have been authorised by the United Nations:

UN Observers in Indonesia 1947–50.
UN Sub-Commission on the Balkans (UNSCOB) 1947–54.
UN Truce Supervision Organisation in Palestine (UNTSO) 1949-present.
UN Military Observer Group in India and Pakistan (UNMOGIP) 1949-present.
UN Emergency Force (UNEF I) 1956–67.
UN Observer Group in Lebanon (UNOGIL) 1958.
UN Operation in the Congo (ONUC) 1960–64.
UN Observers and Security Force in West Irian (UNSF) 1962–63.
UN Yemen Observation Mission (UNYOM) 1963–64.
UN Peacekeeping Force in Cyprus (UNFICYP) 1964-present.
UN India-Pakistan Observation Mission (UNIPOM) 1965–66.
UN Emergency Force (UNEF II) 1973–79.
UN Disengagement Observer Force (UNDOF) 1974-present.
UN Interim Force in Lebanon (UNIFIL) 1978-present.
UN Good Offices Mission in Afghanistan and Pakistan (UNGOMAP) 1988–90.
UN Iran-Iraq Military Observer Group (UNIIMOG) 1988–91.
UN Angola Verification Missions (UNAVEM I and II) 1989-present.
UN Transition Assistance Group (UNTAG) 1989–90.
UN Observer Group in Central America (ONUCA) 1989–92.
UN Mission for the Referendum in Western Sahara (MINURSO) 1991-present.
UN Observer Mission in El Salvador (ONUSAL) 1991-present.
UN Transition Assistance Authority in Cambodia (UNTAC) 1991-present.
UN Iraq-Kuwait Observation Mission (UNIKOM) 1991-present.
UN Protection Force in Yugoslavia (UNPROFOR) 1992-present.
UN Operation in Somalia (UNOSOM) 1992-present.

Wiseman has analysed United Nations' peacekeeping historically.[5] He labels the period 1946–56 as the 'nascent period' of peacekeeping with the creation of four observation teams, the so-called 'generic antecedents' of full peacekeeping forces which emerged in 1956 with the creation of UNEF I. This represented the beginning of what Wiseman calls the 'assertive period' which ended in 1967 with the withdrawal of UNEF I. During this period eight peacekeeping (including observation) forces were created. The withdrawal of UNEF I in 1967 with the ensuing Six Day War called into the question the effectiveness of United Nations' peacekeeping, so that between 1967 and 1973 it went through a 'dormant period' when no forces were created. Paradoxically, it took another conflict in the Middle East, namely the Yom Kippur War of 1973, to spark off a 'resurgent period' in which three full peacekeeping forces were created. After the creation and emplacement of UNIFIL, and the authorisation without emplacement of UNTAG in 1978, the peacekeeping function of the United Nations was frozen for a decade due to a decline in East-West relations.

However, the *rapprochement* between the superpowers in the late 1980s, sparked off a revival, with four forces established between March 1988 and April 1989, culminating in the emplacement of UNTAG over ten years after it had initially been authorised. UNTAG was in many respects a unique force in that it combined peacekeeping, the separation of South African forces and South-West Africa People's Organisation (SWAPO) guerrillas, and peacemaking in the form of supervision and policing of elections that eventually led to the independence of Namibia in 1990. This trend has continued into the 1990s with similar combined forces in Central America, Western Sahara, Cambodia and El Salvador. This new integrated approach, which reflects the trend towards democracy in the 1990s after the collapse of communism, has not replaced the traditional approach whereby peacekeeping is used to keep the parties apart whilst a separate political solution is sought, evidenced by the creation of forces in Yugoslavia and Somalia as well as between Iran and Iraq.

The United Nations has currently twelve forces on station around the globe with the prospect of many more being needed as the world is reshaped in the 1990s with the collapse of communism and the resurfacing of inter-ethnic rivalries. In this respect modern peacekeeping efforts follow a similar pattern to the earlier ones, such as UNTSO and the Middle East forces, needed when the state of Israel emerged after the Second World War, and forces such as ONUC in the Congo emplaced as a result of the decolonisation and independence of States. The latest resurgence of peacekeeping is not only a product of the loosening of political inhibitions in the Security Council but also a product of the numerous conflicts and situations that have rapidly broken out after the end of the Cold War.

Political context

Professor Franck gives a relatively narrow definition of peacekeeping as 'the peaceful interpositioning of UN personnel, in response to an invitation of the disputants, to oversee an agreed cease-fire'.[6] Such a definition is applicable only to inter-State peacekeeping, where a force is placed between two formerly hostile States which have agreed a cease-fire; whereas the United Nations has also undertaken intra-State peacekeeping, for example in the Congo, where a force is placed within one factionalised State. Franck's definition also ignores the technique of observation from which inter- and intra-State peacekeeping evolved. Observation has the limited function of reporting on the state of hostilities whereas peacekeeping has the more intrusive function of separating the parties to the cease-fire without the force generally having the power to enforce the peace. However, the divisions between observation, peacekeeping and enforcement action are unclear, as there are grey areas in which one function merges into another. Nevertheless, these distinctions are important in order to understand the legal principles governing peacekeeping, examined in chapter eight, as well as the political factors examined next.

The main purpose of this section is to give a brief review of the creation of each force to try and analyse the historical and political circumstances under which they arose and to attempt to indicate in what circumstances peacekeeping forces are likely to be established in the future. It may be that the circumstances are different for observation teams compared to peacekeeping forces.

Observation teams

The observation teams created in the nascent period (1946–56) all arose through the change that occurred in the international order following the Second World War. The first force to be created was the UN Observation team in Indonesia in 1947 when a conflict arose involving the Dutch colonialists' attempt to maintain the old order against a rising tide of nationalism in Indonesia. The Security Council, with no direct permanent member involvement once the British withdrew their wartime forces, and with no member willing to stand in the way of decolonisation in this case, was able to authorise UN observers.

The need for such observers was apparent from the confused state of affairs in Indonesia with various cease-fire lines, sporadic fighting and changing areas under the control of each side. Observers were needed to report on the various stages achieved, with the help of quite vigorous Security Council resolutions, towards Indonesian independence.

Decolonisation was also the main cause of the conflict between the newly independent States of India and Pakistan over the disputed Indian state of Jammu and Kashmir which led to the Security Council establishing UNMOGIP in 1949. As with Indonesia, this again was a soft area of the world where none of the permanent members, particularly the superpowers, had sufficient interest in either side to protect them by the veto. As with all peacekeeping forces, UNMOGIP depended upon the cooperation of both parties. Thus such forces are not usually created and emplaced until the fighting has come to an end and the belligerents are willing to accept a cease-fire. However, observation teams are not meant as buffer forces, they only observe the cease-fire and they are not usually large enough nor are they mandated to make the cease-fire effective as are peacekeeping forces proper. Thus UNMOGIP observed throughout the outbreak of hostilities in 1965 and was present to observe the new cease-fire. In 1965, the fighting between India and Pakistan was on a wider front than in 1947 necessitating the emplacement of another team, for a limited period, beyond UNMOGIP's patrol. UNIPOM was in place from 1965–66 again under a Security Council mandate, illustrating that this area of the world was not considered part of a power bloc. UNIPOM was removed after a limited period but UNMOGIP remains because its area of patrol, namely Kashmir, continues to constitute a potential flashpoint where the United Nations needs a constant presence.

Along with UNMOGIP another observation team, UNTSO, created under Security Council auspices in 1949, has lasted for over forty years in an even more troubled area of the world. Unlike UNEF which was emplaced between Israel and Egypt for eleven years between 1956–67 and for a further six years between 1973–79, UNTSO has observed various cease-fires, truces and armistices between belligerents in the Middle East. The peculiar fact is that there is no Security Council resolution directly authorising UNTSO, nor, as with UNMOGIP, is there any periodic renewal of its mandate. It has a loose mandate which is best described as observing and reporting to the United Nations on the situation in the Middle East. Its longevity is probably a testimony to the fact that the Security Council, particularly the permanent members, needs to keep in constant touch with the situation in an area where they have interests, but in which none is paramount, and UNTSO provides them with valuable, neutral information. UNTSO thus acts to some extent as an effective brake on the possibility of escalation based on a hasty, one-sided account of a conflict. In many respects they are similar to fact finding bodies authorised by the Security Council under Article 34, although they are military observers as opposed to civilian personnel. During the period of UNEF'S interpositioning, UNTSO observers worked alongside the peacekeeping force; however, unlike UNEF, UNTSO observers were used after the Six Day War, as it was a political necessity for the United Nations to maintain some presence in the area.

Observation is sufficiently flexible to be used equally successfully in intra-State conflicts such as Indonesia as well as in inter-State conflicts such as in the Gulf War between Iran and Iraq, which after nearly a decade of fighting, stagnated sufficiently to allow a UN observer force (UNIIMOG) into the area in August 1988. It can also be of value where there is a combination of the two situations evidenced by UNOGIL in the Lebanon in

1958 and by UNYOM in the Yemen in 1963. In both cases there arose the problem of outside military interference in a civil war. The countries involved, either directly or indirectly, were again situated in the intermediate areas of the world beyond the direct hemispheric influences of the superpowers, and of any of the other permanent members, thus allowing the Security Council to mandate both forces. Nevertheless, the fact that the Middle East was subject to superpower claims was evidenced by the United States' intervention in Lebanon despite UNOGIL's report that the country was not being undermined by the United Arab Republic.

However, during to the Cold War, when the conflict in question was nearer both politically and geographically to the superpowers to amount to an East-West power struggle, there was less likelihood of an observation team being sent to the area by the Security Council. After the Second World War the world order changed dramatically to an East-West divide based on ideology. Nowhere was this best evidenced than in the Balkans where the pro-Western Greek government alleged military support for the communist insurgents from the surrounding communist countries of Bulgaria, Albania and Yugoslavia. Although the Security Council was able to create a Commission of Investigation, it was left to the General Assembly, in 1947, to create a Sub-Committee which had observation functions. The Soviet Union objected to this. The Cold War motivations behind UNSCOB limited its effectiveness evidenced by the refusal of the Socialist States to allow it on their territory.

Sometimes the United Nations has found it necessary to create a force which combines observation with other duties due to the circumstances of the situation. Although the main Indonesian question had been settled earlier, there were still disputes over several islands in the Indonesian archipelago. One such island was Irian where guerrilla warfare was being carried out by Indonesians parachuted into the jungle and Dutch armed forces in the western part of the island. The Netherlands and Indonesia came to an agreement on 15 August 1962 which provided for the administration of West Irian to be transferred by the Netherlands to a United Nations' Temporary Executive Authority (UNTEA) pending a transfer of the territory to Indonesia. A United Nations' Observer and Security Force (UNSF) was to observe the cease-fire which was to take place before authority was transferred to UNTEA, and then to police the island until the transfer of sovereignty to Indonesia.[7]

Thus the force was really created by the parties although it required the approval of the General Assembly, as the body responsible for questions of self-determination, rather than the Security Council. Surprisingly, taking into account the large role given to the Secretary General in the control of UNTEA and UNSF, the Soviet Union voted for the creation of these bodies. At the time the continuing Congo question had provoked Soviet objections as regards the amount of control the Secretary General had over ONUC and of the ability of the General Assembly to mandate such a force in the absence of Security Council consensus. Nevertheless, the Soviet Union was willing to vote in the Assembly for the creation of a force and an authority whose control amounted to virtual temporary sovereignty over the island.

The reasons for the Soviet Union's support were twofold. Again the crisis was relatively minor and did not involve questions of superpower influence, except to the extent of the Soviet Union's uneasy courtship with the Non-Aligned of which Indonesia was a member. Also, the Soviet assent was due to the agreement of the parties which virtually created the United Nations' force.

Indeed, all observer teams and peacekeeping forces depend on the cooperation of the parties; some arise directly from an agreement between the parties which the Security Council (or more rarely the Assembly, if the agreement calls for it) has the option of approving. Under the armistice agreement of 1949 between Israel on the one hand and Egypt, Syria, Jordan and Lebanon on the other UNTSO was given specific duties;[8] UNYOM directly arose out of an agreement between Yemen, Saudi Arabia and the United Arab Republic negotiated by Secretary General U Thant;[9] UNMOGIP was a direct creation of the Karachi Agreement between India and Pakistan,[10] with which the Security Council had very little involvement; the Agreement on Disengagement between Syria and Israel called for the establishment of UNDOF.[11] Other forces are either requested by the States involved such as ONUC or UNFICYP, or are consented to by the parties on the initiative of the United Nations, for example UNEF. However, to say that only in the latter situation does the initiative for the creation of a force come from the United Nations would be an exaggeration ignoring the often significant contribution of the Secretary General.

Furthermore, the observer forces in Afghanistan and Angola coming towards the end of the Cold War, were the result of express or tacit agreements between the superpowers to allow observer forces into areas of global as well as regional confrontation. UNGOMAP, in Afghanistan to oversee Soviet troops withdrawal, was a product of 1988 superpower accord as well as an agreement between the regional States involved, Pakistan and Afghanistan.[12] UNAVEM, in Angola, was a product of regional agreements of 1988 involving Cuba, Angola and South Africa, but was also backed by the Soviet Union and the United States.[13] Both were primarily a result of the Soviet Union withdrawing from its zones of influence as a prelude to the collapse of the Eastern bloc and ultimately of the Soviet Union in 1991. In the period of the late 1980s when there was a distinct warming in superpower relations, UN observer teams were allowed into what were formerly 'no-go' areas including those areas dominated by the eventual winner of the Cold War, the United States.

The long-standing internationalised civil wars in Nicaragua and El Salvador have been brought to an end by an ongoing Central American peace process started by the States in the region with the Guatemala Accords of 1987.[14] After many years of keeping the United Nations out of its hemisphere, the United States consented to the creation of ONUCA in Nicaragua and ONUSAL in El Salvador. Paradoxically, the United States' aim of overthrowing the left wing government in Nicaragua, which it unsuccessfully pursued for nearly a decade by its heavy support for the Contras, was achieved when the Sandinista government was defeated in UN supervised elections in 1990. It remains to be seen whether its policy of propping up the right wing regime in El Salvador will survive the UN supervised elections promised there in the near future.

Indeed, the current trend in peacekeeping and observation is to combine peacekeeping and peacemaking, in that the parties to the conflict not only agree to a peacekeeping or observer force to keep the parties apart or to monitor a cease-fire, but they also agree to a specific method of settling the dispute. The dominant method chosen in intra-State conflicts has been the choice of a democratic government through free and fair elections reflecting the trend towards democracy in the post Cold War era. Such forces are not too dissimilar from that involved in West Irian in 1962–63, in that they have a separate peacekeeping or observation component and then an additional component established to supervise the chosen method of pacific settlement. In 1989 the Security Council established the United Nations Mission to Verify the Electoral Process in Nicaragua (ONUVEN) at the request of the parties. A similar request by the opposing factions in Angola in 1991 resulted in the establishment of a second UNAVEM team to observe the cease-fire between the factions and to supervise elections scheduled for September 1992. The method is sufficiently flexible to allow for variations. In El Salvador the initial agreement was for observation by ONUSAL of the human rights accord reached by the parties in July 1990 (the San José Agreement)[15] while the parties continued negotiation on a cease-fire and on a peaceful solution. In the long-running dispute over Western Sahara, the initial agreement of 1988 between Morocco and the Popular Front for the Liberation of the Sanguia el-Harura and the Rio de Oro (POLISARIO) brokered by the Secretary General and the Organisation of African Unity (OAU), eventually took the form of an acceptable plan in 1990.[16] Under this plan the UN force, MINURSO, would supervise a cease-fire between the parties and conduct a referendum in which the Western Saharan people would choose between integration with Morocco and independence.

The new observer teams are in the main needed because of the instability caused by the collapse in the bipolar world. One product of this instability is the greater willingness of the United Nations to use force. It did so against

Iraq in 1990–91. When the Iraqis accepted the cease-fire in April 1991, the Security Council established UNIKOM to oversee it on the Iraq-Kuwait border. This was the first time the UN has placed a peacekeeping force between two parties, one of which was in reality the UN authorised Coalition. As well as showing the Security Council's increasingly flexible approach to its powers, it reveals the different conceptions States have of enforcement and peacekeeping. Iraq, while fighting against the Coalition in February and March 1991, accepted the peacekeeping force without much argument, although in reality it had little choice.

The Gulf Crisis also saw the expansion in the use of UN military personnel in an essentially observatory capacity in the provision of humanitarian aid to the Kurdish population in the north. Such a humanitarian function has been undertaken by UN military personnel before, for instance by UNIFIL in Lebanon when the force was powerless to perform its other functions, but such a trend seems set to continue if the increasing number of inter-ethnic wars produces huge waves of refugees attempting to flee from the combat zones.

The end of the Coalition campaign against Iraq saw the Iraqi regime still powerful enough to suppress brutally Kurd and Shia revolts against it starting in March 1991. The Kurdish repression in particular saw a flood of refugees flee across the borders into Iran and Turkey. Western States initially responded by airlifts of food and clothing and eventually by limited military intervention in the north to protect the Kurds and to encourage them to return to Iraq. On 20 May 1991, Iraq consented to the presence of 500 UN guards to replace the 15,000 Western troops in the north of Iraq.

Peacekeeping forces

Observation, supervision and enforcement are the three possible stages of United Nations' military involvement in a conflict. The first two are peacekeeping functions, observation has already been discussed, but it must be remembered that there is often a thin line between observation and full peacekeeping as evidenced by the mandate and functions of UNSF in West Irian and many of the recent forces with integrated or combined mandates performing several functions. Similarly, there is a grey area between peacekeeping and enforcement action highlighted by the actions of ONUC in the Congo.

For the purposes of this section peacekeeping involves not only observation of the cease-fire but also supervision, which in most instances of inter-State conflict entails the creation of a buffer zone between the former belligerents, a function too large, and requiring a different mandate, than for observation teams. Peacekeeping evolved from observation so as to give the United Nations a more active role after the cessation of hostilities. UNEF I was the first 'dramatically innovative venture' into peacekeeping proper.[17] It was created in 1956 by the General Assembly after a joint Anglo/French/Israeli plan to oppose, *inter alia*, Egyptian nationalisation of the Suez Canal. Permanent member involvement prevented the creation of such a force in the Security Council, so the question passed to the General Assembly where UNEF I was created with the substantial assistance of the Secretary General.

It might be argued that the above procedure could have been successfully utilised in other instances of permanent member involvement so as to create peacekeeping forces in the Assembly when such efforts have been vetoed in the Security Council. There are two factors which prevent such a course being chosen more often. First, even though the United Kingdom and France vetoed any attempts to pacify the situation in the Council they only abstained (along with the Soviet bloc) on the Assembly resolution creating UNEF I, and, in fact, they eventually consented to the placement of the force. Although the Assembly could, theoretically, create peacekeeping forces in cases of permanent member intervention, when the Council is blocked by the veto, political reality prevents such a course without the consent of all the parties concerned. In the Suez case, the two permanent members involved had reached a stage where to continue would have brought them under unbearable international pressure, while to withdraw would have been too costly politically; the peacekeeping force was consented to because it maintained the *status quo* achieved so far. To this end it also met the requirements of the other two parties; Egypt because it was being heavily defeated and Israel because it had gained a considerable amount of territory. The circumstances were ripe for a UN peacekeeping force to fill the vacuum.

A second factor which prevented the creation of further forces by the Assembly instead of the Council is the attitude among the permanent members that such forces should only be created by the Security Council. Originally, the French and the Soviet Union took this line in relation to UNEF I and ONUC leading to their challenge of being assessed for financial contributions in the *Expenses* case of 1962. The evidence is that the United States and the United Kingdom adopted this line from 1960 onwards. Evan Luard has accurately summarised the reasons for this.

First, the outright opposition of the Soviet Union and France to the use previously made of the Assembly, their refusal to contribute to the costs of peacekeeping operations the Assembly had authorised, and the prolonged financial crisis which resulted from this constitutional difference in view, all served to induce some caution among other major powers in mobilising the Assembly. Secondly, the increasing size of the Assembly, as well as the change in its composition (in which Afro-Asian Members came to hold more than two-thirds of the votes) meant that it came to be thought a less suitable instrument for use in such situations, by the US as much as by the Soviet Union. Thirdly, the far less use of the Soviet veto in the Council reduced the need for an alternative agency. Finally, the desire of the other permanent members to retain the special influence which they held in the Security Council also encouraged the restoration of the Council's supremacy in security questions.[18]

Communist China has sometimes objected in the past to peacekeeping on the grounds that it was a creation of the superpowers, at other times its supports the emplacement of a force by the Security Council depending on the circumstances of the case. Recently the Chinese have shown a more positive attitude to peacekeeping, illustrated by the fact that it joined the Assembly's Special Committee on Peacekeeping in 1988, and has supported the Council's post Cold War peacekeeping efforts.

The Middle East has been the area in which peacekeeping, whether by the United Nations or by other agencies, has been most utilised. UNEF I was withdrawn in 1967. UNEF II, authorised by the Security Council, was emplaced between Egypt and Israel following the Yom Kippur War of 1973. The danger of superpower intervention as well as the consent of the combatants were direct factors leading to its creation. UNEF II was not only a buffer between the two parties, it was also an indirect buffer between the superpowers backing Israel and Egypt. When Egypt changed its allegiance to become more pro-Western, the United States was able to sponsor negotiations between the Israelis and the Egyptians leading to the Camp David Accords. Although the peace agreement between Israel and Egypt provided for a continued United Nations' peacekeeping presence, the Egyptian defection had practically destroyed the superpower accord behind UNEF II, and so the force was discontinued in 1979 to be replaced by a United States' sponsored multinational force. However, superpower agreement still continued as regards UNDOF created in 1974 as a buffer on the Israeli-Syrian front, as each party remained fairly firmly placed in the Western and Eastern camps. Even with the demise of the Soviet Union, Syria remains Israel's most dangerous enemy necessitating a continued peacekeeping presence.

Middle Eastern peacekeeping forces have the regional function of separating two or more belligerents but they have had wider functions than the maintenance of stable Arab-Israeli relations – they were placed so as to add an extra check on the possibility of escalation in an area where although both superpowers had clients, neither had regional dominance. Similarly, UNIFIL was created in 1978 not only to secure Israeli withdrawal from Lebanon, but also to perform the unstated, global function of separating American-backed Israel and Soviet-supported Syria from engaging in conflict using Lebanon as a battleground, which might have sucked in one or both superpowers. When creating such a force the Security Council only lists the local functions of the force as regards the two belligerents; nevertheless, peacekeeping has played and continues to play a much more global function in the Middle East. The global function has continued with the end of the Cold War, which while producing new opportunities for peaceful settlement of old problems, has led to instability in many areas of the globe where previously superpower pressure resulted in a precarious *status quo*. The Middle Eastern peacekeeping forces, UNIFIL, UNDOF and UNTSO are needed to maintain this stability while the new peace process, which started in 1991, has a chance to succeed.

ONUC, in the Congo, was created in an atmosphere of potential superpower intervention after the Belgians withdrew in 1960. Indeed, it was a Soviet Union's charge that ONUC was leaning towards the pro-Western factions in the Congo which led to the Soviet veto of any continuing Security Council control over the force which in turn led to the General Assembly having control of the operation for a while. However, ONUC managed to tread the neutral tightrope sufficiently to preclude any overt superpower intervention. The members of the Security Council, particularly the superpowers, probably originally authorised the operation because the Congo represented an area in which both superpowers would have liked to have a base, but neither was willing to disturb the global *status quo* by intervening. Thus to concretise this mutual non-intervention, and to assuage each superpower's fear of the other intervening, the United Nations was called to fill the vacuum.

ONUC's operation probably represented the only attempt by the United Nations to modify peacekeeping to suit a case of intra-State conflict. One could argue that UNIFIL in Lebanon, UNFICYP in Cyprus, UNTAG in Namibia and UNPROFOR in Yugoslavia are further examples of United Nations' peacekeeping operations being authorised in intra-State conflicts. However, it is perhaps more realistic to view these forces as a hybrid between intra- and inter-State peacekeeping forces. UNIFIL was created after Israel intervened in 1978 and has acted to a certain extent as a buffer between two factions, pro-Israeli and anti-Israeli, as well as between Israel and Syria. However, each faction is in itself so fragmented that the situation has become one of civil war. Nevertheless, UNIFIL's main function still remains to supervise Israeli withdrawal, rather than to prevent a civil war which was one of ONUC's main tasks.

UNFICYP was created in 1964 after fighting had broken out between the Greek and Turkish Cypriot communities on the island. It was thus a civil war situation akin to that in the Congo, except with fewer parties. Indeed, the fact that there were only two parties enabled UNFICYP to function similarly to an inter-State peacekeeping force, by separating the two communities. This function became particularly evident after the Turkish invasion and occupation of the northern third of Cyprus in 1974. UNFICYP evolved into a true buffer force between two belligerents after this date.

In the case of UNTAG, we saw both the Soviet Union and the United

States consenting, along with the regional powers, to a large UN presence in an economically rich and strategically important area of the world. Although created on paper in 1978, UNTAG was not emplaced until April 1989 as a result of an interim period in which global attitudes between the superpowers and regional attitudes between Angola and South Africa hardened. The new *realpolitik* of the late 1980s meant that the Soviet Union and its allies no longer objected to the linkage of Cuban withdrawal from Angola with South African withdrawal from Namibia.

UNTAG, like UNSF before it, was given a mixture of peacekeeping, observer and police functions, relating to the cessation of hostilities, withdrawal of forces and keeping the peace during a peaceful transition to independence. Such a mixed or integrated approach to peacekeeping has been continued in areas of the world where the end of the Cold War has seen the local factions, in what were internationalised civil wars, so exhausted that political settlement is the only viable option remaining to them. The wars in Central America have already been mentioned, but by far the most ambitious project in this respect is the huge peacekeeping force, UNTAC, sent to Cambodia pursuant to the Paris Peace Accords which were signed by the four factions in the conflict in October 1991.[19]

However, whilst in Namibia and Cambodia the parties to the conflict, which had lasted for many years, were ready to negotiate, the end of the Cold War has set loose new conflicts which require what could be described as old-fashioned peacekeeping simply to keep the parties apart, with any attempts at peaceful solution being a separate and daunting enterprise. The UN operation in Yugoslavia, UNPROFOR, is like ONUC in the Congo in some respects, given that Yugoslavia was a single State until its rapid disintegration started with the civil war in Slovenia and Croatia in June 1991. However, unlike ONUC, whose aim was to keep the Congo intact, UNPROFOR is present to oversee the breakup of Yugoslavia into several nations, with its principal task being a buffer force between Croatia and the remains of Yugoslavia (Serbia and Montenegro) while a peaceful solution to the problem of an international frontier and the Serbian enclaves in Croatia is negotiated. However, as in the Lebanon, the emerging States, particularly Bosnia, have broken down into several factions themselves, leaving UNPROFOR in a vulnerable position, and forcing the peacekeepers to concentrate on the provision of humanitarian assistance to the suffering civilians in Bosnia.

As has been noted in our discussion of observer forces, the provision of humanitarian aid has become an increasing feature in many of the most recent UN forces, as the massive displacement of refugees from internecine conflicts shocks the world's conscience. The most recent force in Somalia, UNOSOM, is a response primarily to the starvation resulting from the increasingly anarchic situation in that country following the overthrow of

President Barre in January 1991. Its functions are to oversee an agreed cease-fire and to provide urgent humanitarian assistance. Although it is urged to help promote a political settlement to end the civil war, the presence of the force is only dependent on the factions agreeing to a cease-fire, not to an agreed method of pacific settlement as in Cambodia.

The collapse of the bipolar world has led to the UN being sucked into the vacuum. In many instances the collapse of the Cold War has also allowed peaceful initiatives in the old conflicts where the factions, no longer propped up by outside States, are ready to settle. Angola, El Salvador, Western Sahara and Cambodia are the newest examples of an approach to peacekeeping that integrates it with a peaceful solution. However, in the conflicts that have emerged out, or escalated as a result, of the Cold War, peace initiatives are separate and usually less successful. In this respect they are like many of the older forces, some of which are still in place, such as UNFICYP in Cyprus. Indeed, there is plenty of evidence to suggest that whereas such forces are essential to maintain the regional and sometimes the global *status quo*, they can hinder a peaceful solution because the parties are happier with that situation than any of the alternatives. Forces such as those emplaced in Cambodia and Western Sahara clearly have an advantage, but since they still depend on consent for their success, such forces cannot always be authorised. It appears there will always be a need for traditional peacekeeping forces. The next could be authorised between the new States that have emerged out of the Soviet Union since 1991. Already Armenia has requested a UN force to be sent to the disputed enclave of Nagorno Karabach in neighbouring Azerbaijan, although the Azeris have not yet agreed to such a force.[20]

Notes

1 *The Blue Helmets: A Review of United Nations Peacekeeping*, 4, 2nd ed. (1991).
2 H. Wiseman, *Peacekeeping: Appraisals and Proposals*, 1 (1983).
3 GA Res. 46/48, 46 UN GAOR (1991). UN doc. A/46/254 (1991), UN doc. 25 August 1992.
4 Boutros Boutros-Ghali, *Agenda for Peace*, para 28 (1992); 31 *I.L.M.* (1992) 953, at 962.
5 Wiseman, *Peacekeeping*, ch. 2.
6 T. M. Franck, *Nation against Nation*, 168 (1985).
7 274 UNTS 6311.
8 42 UNTS 252, 42 UNTS 304, 42 UNTS 327, 42 UNTS 288 respectively.
9 UN docs S/5298, S/5321 (1963).
10 UN doc. S/1430/Add 1 (1949).
11 UN doc. S/11302/Add 1 & 2 (1974).
12 Geneva Accords, 27 *I.L.M.* (1988), 577.
13 UN docs. S/20345, S/20346 (1988).

14 26 *I.L.M.* (1987), 1164.
15 UN doc. S/21541 (1990).
16 UN doc. S/21360 (1990).
17 Wiseman, *Peacekeeping*, 19.
18 E. Luard, *The United Nations*, 46–7 (1979).
19 UN doc. S/23179 (1991).
20 *The Independent*, 6 February 1992.

CHAPTER EIGHT

The legal parameters of peacekeeping

Principles

In this chapter we are going to concentrate on the legal principles governing peacekeeping in the narrow sense of the term, that is the emplacement of a military force of 'blue berets' or 'blue helmets' by the United Nations. The aim is to illustrate the main principles by using examples of UN peacekeeping or observation forces, fuller details of which can be found in chapter nine. We will also mention the attempts at peacekeeping undertaken by regional organisations and individual States, to see if they match up to the generally accepted legal principles as defined by consistent UN practice since 1947, when the Security Council first authorised the emplacement of military observers in the colonial conflict between the Dutch and the Indonesians.

It may appear somewhat odd that the most evident of the UN's functions should not be expressly authorised by the Charter, although any doubts about the legality of peacekeeping by the UN were cleared up by the World Court in the *Expenses* case.[1] One explanation for the emergence of peacekeeping focuses on the failure of the major powers to develop the military enforcement provisions of the Charter contained in Chapter VII.[2] The Cold War effectively stunted the use of military enforcement by the Security Council, with the one main exception of the UN authorised operation in Korea in 1950. To fill the vacuum left in the powers of the UN, peacekeeping gradually emerged. Since military enforcement action was not acceptable to *both* superpowers, military operations developed along different lines, being entirely consensual, non-enforcement, activities. Although there are signs that there may be a partial revitalisation of the enforcement powers of the Security Council, evidenced by the Council's authorisation to use force against Iraq in 1991, it appears that the usefulness of peacekeeping is not diminished. Indeed, there has been a veritable explosion of new forces authorised by the UN since 1988.

The three observation teams sent by the Council to the conflicts in Indonesia, Palestine and Kashmir in the late 1940s established the basic guidelines, though it was not until the General Assembly authorised the First Emergency Force in the Middle East after the Suez Crisis of 1956 that the legal principles governing peacekeeping, whether simple observation or full monitoring and supervision, became firmly established. Indeed, the principles were entrenched to a certain extent by the World Court in the *Expenses* case relying on the Secretary General's report on the setting up of UNEF I as encapsulating the peacekeeping function. The Court quoted the following section of the Secretary General's report:

. . . the functions of the United Nations Force would be, when a cease-fire is being established, to enter Egyptian territory with the consent of the Egyptian Government, in order to help maintain quiet during and after the withdrawal of non-Egyptian troops, and to secure compliance with the other terms established in the [General Assembly] resolution of 2 November 1956. The Force obviously should have no rights other than those necessary for the execution of its functions, in co-operation with local authorities. It would be more than an observers' corps, but in no way a military force temporarily controlling the territory in which it is stationed; nor, moreover, should the Force have military functions exceeding those necessary to secure peaceful conditions on the assumption that the parties to the conflict take all necessary steps for compliance with the recommendations of the General Assembly.[3]

The Court made it clear that the verb 'secure' did not imply enforcement action so as to allow the Force to secure a cease-fire or to halt military movements without the cooperation of the parties.[4] UNEF would only secure such interim measures by cooperation and consent, and, if necessary, by negotiation.

The *Expenses* case also made it clear that the authorisation of such consensual, non-enforcement, military activities is within the powers of the General Assembly as well as the Security Council which, as the World Court explained, has 'primary' but not exclusive competence under Article 24(1) of the UN Charter to maintain or restore international peace and security.[5] Indeed, the first full-scale peacekeeping force, UNEF I, was authorised by the General Assembly after the vetoes of the United Kingdom and France had paralysed the Security Council. Politically, the peacekeeping function of the UN is now firmly in the control of the Security Council, though a great deal of delegation of the organisational and logistical side is given to the Secretary General; legally the General Assembly possesses the power as well.

Although the World Court in the *Expenses* case made it clear that there was a clear line between peacekeeping and enforcement, and that both UNEF I and the UN Operation in the Congo (ONUC) were peacekeeping forces,[6] this does not rule out the possibility of the constitutional basis of such forces originating in Chapter VII. As we have seen, Article 40 of the Charter provides that 'in order to prevent an aggravation of the situation, the Security Council may . . . call upon the parties concerned to comply with such provisional measures as it deems necessary or desirable . . .'. The Security Council has used this power not only to make mandatory demands that States cease firing, or demand that foreign troops be withdrawn from the combat zone, but also to recommend such provisional measures. The power to call for provisional measures is contained in Article 40, and generally peacekeeping forces are created to facilitate the observance of such measures, when they have been accepted by the parties to the conflict. Peacekeeping is often necessary to make the power contained in Article 40 more effective. Peacekeeping is derived from Article 40, although its function does not vary with the nature of the obligation on the parties as regards the provisional measures. The nature of peacekeeping remains consensual and non-offensive whether or not the call for provisional measures is mandatory.[7]

For example, UNEF I was emplaced after the belligerents had accepted the General Assembly's *recommendation* for a cease-fire,[8] a power also possessed by the Assembly by virtue of Articles 10 and 14 of the Charter. Following the breakdown of order in Cyprus and the threat of Turkish intervention in 1964, the Security Council called upon States not to worsen the situation and urged the government to restore order. It then recommended, with the consent of the government of Cyprus, that UNFICYP be created.[9] It was recognised that UNFICYP was established pursuant to non-mandatory provisional measures.[10]

On other occasions, the peacekeeping force has been established following the acceptance of a *mandatory* demand that provisional measures be complied with, made by the Security Council. Iran and Iraq accepted Security Council mandatory resolution 598, adopted on 20 July 1987, over a year later on 20 August 1988,[11] at the point when both armies were exhausted. UNIIMOG was then established with the consent and cooperation of the parties to supervise the cease-fire and withdrawal of troops, and was in place between 1988 and March 1991, withdrawing after Iran and Iraq had agreed on a permanent peace on 15 August 1990.

On other occasions, peacekeeping follows acceptance of provisional measures deriving from an agreement by the parties themselves. Recently, a number of superpower sponsored accords have led to the acceptance of foreign troop withdrawal from internationalised civil war zones. The Geneva Accords on Afghanistan, signed on 14 April 1988,[12] followed negotiations by Pakistan, Afghanistan and the Secretary General's representative, with the Soviet Union and the United States as guaranteeing powers. The parties agreed to a phased withdrawal of Soviet troops which took place over six months, supervised by a small force of UN observers, UNGOMAP, approved by the Security Council.[13] Similar superpower pressure on Angola, Cuba and South Africa, led to a bilateral accord between Cuba and Angola on 22 December 1988,[14] providing for the phased withdrawal of Cuban troops from Angola, which was linked to the tripartite accord between Angola, Cuba and South Africa,[15] providing for the withdrawal of South African troops from Namibia, followed by that country's independence. The bilateral accord provided for the withdrawal of 50,000 Cuban troops to be supervised by a small team of UN observers, UNAVEM, approved by the Security Council.[16] Both UNAVEM and UNGOMAP helped to facilitate the de-escalation of conflicts by the removal of foreign troops, a process which has led to a halt in the civil war in Angola in 1991–92, but not yet in Afghanistan.

Peacekeeping follows from the parties to the conflict accepting a cease-fire or a withdrawal, and then *consenting* to the presence of a force on their soil. Normally consent is obtained from the legitimate governments concerned, which is relatively straightforward when dealing with an inter-State conflict as between Iran and Iraq. However, when dealing with an intra-State conflict, for example, the conflict between the Greek and Turkish communities in Cyprus between 1964–74, it could be argued that the consent of all factions should be obtained, although this is not always possible, and so consent is only obtained from the government, as was the case in Cyprus in 1964.[17] This has led to problems in intra-State peacekeeping operations such as UNIFIL in southern Lebanon, where the initial emplacement of the force in 1978 was gained at the request of the very weak Lebanese government,[18] without the consent or cooperation of the numerous factions that actually controlled southern Lebanon. In its more recent peacekeeping attempts, the UN has tried to gain the consent of all the factions in a civil war, whether governmental or not. This has been the approach in Yugoslavia and in Cambodia for instance, but it still appears that the forces in these countries are under severe pressure with some of the factions breaking their agreements to submit to UN supervision. The lack of accountability of these factions on the international plane may account for their less than cooperative approach.

What is clear is that if the consent of the government concerned is not given or is withdrawn, then the peacekeeping operation cannot remain on that State's territory, unless the UN is prepared to change its mandate to one of enforcement. Such a change of mandate is theoretically possible, as was stated by the Secretary General in his initial report on UNEF I in 1956:

While the General Assembly is enabled to establish the Force with the consent of those parties which contribute units to the Force, it could not request the Force to be stationed or operate on the territory of a given country without the consent of the Government of that country. This does not exclude the possibility that the Security Council could use such a Force within the wider margins provided under Chapter VII of the United Nations Charter. I would not for the present consider it necessary to elaborate this point further, since no use of the Force under Chapter VII . . . has been envisaged.[19]

Despite the possibility of a force initially emplaced as a consensual, non-offensive peacekeeping operation, being converted into an enforcement action under Articles 39 and 42 of the Charter, the likelihood is slim. First of all, States contributing to a peacekeeping force do so on a *voluntary* basis, they would have to give permission for their troops to be used in an entirely different fashion, thus making drastic changes of mandates unlikely. Secondly, peacekeeping forces would have to be rearmed and more than likely would have to be considerably expanded if they were to become effective enforcement units. Finally, such a conversion in mandate would make it less likely that States would willingly accept peacekeeping forces in the future, in other words drastic changes of mandate would jeopardise the neutrality of peacekeeping. It may be because of this that the Secretary General in his report adopted pursuant to the Summit Meeting of the Security Council on 31 January 1992, proposed the establishment of peace enforcement units to be used in cases where a cease-fire has been agreed to but not complied with. The limited aim of these forces would be to secure a cease-fire, by the use of force if necessary. They would not be full enforcement measures under Articles 42 and 43 designed to meet and repulse aggression, nor would they be peacekeeping forces depending upon consent and cooperation.[20]

The need for consent in traditional peacekeeping operations was graphically illustrated in 1967, when Secretary General U Thant ordered the withdrawal of UNEF I, after President Nasser of Egypt made it clear that Egypt's consent had been withdrawn. Although it may be argued that the General Assembly, as the author of UNEF's mandate, was responsible for its status and therefore it, not the Secretary General, had the power to withdraw the force, U Thant's decision *vis-à-vis* Egypt was essentially correct.[21] Indeed, it is highly likely that at least some contributing States would have withdrawn their troops if U Thant had not withdrawn UNEF I.[22] Nevertheless, the withdrawal of UNEF I and the ensuing Six Day War illustrated the limitations of peacekeeping.

Not only is the consent of the host State necessary, its continued *cooperation* with the peacekeeping force throughout the length of its stay is essential. The Israeli occupation of the Golan Heights since 1967 has been a major obstacle to permanent peace between Israel and Syria, but despite the fact that they have been sworn enemies since the establishment of Israel, both manage to cooperate with UNDOF, established by the Security Council,[23] pursuant to the Agreement on Disengagement between Israel and Syria of 31 May 1974,[24] which followed the 1973 Yom Kippur War. This buffer force of over 1,000 lightly armed peacekeepers has been highly successful in maintaining calm on the Israeli/Syrian front despite the fact that Israel has twice invaded Lebanon in 1978 and 1982, acts which, bearing in mind Syrian involvement in Lebanon, could have started a new conflict between the two States. The high level of cooperation with UNDOF is illustrated by the fortnightly inspections of designated demilitarised areas by UNDOF members accompanied by liaison officers from Syria and Israel.[25]

One of the reasons for UNDOF's success is the fact that it is *impartial* or *neutral* in the dispute. Impartiality is another of the essential features of peacekeeping deriving from the non-prejudicial nature of provisional measures as embodied in Article 40 of the UN Charter. Indeed, in the case of the 1,500 strong UN Iraq-Kuwait Observation Mission (UNIKOM), established by the Security Council by resolution 689 of 9 April 1991, the UN managed to maintain its neutrality in peacekeeping even after it had successfully prosecuted a war against one of the parties, Iraq. Indeed, the Security Council imposed further conditions on Iraq after the war ended, including, *inter alia*, the settlement of the boundary between the two countries on the basis of the 1963 Agreement between Iraq and Kuwait.[26] It was quite remarkable that the UN, as one of the parties to the conflict, then had the ability to undertake a neutral peacekeeping operation on the Iraq-Kuwait border, whilst also sending in a team of 500 UN guards to protect the camps established for the Kurds in the north in May 1991, also undertaken with Iraqi consent. The explanation is perhaps the fact that there is a clear legal distinction between the enforcement and peacekeeping functions of the UN and, also on the political plane, the fact that Iraq saw the use of force against it originating not from the UN but from the United States and its Coalition partners.

Another important aspect of peacekeeping, which distinguishes it clearly from enforcement, is that the forces are only authorised to use force in *self-defence*. This limitation is more akin to a personal right of self-defence by individual soldiers if shot at, rather than the much wider right of a State to self-defence.[27] Given that peacekeeping does not infringe the *sovereignty* of any State, it cannot be imbued with rights, such as the right of self-defence contained in Article 51 of the UN Charter, which belong to States. This severe limitation on the use of force by peacekeepers does not unduly hinder the work of inter-State peacekeeping forces when both States have consented to the force, but it does present problems in the intra-State situation when only the host government has given consent, or if the leaders of the factions in the conflict agree to the force but are unable or unwilling to control their forces.

The problem is particularly acute in the case of UNIFIL established at the request of the Lebanese government in March 1978, following the partial withdrawal of Israel from Lebanon. The Secretary General made it clear that the force would only use force in strict self-defence of troops and units, and would not undertake any of the responsibilities of the Lebanese government.[28] Unfortunately, UNIFIL is in a difficult situation in that for most of its life it has operated in a hostile environment, in an area of Lebanon containing various armed factions and not controlled to any degree by the Lebanese government, although in 1991 that government began to assert some authority in the south. Between 1978 and 1990, UNIFIL lost 130 soldiers from hostile acts. This has meant that UNIFIL has been unable as yet to fulfil either aspect of its mandate, first of ensuring the effective restoration of Lebanese sovereignty in the south, and secondly of supervising Israeli withdrawal from Lebanon given Israel's continued maintenance of a security zone in the area south of the Litani river.

The problem is perhaps even more acute in the case of UNPROFOR, recently sent to the disintegrating State of Yugoslavia. Initially, in February 1992, the force was agreed to by Croatia and Serbia since its main task was to oversee a cease-fire between those two former Republics.[29] In this task it is reasonably effectively carrying out the task of a traditional UN peacekeeping force. However, with its headquarters initially in Sarajevo, the capital of Bosnia, another former Yugoslav Republic and nascent State, this inevitably meant that it would be sucked into the internecine conflict between the Serbs, Muslims and Croats in Bosnia. Initially this took the form of Security Council authorisation in May 1992 of a limited force to attempt to secure the airport for the arrival of humanitarian aid.[30] This was dependent on the factions agreeing to a cease-fire, which they apparently did on 5 June 1992. This cease-fire was breached on numerous occasions, putting the lives of the UN force at risk, and often leading to the suspension of aid flights to the beleaguered city.

The deteriorating situation in Sarajevo and in the rest of Bosnia led the Security Council to cross the threshold from peacekeeping to enforcement actions in resolution 770 of 13 August 1992, when it authorised States to 'take all measures necessary' to facilitate the delivery of aid to the city and the rest of Bosnia. This has led, at the time of writing, to plans to sent an expanded force of about 6,000 UN troops to Bosnia, whose aim would be to force the aid convoys through if attacked, probably with the aid of air cover, instead of relying solely on negotiation with the warring factions.[31] This development can be alternatively characterised as either a move towards the Secretary General's envisaged peace enforcement units, on the borderline between enforcement and peacekeeping, or it could be that initial force in Bosnia was unduly restricted in its rules of engagement, in that the force did not appear to be allowed to fire back in self-defence. The expanded mandate seems simply to allow the larger force to do this, in line with traditional rules of engagement for lightly armed peacekeeping forces but not for unarmed observers.[32]

It is to be hoped that the force in Bosnia adopts the latter interpretation to keep it within the acceptable parameters of peacekeeping, for otherwise there would be serious breach of the neutrality principle leading to the blue helmets in the Yugoslav conflict and elsewhere potentially being treated as the enemy.

The latest UN effort in Bosnia reflects a recent trend in peacekeeping towards the provision of *humanitarian assistance*. This is not solely a recent development. UNIFIL in 1982 was directed to assist the people of southern Lebanon when it could not carry out the remainder of its mandate because of the Israeli invasion. Recent internecine conflicts have led to an increase in these activities as the presence of the UN guards in Northern Iraq from May 1991 to protect the humanitarian assistance being given to the Kurds, and the latest UN Operation in Somalia, which was starting to be emplaced in September 1992, amply illustrate.

Functions

The general functions that are characteristic of a peacekeeping force follow from the legal principles that govern it and have already been mentioned in the above section. The consensual, voluntary and essentially pacific nature of peacekeeping means that the force is restricted to observation and supervision of provisional measures accepted by the parties. More specifically the functions of a particular force depend on its mandate which is usually located in the enabling resolutions of the Security Council or General Assembly, and in the reports of the Secretary General, who is delegated the task of setting up the force. Usually the same model, derived from the principles governing UNEF I, is used with slight variations for the particular situation in question. Nevertheless, one can occasionally see a marked difference between the mandates governing inter-State peacekeeping forces and those governing intra-State forces.

Inter-State forces such as UNEF, UNMOGIP, UNIIMOG and UNDOF, are given the relatively clear tasks of supervising a cease-fire, and a withdrawal to positions occupied before the conflict started, both of which have already been consented to by the parties. An examination of inter-State forces reveals that they are almost always successful within the limited objectives of their mandates. In the case of intra-State peacekeeping forces the mandates sometimes have to be different to cope with the more difficult situation. The difficulties of peacekeeping in a civil war-type situation results in the principles of peacekeeping, namely consent, neutrality and limited self-defence, being much harder to achieve as the UN's current experience in Yugoslavia shows. The UN had already faced such an immense problem in its handing of the Congo crisis between 1960–64.

The UN Operation in the Congo (ONUC) was initially sent under the authority of the Security Council at the request of the government of the Congo in July 1960, to provide assistance to that government until the

Congolese security forces could fulfil their tasks following the breakdown of order on Belgian decolonisation.[33] By the time ONUC arrived it was in a precarious position, with fighting continuing in the Congo, rival governments being established, and the attempted secession of the Katanga region of the country with the active assistance of Belgian troops and mercenaries. A simple UNEF-type mandate and operation was clearly insufficient to prevent the collapse of the Congo altogether, although initially Secretary General Hammarskjöld seemed to take the opposite view.[34]

The increasing internationalisation of the civil war led to the General Assembly,[35] and then the Security Council adopting resolutions which seemed to authorise the use of force by the almost 20,000 strong UN force. In resolution 161 of 27 February 1961, the Council found that the situation in the Congo was a 'threat to international peace and security' and urged that ONUC 'take immediately all appropriate measures to prevent the occurrence of a civil war in the Congo, including arrangements for cease-fires, the halting of all military operations, the prevention of clashes, *and the use of force, if necessary, in the last resort*'. In resolution 169 of 24 November 1961, the Council went further by widening ONUC's mandate. The force was directed to maintain the territorial integrity and political independence of the Congo, to assist the central government to restore order, and to 'secure the immediate withdrawal and evacuation from the Congo of all foreign military . . . personnel not under United Nations' command, and mercenaries'. In addition, it welcomed the restoration of the central government in August 1961, and rejected the Katangese claims to secession. To further these ends it authorised the use of force to expel foreign troops and mercenaries 'if necessary'.

Although ONUC, in the main, tried to keep within the principles of peacekeeping, particularly in the period before the adoption of resolution 161, namely by negotiating cease-fires and by not overtly siding with any one of the factions, it eventually had to use force to subdue the Katangese rebellion in April 1961, again in December 1961, and between December 1962 and January 1963.[36] It is very difficult to see ONUC as a true peacekeeping operation, in that it was authorised to use force beyond that necessary for strict self-defence, it was not impartial in the conflict, it received little co-operation, and although it did have the formal consent of the central government, the fact was that for a period until August 1961 there was no real government in the Congo. On the other hand, ONUC was not clearly an enforcement action as undertaken by the UN force in Korea for instance, a view reinforced by the International Court in the *Expenses* case.[37]

One acceptable explanation of the legal basis of ONUC is founded on Article 40 of the Charter, the constitutional basis of most peacekeeping operations. Resolutions 161 and 169 could be said to contain a series of widely drawn provisional measures designed to keep the Congo intact, as well as granting ONUC the authority to enforce those provisional measures if necessary. The enforcement of provisional measures designed not to prejudice any of the parties to the conflict could be said to fulfil the neutralist ideals of peacekeeping, but in practical terms the enforcement of such widely drawn measures in effect meant that ONUC was on the side of the central government against the secessionists. Nevertheless, the Security Council appeared to justify this by concentrating the use of force by ONUC on the foreign elements such as the mercenaries who were assisting the secessionists, and whose presence created the threat to international peace. The removal of the foreign elements was designed to enable the factions to negotiate, and eventually resulted in the parties accepting a Plan of National Reconciliation.[38] The creation of the conditions in which such a reconciliation could occur without foreign intervention could be said to be a fulfilment of the basic ideals of peacekeeping, although the extensive use of force to achieve this seems to stretch those principles to the point were such an operation will not readily be mounted again, although the UN may be being dragged towards such a scenario in Yugoslavia.

Peacekeeping and peacemaking

In the case of ONUC, peacekeeping, in the sense of overseeing a series of provisional measures agreed to by the parties, was superseded by peacemaking, in the sense of enforcing a solution to the crisis. However, the Congo operation was exceptional, the norm being a simple peacekeeping operation in which a force is emplaced once a conflict has stabilised or has stopped, the aim being the maintenance of that *status quo*. Such is the position with those peacekeeping forces still *in situ* after many years, namely UNTSO, UNMOGIP, UNFICYP, UNDOF, and UNIFIL. In all these cases, the peacekeeping forces are not inextricably linked with the process of finding a peaceful solution to the conflict. Peacemaking attempts are undertaken, but they are separate from the emplacement and maintenance of the peacekeeping force. In the case of Cyprus, for instance, UNFICYP was established by Security Council resolution 186 in March 1964. The same resolution contained a recommendation that the Secretary General should use his good offices to achieve a peaceful solution. Peacekeeping and pacific settlement were contained in the same resolution, but they were not linked in the sense that the factions in Cyprus agreed to a specific peaceful solution as well as to UNFICYP. The Secretary General is still using his good offices to seek a peaceful solution to the Cyprus problem.

It would of course be better for world peace and for the effectiveness of the UN if pacific settlement was not left to chance. This could only be brought about if the combination of peacekeeping and peacemaking became institutionalised. This would mean that wherever possible pressure should be brought to bear on the parties to the conflict, not only to accept a peacekeeping force to help keep them apart, but also to accept a recommendation for settlement either by the Security Council, the General Assembly, the Secretary General, or by outside States, organisations or individuals. Thus the force would not only perform the traditional functions of supervising a cease-fire, but would also supervise the implementation of the peace plan.

More precisely, there would be two or three separate operations in the one conflict, or one force with two or three distinct elements, namely a traditional peacekeeping component, perhaps a civilian police force if it is necessary to take over or supervise the police function within a State, and finally a civilian component to supervise the electoral process or other chosen form of pacific settlement. Whilst the peacekeeping element is derived from Article 40 of the Charter, the police and civilian elements are designed more to help the parties towards the agreed solution and are therefore more obviously derived from Articles 36 and 37 of the Charter. This integrated approach, combining various Charter powers in an innovative and flexible way has only been possible in the years after the Cold War with increased permanent member cooperation and greater delegation to the Secretary General.[39]

There is a precedent for this approach in the agreement between the Netherlands and Indonesia of 15 August 1962,[40] which provided a method of settling the conflict between Indonesia and the Netherlands over the remaining Dutch colony of West Irian. The agreement provided for the administration of the colony to be transferred by the Dutch to the UN Temporary Executive Authority (UNTEA), pending a transfer of sovereignty to Indonesia. The supervision of the cease-fire between Indonesia and the Netherlands, and the policing of the territory during the period of UNTEA's authority, were undertaken by the UN Observer and Security Force (UNSF). This plan was approved of by the General Assembly,[41] and went ahead according to the timetable with UNSF being withdrawn in 1963. Nevertheless, the 1962 agreement was not fully complied with by Indonesia because of that State's refusal to hold a plebiscite on self-determination before 1970, a concession originally granted to persuade the Dutch to leave.

Such defects have been remedied by the latest batch of peacekeeping forces which have mushroomed since the end of the Cold War in the late 1980s. The most successful so far have brought independence to Namibia, and an end to civil war in Nicaragua, as well as supervising elections there. This trend is set to continue with a Second UN Angolan Verification Mission (UNAVEM II), being established by the Security Council in May 1991 to supervise the agreement made between the two warring factions (the government and UNITA) in Angola leading to elections,[42] and a similar force to supervise the agreement between the government and the Farabundo Marti National Liberation Front (FMLN) in El Salvador for a cease-fire and a subsequent peaceful solution to the conflict.[43] These forces are in addition to those recently emplaced in Cambodia and Western Sahara, reviewed in chapter nine.

The missions in El Salvador, Western Sahara, Cambodia and Angola all illustrate the necessity of having the consent of all parties to the conflict, both government and opposition to the peacekeeping force and to a pacific solution, the aim being to establish what Secretary General Perez de Cuellar, at the conclusion of the Paris Peace Conference on Cambodia in October 1991 termed a 'neutral political environment' in which the people of the country concerned can decide on their own future. One can see the legal and political direction of peacekeeping, developing the principle of neutrality from its traditional peacekeeping base, namely neutrality between rival factions or States, and extending it to neutrality in the context of the political settlement as a whole. It must be noted, however, that this development will not mean the demise of traditional peacekeeping forces, as the presence of UNIKOM between Iraq and Kuwait, and UNPROFOR in Yugoslavia amply illustrate.

In addition, it is unlikely that this development will be carried to the extent that the UN will be on call as a neutral observer for any electoral process if so requested by a State or the factions within a State. The overseeing of elections, although something of a natural extension of its current activities, would divorce the Organisation from its peacekeeping base. The peacekeeping force traditionally is sent into a conflict zone to secure a cease-fire; it has only recently been used to oversee the implementation of an agreed pacific solution, which has most often taken the form of free and fair elections, though it is not necessary that this will be the mode of settlement chosen by the parties.

However, in October 1990, the General Assembly approved of the establishment of the UN Observer Group for the Verification of Elections In Haiti (ONUVEH).[44] This operation did not have any traditional peacekeeping or observation component and consisted entirely of civilian observers whose function was to report on the electoral process taking place in that strife-torn country. Although peaceful elections took place on 16 December 1990, the elected government was ousted by a military coup in September 1991. It may be tentatively suggested that without the stabilising presence of a UN military component for at least one or two years, the chances of a stable government emerging from the electoral process in such a troubled country are much reduced. Further, the situation in Haiti was purely internal, unlike in Nicaragua, Namibia, El Salvador, Cambodia and Western Sahara, which all had or continue to have international repercussions or implications in terms of outside States' involvement in the conflict.

It may be in recognition of these limitations that the General Assembly accepted a recommendation of its Third Committee on Social, Humanitarian and Cultural Affairs, when it adopted a resolution on 17 December 1991, on the issue of periodic and genuine elections. The Assembly affirmed 'that electoral verification by the United Nations should remain an exceptional activity of the Organisation to be undertaken in well-defined circumstances, *inter alia*, primarily in situations with a clear international character'.[45]

In a slightly different context, as regards the situation in South Africa, where negotiations have started with the aims of abolishing the apartheid system and implementing a universal system of voting, the Security Council has authorised in August 1992 the sending of a team of thirty observers to help create the climate of peace in which a genuine reform process could take place. The team was requested by the African National Congress after it had organised mass demonstrations in protest at the slowness of the government in the negotiations. The government consented to the UN's presence illustrating the fundamental change in South African politics.[46]

It is probable that this small team will be the start of a greater UN involvement in South Africa, perhaps culminating in the supervision of genuine elections in that country to mark the end of apartheid. The General Assembly has for many years recognised the apartheid system in South Africa as constituting a threat to international peace, and the Security Council has made a similar determination in 1977 as regards the acts and policies of the South Africa government. In its 1991 resolution on genuine and periodic elections, the Assembly made it clear that the situation in South Africa was within the exception to the rule that electoral supervision was not available as of right to requesting States, it being 'international' in character.

Peacekeeping outside the UN

If a peacekeeping operation conforms to the legal principles outlined above, then it can be lawfully undertaken by a regional organisation, or on an *ad hoc*, collective basis, or indeed by individual States. Consensual, non-offensive operations do not breach the ban on the use of force contained in Article 2(4) of the UN Charter, nor are they actions which require the authorisation of the Security Council under Article 53 of the UN Charter, which is confined to enforcement actions. An example of a true peacekeeping operation was that undertaken by the 2,500 strong Multinational Force in the Sinai (MFO). Although American dominated, this force has successfully undertaken observation of the requirements of the 1979 peace treaty between Egypt and Israel.[47]

On the other hand, there have been military operations that quite clearly have not conformed to the principles of peacekeeping, even though the States concerned may use the term. The Syrian involvement in Lebanon since 1976 at times has had the consent of the various powerless governments that have ineffectually attempted to rule a country in a state of civil war. Although this possibly gives the Syrian intervention the air of consensuality necessary for a peacekeeping force, it is quite clear that the heavily armed force has acted aggressively against several of the factions in Lebanon on many occasions during its prolonged stay.[48] Although its unlawful use of force may have eventually produced a more stable Lebanese government in 1990, Syria cannot excuse its unlawful action by misusing the concept of peacekeeping.

Similarly, the Indian 'peacekeeping' force in Sri Lanka, emplaced at the request of the beleaguered Sri Lankan government in 1987,[49] apart from initially having the consent of the government, failed to act in the impartial and non-offensive manner required of a true peacekeeping force. By mid-1988, the 50,000 strong, heavily armed Indian force had launched a major offensive against the Tamil rebels in the north of the country. However, the political situation in Sri Lanka did not improve and the government requested in July 1989 that India leave. India refused until March 1990. It is quite clear that the Indian intervention was not a peacekeeping operation in that it used aggressive force against one of the factions, and during 1989–90, operated without host State consent. In the absence of any evidence that the force was of a non-enforcement, consensual, character, and in the absence of any other evidence of an armed attack, whether direct or indirect, against Sri Lanka, it is quite clear that the Indian military operation amounted to a serious breach of Article 2(4) of the UN Charter.

It is clear from the operations in Lebanon and Sri Lanka, that the term 'peacekeeping', like so many legal concepts, is abused by States. The surest way of maintaining the integrity of the peacekeeping function is to retain it within the United Nations. Although it is not essential for outside peacekeeping operations mounted by regional bodies or individual States to have the authorisation of the Security Council, it would be wise for proposers of such operations to seek advice from the UN and if possible to secure Security Council approval.

Notes

1 *Certain Expenses of the United Nations* case, I.C.J. *Rep.* 1962, 151.
2 See also A. James, 'United Nations peacekeeping and non alignment', in M.S. Rajan *et al.*, *The Non Aligned and the United Nations*, 93–9 (1987).
3 I.C.J. *Rep.* 1962, 171.
4 *Ibid.*, 170.
5 *Ibid.*, 162.
6 *Ibid.*, 166.

7 See further D. W. Bowett, *United Nations Forces*, 274–312 (1964).
8 GA Res. 997, 1 UN GAOR ESS (1956).
9 SC Res. 186, 19 UN SCOR Resolutions (1964).
10 UN doc. S/5653 (1964). But see R. Higgins, *United Nations Peacekeeping: Documents and Commentary, vol. 4: Europe 1946–1979*, 143–4 (1981).
11 SC 2823 mtg, 43 UN SCOR (1988).
12 27 *I.L.M.* (1988), 577.
13 SC Res. 622, 43 UN SCOR Resolutions (1988).
14 UN doc. S/20345 (1988).
15 UN doc. S/20346 (1988).
16 SC Res. 626, 43 UN SCOR Resolutions (1988).
17 SC 1095 mtg, 19 UN SCOR (1964).
18 SC Res. 425, 33 UN SCOR Resolutions (1978).
19 UN doc. A/3289 (1956).
20 Boutros Boutros-Ghali, *Agenda for Peace* para. 44 (1992); 31 *I.L.M.* (1992) 953, at 966.
21 UN doc. A/6370 (1967). See further A. Di Blase, 'The role of host state consent with regard to non-coercive actions by the United Nations', in A. Cassese (ed.), *United Nations Peacekeeping: Legal Essays*, 55 (1978).
22 R. Higgins, *United Nations Peacekeeping: Documents and Commentary, vol. 1: Middle East 1946–1967*, 339 (1969).
23 SC Res. 350, 29 UN SCOR Resolutions (1974).
24 UN doc. S/11302 (1974).
25 See for example UN doc. S/12710 (1978).
26 485 UNTS 321; SC Res. 687, 46 UN SCOR Resolutions (1991).
27 M. von Grunigen, 'Neutrality and peacekeeping', in Cassese (ed.), *United Nations Peacekeeping*, 137–8.
28 UN doc. S/12611 (1978).
29 SC Res. 743, 47 UN S/PV (1992).
30 SC Res. 758, 47 UN S/PV (1992).
31 *The Observer*, 20 September 1992.
32 *Ibid.*
33 SC Res. 143, 15 UN SCOR Resolutions (1960).
34 UN doc. S/4389 (1960).
35 GA Res. 1474, 4 UN GAOR ESS (1960).
36 UN doc. S/5240 (1963).
37 I.C.J. *Rep.* 1962, 177.
38 UN doc. S/5053/Add.13, Annex 1 (1962).
39 See further H. Caminos and R. Lavalle, 'New departures in the exercise of inherent Powers by the UN and OAS Secretaries General: the Central American situation', 83 *A.J.I.L.* (1989), 395; R. Lavalle, 'The inherent powers of the Secretary General in the political sphere: a legal analysis', 36 *N.I.L.R.* (1990), 22.
40 274 UNTS 6311.
41 GA Res. 1752, 17 UN GAOR (1962).
42 SC Res. 696, 46 UN SCOR Resolutions (1991).
43 SC Res. 693, 714, 46 UN SCOR Resolutions (1991).
44 GA Res. 45/2, 45 UN GAOR (1990).

45 GA Res. 46/137, 46 UN GAOR (1991).
46 SC Res. 765, 772, 47 UN S/PV (1992).
47 For a contrast between the MFO's success and the failure of the Multi-National Force (MNF) in Beirut in 1982–84 see R. C. R. Siekmann, 'The multinational peacekeeping force in the Sinai in the light of United Nations practice on peacekeeping forces', 24 *I.J.I.L.* (1984), 504, and B. L. Zimbler, 'Peacekeeping without the UN: the multinational force in Lebanon and international law', 10 *Yale Journal of International Law* (1984), 222.
48 A. James, *Peacekeeping in International Politics*, 337 (1990).
49 27 *I.L.M.* (1987), 1175.

CHAPTER NINE

A review of peacekeeping

It has been demonstrated in chapters seven and eight that UN peacekeeping is limited by political and legal factors. The purpose of the present chapter is to provide a review of all the UN forces in terms of their mandate, functions and effectiveness. As regards the latter, the principal aim will be to ascertain the success of the force in fulfilling its mandate, although we shall also attempt to assess the effect that peacekeeping has on the final resolution of a dispute. The determination of the effectiveness of peacekeeping should be strictly confined to the purposes for which the individual force was created, which are often very limited, and do not generally extend to the peacemaking process. Nevertheless, peacekeeping has an effect on pacific settlement, and lately, these two distinct functions have been linked, and so this chapter will attempt to assess the relationship between the two.

United Nations observation teams

UN Observers in Indonesia 1947–50

The creation of an observation team in Indonesia illustrates how early on in its life the United Nations realised the necessity of having accurate, neutral information about a conflict with which it was dealing. Initially, the Security Council, in resolution 27, called upon the Netherlands and Indonesia 'to cease hostilities forthwith' and to settle their disputes by peaceful means.[1] The resolution was based on an Australian draft but with references to Articles 39 and 40 deleted. With varying cease-fires and demarcation lines being established on the islands the Security Council needed accurate information as to the state of hostilities before it could take more positive peacemaking steps. Dutch objections based on Article 2(7) meant that the establishment of an independent commission was not authorised,[2] but instead the Council requested, in resolution 30, that career consuls in Batavia report on the observance of the cease-fire called for in the earlier resolution.[3]

The same resolution also established a Consular Commission to attempt peacemaking. The Consular Commission itself interpreted the functions of the military observers, namely 'to observe any possible violations of the cease-fire; to investigate, where possible, allegations of violations of cease-fire orders; and to gather any other data that might be of value to the Commission and to the Security Council'.[4] These functions remained basically the same with the creation of the Good Offices Committee which became the United Nations' Commission on Indonesia,[5] although instead of observation of temporary cease-fire lines, the team was given the task of observing the demilitarised zone created under the Renville Agreement.

Although resolution 27 had references to Chapter VII deleted some members still believed that it contained a mandatory call under Article 40 of that Chapter.[6] Resolution 30 was adopted to supplement resolution 27. Nevertheless, this does not mean that the observer force was in some way an enforcement measure. The Consular Commission's interpretation of its functions illustrated the essential limitation of the force to observation of a previously implemented cease-fire. The force was not authorised to prevent breaches of the cease-fire. Indeed, both parties clearly consented to its presence.[7]

Overall the United Nations' observers were given a broad mandate to lend assistance to the Consular Commission, the Good Offices Committee and the United Nations' Commission on Indonesia. These bodies were assigned the task of achieving an end to hostilities between the Dutch and the Indonesians and of facilitating a rapid progress towards Indonesian independence. The observers, through fulfilling their mandate of reporting on each stage, contributed to the eventual success in achieving these objectives.[8]

UN Sub-Commission on the Balkans (UNSCOB) 1947–54

Although UNSCOB was created by the General Assembly, it had its origins in the report of the Commission of Investigation established under Article 34 by the Security Council to investigate Greek allegations of illegal border incursions from Albania, Bulgaria and Yugoslavia.[9] The question came before the General Assembly after having been removed from the Council's agenda. With the report of the Commission of Investigation before it,[10] the Assembly decided to establish UNSCOB to assist the governments concerned to comply with its recommendations which, *inter alia*, called on Albania, Bulgaria and Yugoslavia not to furnish aid to the guerrillas and as regards observation called on UNSCOB to send a team to observe the frontiers.[11]

UNSCOB gave a general interpretation of its own mandate in relation to its observation function as the 'continuous observation of the general circumstances prevailing in the frontier areas'.[12] This was later refined by the

Assembly to observation and reporting 'on the response of Albania, Bulgaria and Yugoslavia to the call not to furnish aid to the Greek guerrillas'.[13]

The Eastern bloc countries, including Albania, Bulgaria and Yugoslavia, argued that UNSCOB had been constituted illegally. They contended not that the Assembly was taking upon itself powers reserved to the Security Council, but rather that the very establishment of a Special Committee was an infringement of Albanian, Yugoslavian and Bulgarian sovereignty.[14] Professor Higgins answers these contentions by saying that this confused the establishment of UNSCOB with its operation: 'The General Assembly acknowledged that UNSCOB could not operate in the territory of any State without that State's consent; but its establishment was nonetheless clearly within the terms of Articles 10, 11, 14 and 22 of the Charter'.[15]

For the Eastern bloc's arguments to be correct, would necessarily imply that the Assembly had created a force which could forcefully enter the territories of Albania, Bulgaria and Yugoslavia to carry out its functions. The use of force by the Assembly would indeed raise constitutional problems, but the fact was that UNSCOB's presence was based on consent.

Only one of UNSCOB's functions was observation, the others were set out in General Assembly resolution 109, namely to promote the cessation of external support for the Greek guerrillas and the establishment of normal diplomatic and friendly relations in combination with the pacific settlement of frontier incidents. Most of these objectives had been achieved by the mid-1950s, although it is doubtful whether UNSCOB's observation team made any great contribution to this. It was severely limited by only having Western support, and Greek consent, which resulted in its presence on Greek soil only. The detailed reports of the observers certainly cannot be said to have impeded a solution of the problem,[16] but because UNSCOB was motivated by Cold War factors, it can have had little influence on events. Yugoslavia's defection from the Communist camp was of far greater significance.

UN Truce Supervision Organisation in Palestine (UNTSO) 1949-present
As has already been explained in chapter seven, UNTSO's longevity arises out of the political necessity for the United Nations to have a constant presence in the most volatile area of the world. Its duties have ranged from observation of the 1949 truce and subsequent armistice agreements, to general observation in the whole Middle Eastern theatre, with specific roles being granted to it after the 1956, 1967 and 1973 conflicts.

One would have thought that this would have required constant adjustment of UNTSO's mandate by the Security Council, but this does not appear to be the case. Even its original creation seems to have arisen indirectly from a Council decision. In 1948 the Security Council established a Truce Commission directed to negotiate and supervise a truce between Israel and the Arab States in resolution 48.[17] Resolution 54 made the Council's call for a truce mandatory under Articles 39 and 40, and gave the Truce Commission wide powers to take any necessary steps to make the cease-fire effective.[18] UNTSO arose from the team employed by the Truce Commission to observe and supervise the cease-fire and truce.[19] UNTSO was then referred to in the armistice agreements and given the specific function of observing the armistice lines. This function was recognised by the Council in 1949.[20]

The continuing functions of UNTSO are those of observation and reporting. Its success should be measured in the fulfilment of these functions which it has done admirably since the 1949 armistice. UNTSO, like all peacekeeping operations, was not designed to stop wars and so its effectiveness should not be measured by the frequency with which conflicts occur in the Middle East.

Indeed, it is precisely because of that frequency that UNTSO is so important. This was amply illustrated by the outbreak of the Yom Kippur War in 1973. The Secretary General reported to the Council that Egypt had struck first. Egypt had asserted the opposite,[21] but so accurate was the Secretary General's report that the Egyptian government abandoned its version.[22] At a time of heightened international tension with the danger of hostilities escalating, the correct ascertainment of the facts was essential.

A body of UNTSO observers was sent to Beirut in 1982 by the Security Council to observe on three things: namely, the multinational force, Israeli withdrawal, and the situation in the refugee camps.[23] Known as the Observer Group in Beirut (OGB), their success has been summarised by the Secretary General:

Although their numbers are small and unarmed, the observers are an important source of information in a most sensitive area. The presence of OGB in and around the city also represents the concern of the international community and its desire to be of assistance to the heavily afflicted people of the area.[24]

The function of the Observer Group in Beirut is observation and it has been successful in achieving that. However, its presence contributed little to the amelioration of the lawlessness in the city evidenced by kidnappings, street fighting and starvation in the refugee camps leading to Syrian military intervention in February 1987 and the eventual restoration of some order.

UN Military Observer Group in India and Pakistan (UNMOGIP) 1949-present

Following India's complaint of Pakistani aid to insurgents in the Indian states of Jammu and Kashmir,[25] the Security Council adopted resolution 39 in 1948, establishing a UN Commission for India and Pakistan (UNCIP) with the dual functions of investigating the facts under Article 34, and of exercising a mediatory influence.[26] The creation of an observation team was essentially distinct, although Council resolution 47 of 21 April 1948 allowed UNCIP to use observers; they were not emplaced until after a bilateral agreement on a cease-fire between India and Pakistan was reached on 27 July 1949.[27] Thus observation of the cease-fire in the period 1949–65 was a direct result not of a Security Council resolution but of the functions granted to UNMOGIP by a bilateral accord.

When new hostilities broke out in 1965 the Security Council, in resolution 209, ordered a new cease-fire and the withdrawal of both belligerents behind existing cease-fire lines.[28] India and Pakistan were called on to cooperate with UNMOGIP in its task of observing the cease-fire. This was supported by Council resolution 211 of 20 September 1965 which demanded a cease-fire and withdrawal. UNMOGIP played a significant role in observing the cease-fire and withdrawal finally agreed upon at Tashkent by India and Pakistan.

UNMOGIP successfully carried out its mandate of observing the cease-fire line in Kashmir. Although its presence may well have helped to restrain the parties, the cease-fire line was breached in 1965 and 1971 during conflicts on a wider front than that patrolled by UNMOGIP.[29] Nevertheless, the 1965 hostilities and, in particular the 1971 conflict, were not disputes directly over the status of Kashmir and so it appears to be a reasonable assumption that without UNMOGIP there may well have been more wars over the disputed area.

Paradoxically, although UNMOGIP may have contributed effectively to preventing either side from resorting to force to settle their dispute, it has effectively helped to cement the *status quo* during which the dispute is unlikely to be resolved. The cease-fire line patrolled by UNMOGIP is seen by both sides as preferable to either of them giving concessions following diplomatic negotiations. Peacekeeping has had the effect of making provisional measures permanent by hindering the peacemaking process. On the other hand, it has helped to prevent the occurrence of more conflicts.

UN Observer Group in Lebanon (UNOGIL) 1958

With the crisis in Lebanon UNOGIL was established by Council resolution 128 of 11 June 1958 which decided to despatch 'an observation group to proceed to Lebanon so as to ensure that there is no illegal infiltration of personnel or supply of arms or other *matériel* across the Lebanese borders' from the United Arab Republic.

The use of 'ensure' in paragraph 1 of the enabling resolution suggests that UNOGIL was being directed forcibly to prevent infiltration. Practically, such a mandate would be impossible for an observation team, numbering 100, to perform. Indeed, the Secretary General's interpretation of

UNOGIL's mandate, which was not contested in the Council, emphasised that its role was strictly limited to observing whether illegal infiltration occurred, and that it was there with the consent of the Lebanese government.[30]

Even after the United States had intervened in mid-July, UNOGIL's functions probably remained as investigatory and observational as envisaged by Article 34. It was essentially different from most other types of peacekeeping forces which are usually created to perform some role in relation to provisional measures called for by the Assembly or the Council; whereas UNOGIL's mandate was to ascertain the facts before the United Nations could adopt any further measures. Although UNOGIL consisted of a team of military observers and therefore is included in this analysis, it could easily be classified with non-military investigatory teams established by the Council.

UNOGIL observed and reported that there was no significant infiltration of Lebanon from the United Arab Republic and to that extent it had fulfilled the terms of its mandate.[31] However, on a wider view, its reports did not prevent military intervention by the United States, although its continued presence along with the American marines in addition to the establishment of a new government under General Chehab, probably had the effect of stabilising the situation.

UN Observers and Security Force in West Irian (UNSF) 1962–63

Most peacekeeping forces heavily involve the Secretary General. It will be seen that earlier forces such as ONUC were really the creation of the Secretary General, whereas later forces such as UNIFIL reflected the Soviet Union's view that the Secretary General's task should not be the creation and direction of such forces, but the administration of them after the Security Council has mandated them, mandates which are regularly reviewed by the Council. UNSF along with ONUC are probably illustrative of the highpoint of the Secretary General's role in the Organisation's peacekeeping function during the Cold War period.

Although the agreement between the Netherlands and Indonesia required the approval of the General Assembly for the creation of the UN Temporary Executive Authority (UNTEA) and UNSF in West Irian,[32] it was the agreement itself which detailed the functions of these bodies and granted the power of control over them to the Secretary General.

The functions of UNSF contained in the agreement relate to two different aspects of the planned transfer of sovereignty: first, an observation role as regards provisional measures agreed upon by the parties such as a cease-fire pending the transfer of sovereignty to UNTEA; and secondly, to act as an internal security force during the temporary administration by UNTEA pending transfer of authority to Indonesia. Loosely, UNSF could be described as facilitating provisional measures, on this occasion adopted by the parties, until the end result (transfer of sovereignty to Indonesia) could be achieved.

UNSF was wholly successful in fulfilling its mandate. It managed to secure an effective cease-fire on West Irian in just over one month. It then went on to maintain law and order effectively during the transition period as well as completing the establishment of a viable police force capable of taking over on UNTEA's withdrawal.[33] Such success was guaranteed by the complete cooperation of the parties who had agreed on the pacific settlement of the dispute. Nevertheless, UNSF, which was withdrawn in 1963, had little influence on the refusal by Indonesia to hold a plebiscite before 1970 as agreed with the Netherlands. Although a solution to the dispute was achieved it was not the solution intended.

UN Yemen Observation Mission (UNYOM) 1963–64

With Saudi Arabia supporting the Royalist faction and the United Arab Republic supporting the Republican faction in Yemen, it was politically necessary not only to obtain the consent of Yemen to a United Nations' presence, but also the cooperation of Saudi Arabia and the United Arab Republic. Secretary General U Thant negotiated with the Republican government of Yemen, and the governments of Saudi Arabia and the United Arab Republic. They agreed on disengagement and on a United Nations' presence;[34] and they defined UNYOM's functions as observation only by about 100 personnel in the Saudi Arabian-Yemen area.[35]

The Council approved the Secretary General's reports in a resolution adopted on 11 June 1963,[36] and requested the Secretary General 'to establish the observation operation as defined by him'. The Secretary General further refined the functions of UNYOM in subsequent reports. These functions were limited to observing, reporting and certifying the disengagement between Saudi Arabia and Yemen,[37] and to observing on the departure of the United Arab Republic from Yemen.[38] This constituted a limited observation mandate not allowing UNYOM to take any steps to resolve the conflict.[39]

UNYOM had a very limited purpose, namely the observation and certification of the disengagement agreement. 'The parties themselves' were 'totally responsible for fulfilling the terms of the disengagement'.[40] Nevertheless, UNYOM was too small even to carry out its limited mandate.[41] UNYOM not only failed in this respect, but after its departure in September 1964, the civil war continued for several years with the continuing involvement of Egypt and Saudi Arabia.

UN India-Pakistan Observation Mission
(UNIPOM) 1965–66

Large-scale violations of the Karachi Agreement were reported by

UNMOGIP on 5 August 1965.[42] The necessity for another observer force lay in the fact that the conflict broke out on a much wider front than that covered by UNMOGIP. On 4 September the Security Council adopted resolution 209 which called for an immediate cease-fire and requested the cooperation of India and Pakistan with UNMOGIP. The fighting continued leading to a repeated cease-fire call on the 6 September in Council resolution 210, which also contained a request to the Secretary General to strengthen UNMOGIP. Resolution 211 of 20 September gave a specific time for the cease-fire to become operative and asked the Secretary General 'to provide the necessary assistance to ensure supervision of the cease-fire and withdrawal of all armed personnel'.

The Security Council probably envisaged an enlarged UNMOGIP when adopting resolution 211. Indeed, India insisted that only one operation was authorised.[43] However, the Security Council neither censured the Secretary General for creating UNIPOM nor did it specifically grant him authority to do so. Only the Soviet Union made a somewhat oblique criticism: 'Only the Security Council is competent to adopt measures on concrete questions connected with observers of the United Nations, namely, with their functions, their numbers, the command, the method of financing their activities, and so on.'[44]

To a large degree UNIPOM was the Secretary General's creation. He reconciled his action with the constitutional requirements by insisting that to extend UNMOGIP beyond Kashmir would have been a breach of its mandate and a usurpation of the functions of the Security Council. Thus he argued that he needed to create UNIPOM in order to satisfy the requirements of Council resolution 211. The Secretary General also probably had the idea that UNIPOM would be the more transient requirement, whereas UNMOGIP would need to be kept in place for many years as it was Kashmir that was the flashpoint.

UNIPOM's functions were derived from the mandate in resolution 211, namely to provide, by observer duties, assistance as regards the cease-fire and withdrawal in the areas outside UNMOGIP's control. Under the agreement reached by India and Pakistan in January 1966, the functions of both forces were given greater definition as regards disengagement.[45] Nevertheless, UNIPOM's creation was the reverse of UNMOGIP. The latter was created by agreement between the parties and sanctioned by the Security Council. UNIPOM was created by the Council, or more correctly a combination of the Council and the Secretary General, consented to by the parties, and later sanctioned by them.

UNIPOM was concerned with overseeing the implementation of the cease-fire and withdrawal orders of the Security Council along the international frontier beyond Kashmir. The observers worked well in helping to implement the cease-fire between forces which were sometimes only 50 metres apart,[46] although sporadic fighting continued for some time.

Nevertheless, before UNIPOM could supervise the cease-fire both parties had to agree upon it.[47] As with all peacekeeping initiatives, success depends on the parties accepting and maintaining a cease-fire. On 10 January 1966 a solution to the conflict, apart from the area of Kashmir, was agreed by the parties at Tashkent, whereby all the military personnel of India and Pakistan would be withdrawn to positions held before 5 August 1965. The withdrawal, under UNIPOM's supervision was carried out on schedule.[48] Peacekeeping was accompanied by peacemaking on this occasion although it must be remembered that the central problem of Kashmir remained requiring the continued presence of the United Nations in the form of UNMOGIP.

UN Good Offices Mission in Afghanistan (UNGOMAP) 1988–90

After nearly six years of negotiations involving Pakistan, Afghanistan and the Secretary General's representative, with the Soviet Union and the United States behind their respective States, the Geneva Accords were finally signed on 14 April 1988. The Accords contained, *inter alia*, an agreement between Afghanistan and Pakistan on mutual non-intervention; guarantees by the Soviet Union and the United States not to interfere or intervene in the internal affairs of Afghanistan or Pakistan; an agreement on the phased withdrawal of Soviet troops to be completed within nine months; and finally an annexed memorandum of understanding provided that the UN Secretary General would send an inspection team, divided into two units, to be sent to Kabul and Islamabad, to report on the withdrawal of foreign troops and on any violation of the Accords.

The memorandum to the Accords established the mandate of the force which was quickly dispatched to the area. In letters written to the President of the Security Council shortly after the conclusion of the Accords,[49] the Secretary General informed the members of the Council that he intended to dispatch a team of fifty unarmed observers drawn from existing UN forces for an initial period of ten months, and asked the President to 'inform me of the members' concurrence'.

Strangely, it was not until the end of October 1988, that the Security Council formally confirmed its agreement to the measures envisaged and executed by the Secretary General, 'in particular the temporary dispatch to Afghanistan and Pakistan of military officers'.[50] No explanation was given in the Security Council. It appears that the Secretary General had the consent of the Security Council to redeploy existing UN observers to Afghanistan and Pakistan without formal authorisation. Given the exigencies of the situation, and the fact that both superpowers wanted a UN presence, the necessity for establishing a clear constitutional base for UNGOMAP seems to have been overlooked. As with UNTSO in 1948, UNGOMAP was in reality created by parties to an agreement and later sanctioned by the Security Council.

The Geneva Accords were concerned with provisional measures, not a cease-fire, but a withdrawal of Soviet troops, with no further external intervention, pending the establishment of a political solution. UNGOMAP was created to facilitate these measures by providing neutral information on compliance. Despite the continuing struggle between the various factions in Afghanistan, UNGOMAP successfully completed its first task of reporting on the withdrawal of all Soviet troops from Afghanistan in February 1989 in accordance with the Geneva Accords.[51] However, it encountered difficulties in fulfilling the second part of its mandate, namely reporting on violations of the Accords. This was not all that surprising since both the Soviet Union and the United States as well as Pakistan breached their undertakings not to intervene in the internal affairs of Afghanistan. Afghanistan made an unsuccessful complaint against Pakistan in April 1989,[52] when it alleged that Pakistan had violated the Accords on 1,200 occasions. Pakistan replied that no violations had been reported by UNGOMAP. There appeared to be no UNGOMAP report to justify any of these allegations and there were no other speakers at the meeting.[53] This was symptomatic of the intractable nature of the conflict in Afghanistan. UNGOMAP, envisaged as a temporary measure anyway, served no useful purpose in this environment and was withdrawn in March 1990.[54] It was not until the Soviet Union, in its death throws, agreed with the United States not to provide arms to the factions in Afghanistan from 1 January 1992 that there emerged signs of an end to the civil war with the overthrow of the formerly Soviet-backed regime of Najibullah in April 1992.

UN Iran-Iraq Military Observer Group (UNIIMOG) 1988–92

Following Iranian and Iraqi acceptance of the cease-fire called for in operative paragraph 1 of Council resolution 598 on 20 August 1988,[55] the Secretary General produced a report interpreting the provisions of operative paragraph 2 of that resolution, which requested the Secretary General to 'dispatch a team of United Nations' observers to verify, confirm and supervise the cease-fire and withdrawal'.

In his report the Secretary General referred to the mandate and then provided more detailed terms of reference, stating that UNIIMOG would: establish cease-fire lines in cooperation with the parties; monitor compliance with the cease-fire; investigate violations; prevent, through negotiation, a change in the *status quo*; and supervise withdrawal to internationally recognised boundaries.[56] The Security Council approved the report and decided to establish UNIIMOG for an initial period of six months.[57]

Resolution 598 of 1987 was clearly a mandatory call for a cease-fire within the meaning of Chapter VII, Articles 39 and 40. UNIIMOG was established pursuant to that call, but it was in no way authorised to enforce it. Its presence depended upon the consent of both parties and its mandate depended on an existing cease-fire. These facts, in addition to the small size of the force (350 observers), made it clear that this was a typical consensual UN observation operation.

UNIIMOG was very successful in monitoring the cease-fire between Iran and Iraq, which held from August 1988. For instance, in a report on the situation in October 1988, the Secretary General stated that UNIIMOG was working effectively in helping the parties to settle peacefully the minor violations of the cease-fire that had occurred, and had received the full support and cooperation of both parties.[58] In fact the success of UNIIMOG helped to stall the negotiations between Iran and Iraq on a permanent peaceful solution, and it was fortuitous that the Iraqi invasion of Kuwait in August 1990 forced Iraq to agree on 15 August to Iranian terms to enable it to concentrate its forces not on the Iranian border but on repelling any Coalition counter-attack against Kuwait or Iraq. It was curious that while the Coalition under Security Council authorisation was preparing for and using force against Iraq, UNIIMOG was peacefully supervising the final phases of Iraqi troop withdrawal to the internationally recognised frontier as agreed to by Iraq and Iran. This process led to the termination of UNIIMOG's mandate on 27 February 1992.[59]

UN Angola Verification Missions (UNAVEM I and II) 1989-present
UNAVEM I was established after Cuba and Angola signed a bilateral accord on 22 December 1988,[60] providing for the withdrawal of Cuban troops from Angola, which was linked to the tripartite accord between Angola, Cuba and South Africa concerning the withdrawal of South African troops from, combined with the eventual independence of, Namibia, signed the same day.[61] The latter will be discussed when UNTAG is examined.

The bilateral accord provided that the 50,000 Cuban troops present in Angola, 'in accordance with Article 51 of the UN Charter' shall be withdrawn by 1 July 1991, after phased withdrawal within Angola to the 15th and 13th parallels, providing that no flagrant violations of the tripartite agreement occurs. Angola and Cuba then requested the Security Council to verify 'the redeployment and the phased and total withdrawal of Cuban troops' from Angola. In anticipation of this agreement, on 20 December 1988, the Security Council decided to establish UNAVEM for a period of thirty-one months, to carry out the mandate provided for in the agreement between Angola and Cuba.[62]

In fact Cuban troop withdrawal was complete ahead of schedule by the beginning of June 1991.[63] However, UNAVEM did not become redundant in that with the outside props removed, in the form of Cuban support for the Angolan government and South African support for UNITA, these two opponents in the civil war reached an agreement in Lisbon on 31 May 1991 on a cease-fire and the holding of elections by 30 November 1992. The parties requested UN supervision of the cease-fire and of the elections, leading to a revised mandate for UNAVEM, rechristened UNAVEM II, by Security Council resolution 696, unanimously adopted on 30 May 1991. Unlike UNGOMAP in Afghanistan, UNAVEM has become integral in the second stage of peacekeeping, the implementation of an agreed peaceful solution, involving not only traditional peacekeeping functions, the over-seeing of the cease-fire to be carried out by the military component of the force, but also the supervision of the Angolan police force, and of the elections, to be carried out by police and civilian elements.[64] To this end the size of the force was increased from 70 military observers, to 350 military observers, 90 police observers, and 71 civilian election observers. In a report dated 24 June 1992, the Secretary General warned that 'the political and security atmosphere throughout Angola remains tense and could yet derail the process if not contained', although he was still optimistic that elections would take place.[65] At the time of writing (end of September 1992), elections have just occurred with the MPLA faction winning. The success of the process, however, has been undermined by UNITA's threat to resume hostilities.

UN Observer Group in Central America
(ONUCA) 1989–92

The first major step to ending the internationalised civil wars that had raged in Central America in the 1980s was the signing of the Guatemala Agreements in August 1987 by El Salvador, Honduras, Nicaragua, Costa Rica and Guatemala.[66] The agreements were characterised by general pledges, which, inter alia called for: national reconciliation; the cessation of hostilities within the countries concerned; democratisation including free-dom of the press, political pluralism and the ending of states of emergency; free elections in all five countries; the cessation of assistance to irregular forces; and finally, the non-use of territory for aggression against other States.

In furtherance of these Accords, President Ortega of Nicaragua agreed to hold elections in that country following a summit meeting of the heads of State of the five Central American countries in February 1989. As part of this agreement, the Central American countries requested UN supervision of the electoral process as well as announcing that they had agreed with the UN Secretary General that a multinational force be placed in the region to help prevent cross-border attacks, weapons infiltration and any other kind of external interference with the electoral process.[67]

The speed of the UN's reaction to this request was impressive, reflecting the fact that the Secretary General was involved through the peace process pursuant to a very vague mandate initially granted by Security Council resolution 562 of 1985, which simply requested that the Secretary General keep the Council apprised of any developments in the Central American peace process. After the initial request in February 1989, the Secretary General announced in July that a UN Observer Mission to Verify the Electoral Process in Nicaragua (ONUVEN) would be established to supervise the elections.[68] This was retrospectively endorsed by the Security Council in resolution 637 of 1989 which merely noted with 'appreciation the Secretary General's agreement with Nicaragua to deploy a United Nations election observer mission in that country'. A similar approach was taken to the military observer force whose function it would be to supervise a regional cease-fire as well as a local one between the Contras and the Nicaraguan government troops. Again the Council appeared content to endorse the Secretary General's efforts when it adopted resolution 644 in 1989 formally authorising the creation of ONUCA.

As has been stated the Secretary General's good offices mission to Central America derived from Council resolution 562 of 1985, but took on a much wider aspect than that envisaged in the resolution. However, it may be that the Secretary General perceived his mandate to be granted not only by the Security Council but also by the unanimous support of the General Assembly expressed at its 42nd session in October 1987. Resolution 42/1 requested that the Secretary General afford the fullest support to the five Central American governments in their efforts to achieve peace, especially by granting the assistance requested in the setting up of the verification machinery.

ONUVEN reported throughout the build-up to the election in Nicaragua and despite some irregularities it was able to report, along with other observers, that a free and fair election took place in Nicaragua on 25 February 1990, which resulted in a surprising defeat for the Sandinista government.[69] ONUCA successfully oversaw a cease-fire in the region in the election period,[70] and was then redeployed to assist in the demobilisation of the Contra rebels,[71] the final step in the pacific settlement of the war. Having completed its mandate, ONUCA was removed from Nicaragua and its mandate was terminated on 16 January 1992, enabling the transfer of its equipment and personnel to ONUSAL in El Salvador as a continuation of the regional peace process.[72]

UN Mission for the Referendum in Western Sahara
(MINURSO) 1991-present

The conflict between POLISARIO guerrillas and Moroccan troops, which started in earnest in 1976 when Spain withdrew from its former colony of Western Sahara, seemed to be another intractable problem in which the United Nations was marginalised. However, the Secretary General, alongside his opposite number from the OAU, persisted in their good offices and made a significant breakthrough on 30 August 1988, when their settlement proposals were accepted by the parties. The Security Council instructed the Secretary General's Special Representative to formulate a referendum plan.[73]

An acceptable referendum plan was not approved by the Security Council until 27 June 1990, when in resolution 658 it accepted the Secretary General's report in which he detailed the settlement process,[74] whereby the Western Saharan people would choose between independence and integration with Morocco. The referendum was originally scheduled for January 1992, but has been postponed because of cease-fire violations and disagreements on the composition of the electorate in Western Sahara.

The UN Mission for the Referendum in Western Sahara, known by its French acronym, MINURSO, was authorised by the Security Council on 29 April 1991 in resolution 690, and was emplaced in September 1991, following a cease-fire agreed to by both parties. Despite the consent of the factions, MINURSO is experiencing tremendous difficulties, not only in covering the vast territory with only 349 military observers, as well as police and civilian personnel, but mainly because the necessary cooperation from the parties has been lacking. There have been numerous cease-fire violations, but the main problem has been over the census list of those entitled to vote in the referendum, with both sides disagreeing and with POLISARIO accusing the UN of favouring Morocco.[75]

In these circumstances, with two of the basic principles of peacekeeping in jeopardy, namely unconditional acceptance of the provisional measures by the parties, and neutrality, not in this case in the UN's supervision of the cease-fire, but in the administration of the peace process, serious doubts have been raised against the prospect of obtaining a successful outcome to this long-running dispute. The Secretary General expressed these doubts in February 1992,[76] despite the fact that the Security Council had commissioned a new report on voting criteria which continues to form a basis for discussion between the two parties.[77] The Security Council extended MINURSO's mandate until the end of August 1992 in the hope that agreement would be reached by then.[78]

UN Observer Mission in El Salvador
(ONUSAL) 1991-present

The continuation of the Central American peace process into El Salvador required a modification of the approach used by the UN in Nicaragua. Whilst the Nicaraguan operation required supervision of a cease-fire and elections, ONUSAL was initially set up to verify that the parties to the long-running civil war, the government and the FMLN, comply with the human rights accord they signed at San José in July 1990.[79] Although not the normal sort of provisional measure that the UN is requested to oversee, one can see that the observance of human rights by both parties to a dirty civil war is an interim measure or a first step towards a lasting political settlement. In this way one can see ONUSAL as fitting into the UN peacekeeping model.

The Security Council, in establishing ONUSAL and outlining its initial mandate in resolution 693 on 20 May 1991, urged the parties to agree on a cease-fire and on a final pacific solution to the conflict, and stated that upon these agreements ONUSAL would then become an integrated peacekeeping operation, verifying the provisional measures as well as over-seeing the peaceful solution.

Such an approach illustrates the highly flexible and dynamic nature of peacekeeping in the post Cold War era. The major element of ONUSAL was formed from the disbanding of ONUCA, illustrating how UN peacekeeping has been tied into the Central American peace process. The parties formally ended the civil war by agreements made on 31 December 1991 and on 16 January 1992, and the peaceful solution was detailed in the latter agreement and in negotiations lasting until June 1992.[80] The agreement contained a cease-fire commencing on 1 February 1992, continuing for nine months until the FMLN's military structure is dismantled with its members being integrated into the civil and political life of the country, including its institutions. Later negotiations revealed the extent of the government's concessions which include the establishment of a new police force, a reformed electoral code to legalise the FMLN as a political party, as well as government purchase of land for peasants. The aim of the agreements is to address the social inequalities that led to the civil war, to create a 'revolution by negotiation' according to the Secretary General.[81] In order to service these agreements the Security Council expanded ONUSAL's mandate, by dividing the force into two with a military division to verify cease-fire arrangements and a police division to monitor public order pending the formation of a new national police force.[82] Although there is as yet no agreement to hold UN supervised elections, the intention is clearly to integrate the FMLN into the political process, and to allow proper free and fair elections in the future.

UN Iraq-Kuwait Observation Mission
(UNIKOM) 1991-present

At the end of the conflict between Iraq and the UN authorised Coalition, the Council adopted resolution 687 on 3 April 1991 detailing the cease-fire arrangements between the belligerents. Paragraph 5 requested the Secretary General, 'after consulting with Iraq and Kuwait', to submit a plan for the deployment of a UN observer force to monitor the 'demilitarized zone, which is hereby established, extending 10 kilometres into Iraq and 5 kilometres into Kuwait' from the boundary agreed to by the two States in 1963.[83] To this end the Coalition States would withdraw their armies from this area as soon as UNIKOM was emplaced.

The Security Council approved the Secretary General's plan in resolution 689 of 9 April 1991. The Secretary General proposed a force of about 1,500 observers to monitor the demilitarised zone, to deter violations of the boundary by its presence, and to observe any hostile or potentially hostile action mounted by one State against the other. The Secretary General made it clear from his report that UNIKOM would simply 'be required to monitor and observe and would not be expected and, indeed, would not be authorised to take physical action to prevent the entry of military personnel or equipment into the demilitarized zone'.[84] UNIKOM is a non-enforcement measure, although Iraq appeared to be under an obligation to accept it not only because it had been defeated but formally because resolution 687 appeared to be adopted under Chapter VII and Iraq had to agree to all its terms. Although Iraq had little choice but to consent to UNIKOM's presence as well as to the UN guards which replaced the Western troops in northern Iraq in June and July 1991, there remains the problem of Iraq withdrawing its consent to their presence. Presumably, at least in UNIKOM's case, the Council would take this to be a breach of the cease-fire terms requiring enforcement action perhaps of a military nature, although the Council would also have to withdraw UNIKOM.

There is also ambiguity about the length of time UNIKOM will be *in situ*. One possibility will be that it will remain there indefinitely performing a role similar to that of UNMOGIP or UNTSO. Alternatively, it could be withdrawn after the UN's boundary Commission has finally demarcated the boundary between Iraq and Kuwait. The former appears the more likely given the volatile state of relations between Iraq and Kuwait and Iraq and the UN.

United Nations peacekeeping forces

First UN Emergency Force in the Middle East (UNEF I) 1956-67
Pursuant to a joint Anglo/French/Israeli plan, Israel attacked Egypt in the

Sinai on 29 October 1956. The United States urged the Council to find a breach of the peace and demand a cessation of the attack, combined with immediate Israeli withdrawal. The Soviet delegate agreed that the Israeli action came within Article 39, but preferred to use the more emotive classification of an act of aggression.[85] No resolution was forthcoming although after the Anglo/French ultimatum had been delivered both the United States and the Soviet Union introduced draft resolutions calling on Israel to cease firing and to withdraw her troops.[86] These drafts did not contain references to Chapter VII in a deliberate attempt to forestall the threatened Anglo/French intervention. No recommendatory measure could circumvent the vetoes of the United Kingdom and France.

On 31 October 1956, British and French forces intervened, an action which was classified by the Yugoslavian delegate as an act of aggression. He formally proposed that an emergency special session of the General Assembly should be convened under the Uniting for Peace procedure. A procedural vote was taken and the resolution was adopted despite the negative votes of the two permanent members involved.[87]

Despite the classification of the conflict by several members of the Council as coming within Chapter VII, and the use of the Uniting for Peace resolution, which, by its terms, necessarily implies that the situation comes within Article 39, the General Assembly's first resolution on the conflict made no significant jurisdictional finding. Assembly resolution 997,[88] based on a United States' draft, urged the parties to cease-fire, to withdraw to their previous positions, and recommended that all member States refrain from further acts. Canada abstained and New Zealand voted against the resolution because it lacked any method which would create conditions under which a cease-fire and a withdrawal would be acceptable to all the parties.[89]

Canada acted to rectify the failure of resolution 997, by proposing what was to become resolution 998, which requested the Secretary General to submit a plan 'for the setting up, with the consent of the nations concerned, of an emergency international United Nations' Force to secure and supervise the cessation of hostilities in accordance with the aforementioned resolution'.[90] On the same day a nineteen power draft was adopted as Assembly resolution 999.[91] This placed emphasis on the necessity of achieving an immediate cease-fire, and authorised the Secretary General to arrange immediately with the parties concerned a cease-fire and a withdrawal of forces behind armistice lines. The intention was to create the conditions under which UNEF I could fill the vacuum created by compliance with the cease-fire and withdrawal. The Secretary General's plan for UNEF I was approved by the Assembly as was his report on the guiding principles for the functioning of UNEF.[92]

Despite proposals that UNEF I should guarantee passage through the Suez Canal and the Gulf of Aqaba,[93] UNEF's mandate and functions derived from the General Assembly's resolutions which basically called for four things: a cease-fire, the cessation of hostilities, abstention from military raids and incursions, and scrupulous observance of the armistice agreements. UNEF's supervision of these elements depended upon the establishment of a cease-fire and upon the consent of the Egyptian government to allow it to be emplaced on Egyptian soil.

Egypt's consent to UNEF I is illustrative of the basis of all observer and peacekeeping functions. It also demonstrates their weakness for Secretary General U Thant viewed President Nasser's request in 1967 that UNEF I be withdrawn as necessitating the removal of the force.[94]

There were objections to the Secretary General's view. Israel, New Zealand and Australia argued that the withdrawal of UNEF I should be a decision of the Assembly not of Egypt.[95] U Thant's decision has been challenged on the basis of an *aide-mémoire* written by the Secretary General at the time of the creation of UNEF I, Dag Hammarskjöld, but not published until 1967.[96] The former Secretary General stated that Egypt's acceptance of UNEF contained more than just unilaterally revokable consent in that the Egyptian government had consented to UNEF's presence on its territory until its mandate had been completed. To this extent, argued Hammarskjöld, this so called Good Faith Accord had limited Egypt's sovereignty. It has been argued that this Accord should have at least forced Egypt to negotiate with the United Nations.[97]

These arguments seem to forget that without Egypt's consent UNEF's continued presence would have been hostile as regards Egypt, and if attacked, as it in fact was,[98] UNEF could have used self-defence which was an integral part of its mandate, but if it was to carry out its functions in the face of Egyptian hostility it would have had to use force beyond that required for self-defence. Thus UNEF would have come dangerously close to constituting enforcement action.

The Good Faith Accord could not derogate from the basic principle of peacekeeping, namely host State consent. The only condition attaching to Egypt's right to demand withdrawal was that of giving notice which in the face of such a demand and the increasing hostility towards UNEF proved to be unenforceable by the United Nations. The Secretary General recognised the stark reality of the situation when he withdrew UNEF without reference to the Assembly. The emplacement of a peacekeeping force does not limit the host State's sovereignty. The positioning of UNEF I was clearly predicated on Egyptian consent and on both parties' voluntary compliance with the Assembly's call for a cessation of hostilities. The argument that UNEF I was entitled to stay on Egyptian soil until its mandate was completed was unsound because this would appear to have given UNEF an enforceable right to stay. Such enforceable rights are incompatible with a consensual peacekeeping force such as UNEF I.

UNEF I's mandate had four aspects: to secure the cease-fire, rapidly achieved with the cooperation of the parties to the conflict; to supervise the withdrawal of foreign troops, achieved relatively slowly due to the reticence of Britain and France;[99] to observe the armistice agreement; and to patrol the armistice lines. As regards the latter, UNEF took over most of UNTSO's patrols and was reasonably efficient taking into account Israel's repudiation of the Israeli-Egyptian Armistice in 1956 and its consequent withdrawal from the Mixed Armistice Commission.[100] This withdrawal had a potential influence on the third aspect of UNEF's mandate, namely to observe the armistice agreement.

Nevertheless, although no longer recognising the Agreement *de jure*, Israel continued to recognise it *de facto*, which contributed to UNEF's success in reducing the number of fedayeen raids from the Gaza Strip and in keeping the number of border incidents to a minimum level during the force's stay.

UNEF I 'ranked among the most effective of United Nations' peacekeeping operations' in that it not only fulfilled its mandate, but also helped to secure over a decade of relative peace in the Middle East.[101] On the other hand, it could be said that UNEF I did not contribute a great deal towards a peaceful solution of even part of the Middle Eastern question. One could perhaps go further and argue that the parties, particularly Egypt, used the decade in which UNEF was *in situ* as a breathing space in which to rearm in preparation for the next conflict, using UNEF's buffer to hide behind. Certainly UNEF's contribution to peace was severely questioned when President Nasser withdrew Egypt's consent to the presence of UNEF which led to its removal; an action which, in itself, suggested that Egypt no longer wanted peace and therefore no longer required UNEF. Despite arguments to the effect that Egypt had no right to withdraw consent, it is doubtful whether a peacekeeping force could remain on a State's territory without that State's consent.

UN Operation in the Congo (ONUC) 1960–64

The Republic of the Congo achieved independence from Belgium on 30 June 1960. As with many colonies, the Congo was something of an artificial construction consisting of many tribal areas. The Belgian authorities had done little to unify the colony before independence and so within a few days of its achievement disruptions between the various factions occurred resulting in Belgian intervention which was characterised as humanitarian by the Belgian government.

President Kasavubu and Prime Minister Lumumba sent a cable to the Secretary General requesting United Nations' military assistance to protect the Congo 'against the present external aggression which is a threat to international peace'.[102] The Secretary General, utilising Article 99 of the

Charter, asked that the President of the Council convene that body.[103] The resultant resolution was the work of Dag Hammarskjöld, as were the two subsequent Council resolutions.

On 14 July 1960 the Council adopted resolution 143, which made no jurisdictional finding but called upon Belgium to withdraw and decided to authorise the Secretary General to take the necessary steps to provide military assistance, 'in consultation with the Government of the Congo' until the Congolese security forces could fully meet their tasks. To all intents and purposes this appears to be another case of the United Nations filling the vacuum created by the breakdown in security, but the simplicity of this belies the complexity of the civil war situation facing the United Nations. ONUC was to assist the government in restoring law and order 'but which government? that of Lumumba? Kasavubu? Ilea? Mobutu?'.[104]

Despite the creation of ONUC, the situation deteriorated and on 11 July 1960 Tshombe, President of the Katangese provincial government, declared Katanga's secession. Belgian troops remained despite resolution 143. Again on the Secretary General's initiative the Security Council adopted resolution 145 on 22 July 1960. The resolution recognised the unity of the Congo, again called on the Belgians to withdraw while authorising the Secretary General 'to take all necessary action to this effect'. It also requested that all States refrain from interference which might undermine the territorial integrity and political independence of the Congo.

Belgium refused to withdraw from Katanga with the consequence that ONUC could not enter the province without using force, an event which the previous resolutions had not catered for. Under these circumstances the Council adopted resolution 146 on 9 August 1960. The resolution called on the government of Belgium to withdraw its troops from Katanga; declared that ONUC should enter Katanga; reaffirmed that ONUC 'will not be a party to or in any way influence the outcome of any internal conflict, constitutional or otherwise'; and called upon Members 'to accept and carry out the decisions of the Security Council' in accordance with Articles 25 and 49.

By September 1960 the Congo was in a state of constitutional as well as military upheaval with Kasavubu and Lumumba dismissing each other from office followed by the coup by the army chief of staff General Mobutu on 14 September. This combined with the continuing attempt to secede by Katanga and the problem of how much force was to be used to enable ONUC to carry out its mandate divided the Council. The Soviet Union was particularly critical of the Secretary General who had so far masterminded the operation.[105] This resulted in the Soviet veto of another Hammarskjöld-proposed resolution.[106] The deadlock in the Council was a reflection of the increasing internationalisation of the civil war, with the Soviets supporting Lumumba, the Americans supporting Kasavubu, whilst the French, British and Belgians showed support for Tshombe.

The United States proposed that the matter be transferred to the General Assembly under the auspices of the Uniting for Peace resolution. This proposal was adopted by procedural vote,[107] despite the negative votes of the Soviet Union and Poland who stated that the Uniting for Peace resolution was illegal. Besides, they argued, the Assembly was about to start its regular annual session anyway.

Although opposed by the Eastern bloc the Assembly adopted a resolution on 20 September 1960. This resolution stated, *inter alia*, that to safeguard international peace it was 'essential for the United Nations to continue to assist the Central Government of the Congo' and to this end requested the Secretary General to take 'vigorous action' to restore law and order and to preserve the unity, integrity and political independence of the Congo. It also requested all States to refrain from intervening and reminded members of Articles 25 and 49.[108] However, the Assembly then split into factions none of which could form the necessary majority to adopt a significant resolution.

The death of Lumumba and the deterioration of the situation into civil war finally united the Council sufficiently to enable it to adopt resolution 161 on 27 February 1961 which contained two parts. Part A categorised the crisis as a 'threat to international peace and security' and a 'serious civil war situation'. It urged that 'the United Nations take immediately all appropriate measures to prevent the occurrence of a civil war in the Congo, including arrangements for cease-fires, the halting of all military operations, the prevention of clashes, and the use of force, if necessary, in the last resort'. It also urged the withdrawal of all Belgian troops and advisers as well as mercenaries; and decided to investigate the death of Lumumba. Part B also found a 'threat to international peace and security'. It also noted the violation of human rights and fundamental freedoms in the Congo and urged self-determination through free and fair elections without outside interference.

On 24 November 1961 the Security Council adopted resolution 169 which reaffirmed the mandate of ONUC in the following terms:

(a) To maintain the territorial integrity and political independence of the Republic of the Congo;
(b) To assist the Central Government of the Congo in the restoration and maintenance of law and order;
(c) To prevent the occurrence of civil war in the Congo;
(d) To secure the immediate withdrawal and evacuation from the Congo of all foreign military, paramilitary and advisory personnel not under United Nations' command, and mercenaries;
(e) To render technical assistance.

It welcomed the restoration of a Central Government on 2 August 1961 in accordance with the *Loi Fondamentale*, and deplored armed action against the government specifically by the secessionists in Katanga aided by external resources and mercenaries. It completely rejected the claim that Katanga was a 'sovereign independent nation'. To this end the resolution authorised the Secretary General to take 'vigorous action', including the requisite measure of force 'if necessary' for the expulsion of foreign military personnel not under United Nations' command.

The Council resolutions establishing and mandating ONUC (143, 145, 146) were essentially the work of Secretary General Hammarskjöld. It is important, therefore, to ascertain his views as to their basis. His use of Article 99 to start the Council in motion gives the first indication as to the possible constitutional base of the action for he believed that his use of Article 99 necessarily implied a finding by himself of a situation falling within Article 39 of the Charter.[109] However, he did not want to categorise the Belgian intervention as aggression in order to obtain the support of the Western powers on the Council. On the other hand, a characterisation of the situation as a mere breakdown in internal law and order would have indirectly justified Belgian intervention and would not have been acceptable to either the Socialist or Afro-Asian members of the Council. The Secretary General found a path through this minefield by proposing to create such conditions as to facilitate Belgian withdrawal with a United Nations' force filling the vacuum.[110]

It must be noted that the first three enabling resolutions made no finding under Article 39 despite the Secretary General's belief that Article 99 necessarily implied a 'threat to the peace'. The Secretary General was intent on obtaining a mandate for the force, hence the resolutions had to be constitutionally ambiguous in order to obtain sufficient consensus. However, they do contain inferences as to where they could be placed under the Charter. Resolutions 143 and 146 contained provisions indicating that the force was to comply with Article 2(7), in that ONUC was to provide military assistance in consultation with the Congolese government and would not intervene or influence the outcome of any internal conflict. Indeed, the Secretary General initially seemed to view ONUC as similar to interpositional, consensual peacekeeping as being undertaken at the time by UNEF I.[111] This would seem to suggest that ONUC was either created under the recommendatory powers of Chapter VI or under the doctrine of implied powers, since Chapter VI does not contain any specific provision under which a peacekeeping force could be established.

However, the last of Hammarskjöld's inspired resolutions, 146, contained references to Article 25 suggesting that the resolutions were 'decisions' not recommendations and so were mandatory without containing an express or implied finding under Article 39. As the situation deteriorated so the Council began to cross the threshold into Chapter VII. References to non-intervention in resolution 146 probably signified that the authorisation to ONUC to enter Katanga was, theoretically, not seen as enforcement action under Article 42 but as a provisional measure under Article 40.[112] This certainly accords with the Secretary General's revised view.[113] Without a determination within the terms of Article 39, which necessarily internationalises the situation, provisional measures under Article 40, although made mandatory by reference to Article 25, cannot escape the limitation in Article 2(7), because they are not enforcement measures.

Assuming, after resolution 146, that ONUC was operating under Article 40, could the General Assembly then take over the operation of the force when the Security Council became paralysed by the veto? The day-to-day operation of the force did not require supervision by the Security Council or by the General Assembly; the only action required by either organ was when the mandate of the force needed adjusting. Thus if the mandate provided by the Security Council was sufficient for the force to continue day-to-day operations, there would be no legal need for the General Assembly to adopt a resolution. However, there was a political need to show that a majority of members supported the action.

The problem is whether the General Assembly, acting under the Uniting for Peace resolution, altered the mandate in its resolution 1474. There are suggestions that it did for it requested that the Secretary General take 'vigorous action' to restore the unity and independence of the Congo. By itself, this request could, at the most, be classified as a recommendation of enforcement action, which would have been within the Assembly's powers, but would have constituted an alteration of the mandate. The Security Council had only called for mandatory provisional measures under Article 40. The General Assembly could be seen as recommending enforcement action similar to the power exercised by both the Security Council and the General Assembly during the United Nations' action in Korea. This would put ONUC beyond the pale of a peacekeeping force and would have made it an enforcement action.

However, there are suggestions in Assembly resolution 1474 that all that body intended was a reaffirmation of the Security Council's resolutions; in other words, it did not intend to alter the mandate. References in the resolution to Articles 25 and 49 indicate a confirmation of Council resolution 146 for such Articles do not apply to Assembly recommendations. If the Assembly was trying to take mandatory enforcement action that would have been unconstitutional. This was affirmed in the *Expenses* case in which the World Court opined that the Assembly had not taken enforcement action as regards its handling of ONUC.[114] Although its reasoning is not clear, the Court's judgement also suggests that the Assembly's contribution to ONUC's mandate was not recommendation of enforcement action, but simply a reaffirmation or possibly a reinterpretation of the mandate created by the Security Council.

The following Council resolution, 161, made arguments relating to the legality of the Assembly's contribution somewhat academic, for it comprehensively reinterpreted ONUC's mandate in terms which went beyond those in the Assembly's resolution. The Council found a threat to the peace. Such an implied finding within the terms of Article 39 placed the whole operation under Chapter VII. So even if the operation remained under Article 40, there was the possibility of making it into enforcement action at a later stage. Also, it is arguable that such a finding renders the limitation contained in Article 2(7) redundant.

There appear to be two alternatives: either resolution 161 went beyond provisional measures, or the finding of a threat to the peace was merely a sign of a deteriorating situation rather than a method by which the mandate could be changed. It appeared to go further than previous Council resolutions in that the emphasis was no longer on helping the Congolese government which appeared to have disintegrated; instead it was reduced to maintaining the Congo's integrity, to prevent its breakup by factionalisation and secession, a Congo in which a new government could be elected. To this end it authorised the use of force in the last resort. The International Court was of the opinion that this did not amount to enforcement action. Nevertheless, for one thing, Article 2(7) no longer seemed important to the Council, to the extent of involving the consent of the Congolese government, for one did not exist at the time. For another, resolution 161 authorised the use of force by ONUC 'in the last resort', in other words the use of force was not limited merely to self-defence. This last factor seems to push ONUC beyond a force overseeing the implementation of provisional measures to a force authorised to use enforcement measures. However, such a mandate can be reconciled with Article 40. The authorisation to use force in the last resort came at the end of a list of provisional measures, 'cease-fires', 'halting of all military operations', and 'the prevention of clashes', and so can be seen as coming within an authorisation merely to enforce provisional measures as provided by the last sentence of Article 40 which reads, 'the Security Council shall duly take account of a failure to comply with such provisional measures'.

Security Council resolution 169 contained a comprehensive restatement of ONUC's mandate. It was able to contain a reassertion that ONUC was assisting the Congolese government because the central government had been restored. The force therefore returned, to some extent, to the consensual type of peacekeeping force exemplified by UNEF. However, the mandate also referred to the prevention of civil war as one of the force's purposes. This must be read in conjunction with the mandate's requirement (d) of ensuring the withdrawal of foreign military personnel and mercenaries, for it was the internationalisation of the civil war that constituted the threat to the peace.

The mandate contained in resolution 169 was in the nature of a series of widely drawn provisional measures. It was meant to enable ONUC to preserve the Congo intact to enable a peaceful settlement between all the factions to occur. It was not an authorisation for ONUC to enforce a political solution. Efforts to prevent secession may have appeared as if ONUC was being used by the central government to enforce its will on the secessionists. However, the basis of ONUC's action towards secession was that it arose because of foreign intervention and foreign engineering of a revolt, which was not in accord with the widest interpretation of ONUC's mandate, namely the protection of the territorial integrity and independence of the Congo.

The Congo was to remain as a whole, but if the secession was wholly or mainly indigenous, ONUC's action would have been an enforcement of that aim. However, the Council resolutions made it clear that that organ believed that the secession was being caused from outside the country. This was evidenced by resolution 169 which authorised the use of force solely for the expulsion of foreign military elements. Whether there would have been a Katangese secession anyway remains conjecture; the fact remains that foreign military involvement provided the situation with the necessary international element to have allowed ONUC to operate without it technically becoming an enforcement action under Article 42, in that its use of force was confined to the enforcement of the provisional measures outlined in the mandate.

Nevertheless, enforcement of provisional measures is in many respects similar to enforcement action under Article 42, particularly when the provisional measures are so widely drawn as to include the maintenance of the integrity of a nation. This has led Bowett to describe ONUC's constitutional base as being somewhat wider than Article 40, seeing it as a force 'for the purpose of supervising and enforcing compliance with the provisional measures ordered under Article 40 and for other purposes which were consistent with the general powers of the Council under Article 39'.[115] This involves recognising that ONUC had gone beyond Article 40, but not as far as Article 42, by suggesting that the general powers of Article 39 were utilised. It must be pointed out, however, that the provisions of Article 39 have been used as authority for the recommendation of enforcement action as in the Korean war.

It would be best to summarise ONUC's actions as having the enforcement of provisional measures under Article 40 as their constitutional base, but since these measures were increasingly widely drawn so as to cope with an ever-deteriorating crisis, they, in fact, amounted to *de facto* enforcement action. It could be argued that ONUC was acting in defence of its purposes. However, this is an unacceptably wide interpretation of self-defence, going far beyond that authorised for other peacekeeping operations, which are only allowed to use self-defence when fired on. Allowing a force to take positive action in defence of its purposes is no different from allowing it to enforce them.

The effectiveness of ONUC in fulfilling its mandate can be determined by examining the Secretary General's report on the implementation of the Security Council's resolutions relating to the Congo.[116] He refers to the purposes listed (a) to (e) in Council resolution 169.

As regards the directive to ONUC to maintain the territorial integrity and political independence of the Congo, the Secretary General states that the most serious threat to this was from the Katangese secessionists. Although integrity was restored in a symbolic sense in August 1960 with Tshombe's consent to ONUC's entry into Katanga, further secessionist activities meant that the full integration of the province was only achieved when a public renunciation of secession was announced by Tshombe combined with the complete freedom of movement achieved by ONUC throughout Katanga, the neutralisation and disarming of the Katangese gendarmerie, the elimination of Katanga's airforce and the flight of the mercenaries.

In relation to assisting the Congolese government in the restoration and maintenance of law and order, the Secretary General noted that until the formation of a recognisable central government in August 1961, ONUC was unsuccessful in this part of its mandate. After that date, particularly with the termination of Katanga's secession, ONUC restored law and order to the whole of the Congo by 1963. The formation of a central government acceptable to all the parties, including, eventually, Katanga, also helped ONUC to carry out successfully the third part of its mandate, namely the prevention of civil war in the Congo. The ending of the Katangese provincial government's secession necessarily entailed ONUC effectively carrying out the fourth part of its mandate, namely the removal of foreign military and paramilitary personnel and mercenaries.

It can be seen from the above that ONUC's success depended heavily on it ending the Katangese secession and as we have seen, ONUC's operation to carry this out came perilously close to being enforcement action. It is submitted that ONUC was successful because it overstepped basic peacekeeping principles. Its mandate was so widely drawn that its fulfilment entailed going beyond the maintenance of the *status quo*, which is the normal purpose of peacekeeping forces, to providing a solution to the conflict.

From the once disintegrating Congo there has arisen a stable African State, Zaire, a fact that must, in part, be due to the United Nations' operation in the Congo. Despite its operational difficulties, in terms of its contribution to the settlement of a crisis and to international peace, ONUC must be judged one of the most successful peacekeeping operations undertaken by the United Nations.[117]

UN Peacekeeping Force in Cyprus (UNFICYP) 1964-present
Violence broke out between the Greek and Turkish Cypriot communities
after the President of Cyprus, Archbishop Makarios, had proposed constitutional amendments on 30 November 1963. The threat of Turkish intervention arose.[118] This led to proposals for a joint British/Turkish/Greek
'peacemaking' force to be interposed between the two communities.[119] The
Soviet Union characterised this proposal as enforcement by NATO and
stated that only the Security Council could take any practical measures.[120]
The Cypriot government wanted a United Nations', not a guaranteeing
powers', presence.[121]

The non-permanent members of the Council, excluding Czechoslovakia,
sponsored resolution 186 which was adopted by the Council on 4 March
1964. The resolution noted that the situation 'with regard to Cyprus is likely
to threaten international peace and security'; called on Members 'to refrain
from any action or threat of action likely to worsen the situation in Cyprus,
or to endanger international peace'; asked the government of Cyprus which
had 'the responsibility for the maintenance of law and order' to take
measures to stop the violence; recommended the creation 'with the consent
of the government of Cyprus' of UNFICYP; and recommended that the
'function of the force should be, in the interests of preserving international
peace and security, to use its best efforts to prevent a recurrence of the
fighting, to contribute to the maintenance and restoration of law and order
and a return to normal conditions'.

The Secretary General's interpretation of UNFICYP's mandate made it
clear that what was contemplated was a consensual type-peacekeeping
operation based on UNEF I, avoiding any action 'designed to influence the
political situation in Cyprus except through creating an improved climate in
which political solutions may be sought'.[122] This neutralist policy was meant
to allay fears of enforcement. Nevertheless, ONUC's actions under a
neutralist stance came perilously close to enforcement, and the Secretary
General's interpretation of the use of force by UNFICYP had a similar
potential, envisaging the possible use of force by UNFICYP to carry out its
mandate.[123] As with ONUC, UNFICYP's mandate, outlined in resolution
186, contained a series of widely drawn provisional measures. However,
unlike in the Congo situation where the Council was faced with a threat to
the peace, here the Council did not make a crucial Article 39 finding. Thus
UNFICYP was created following non-mandatory provisional measures and
so could not undertake enforcement action without a finding in the terms of
Article 39.

Between 1964 and 1974, UNFICYP did not act as a buffer force between
the two communities, but rather as a police force since there were not, as

such, definable cease-fire lines. This situation changed in 1974. A Greek-backed coup against Makarios and the imminent invasion by Turkey led the Council to meet on 16 July 1974 at the request of Secretary General Waldheim and the Cypriot representative.[124] In the Council's first meeting some of the members stated that there was a threat to international peace.[125] Indeed, resolution 353, adopted on 20 July 1974, the day Turkey invaded, stated that there was a 'serious threat to international peace and security', and demanded 'an end to foreign military intervention' in Cyprus. This implied finding under Article 39 combined with the peremptory language and a call for a cease-fire suggested mandatory provisional measures under Article 40.

None the less, UNFICYP's original constitutional basis, founded on non-mandatory provisional measures, was not changed and brought within Chapter VII, although its functions were to change from it being an intra-State to, factually speaking, an inter-State peacekeeping force. The Secretary General reported on the measures proposed by the foreign ministers of Greece, Britain and Turkey (but not Cyprus), that UNFICYP should create a security zone between the Turkish forces in the north of the island and the Greek Cypriot forces in the south. The Security Council requested that he implement his report.[126]

Although the Cypriot government had consented to the original emplacement of UNFICYP in 1964, it objected somewhat to the new deployment saying that it appeared to perpetuate foreign military intervention.[127] It did not go as far as to withdraw its consent but its cooperation seemed to become unimportant with all the negotiations about the security zone taking place between Greece, Britain, Turkey and the Secretary General. However, although there was no effective government for the whole island, there was a need to involve the two Cypriot factions as well as the guaranteeing powers to obtain a lasting cease-fire and to allow UNFICYP to perform its new functions.[128]

If we turn now to the effectiveness of UNFICYP, in the period 1964 to 1974, after initial difficulties, it succeeded in securing a virtual end to the fighting on the island, although its attempts at creating a return to normal conditions on Cyprus were a limited success.[129] As early as 1967, the Secretary General warned that excessive confidence in the presence of UNFICYP had reduced the parties' willingness to negotiate a settlement.[130]

In the period before the Turkish invasion, UNFICYP's major pre-occupation was to try to maintain the *status quo* on the island. This remained its position towards the new *status quo* imposed on the island following the Turkish invasion and occupation of the northern part of the island in 1974. UNFICYP was powerless to prevent the invasion, instead its functions were changed to that of a buffer force. In carrying out its revised mandate successfully, UNFICYP has helped to entrench the post 1974 position on the island, with the cease-fire line becoming 'more and more an international frontier'.[131]

The Security Council has encouraged peacemaking through the Secretary General's good offices and has called upon all States not to recognise any Cypriot State other than the Republic of Cyprus.[132] A parallel can be drawn with the Congo situation where the Council was also concerned to keep the nation intact. However, in that case the Council took positive action through its peacekeeping force to maintain the integrity of the Congo, whereas UNFICYP is used to maintain a division of the island State whilst any progress towards reintegration must come about via separate peacemaking attempts by the Secretary General.

Second UN Emergency Force in the Middle East (UNEF II) 1973–79
Unlike the preceding three Middle Eastern wars, the Yom Kippur War of 1973 did not follow a period of heightened tension in the region. Consequently, the international community was largely unprepared when on 10 October 1973 the armed forces of Egypt and Syria launched a coordinated attack against Israeli positions in the Sinai and the Golan Heights. The tactic of surprise enabled Egypt and Syria to be initially successful in their main aim, the recapture of territories lost in 1967.

The outbreak of war also took the Security Council by surprise. Although the Council was convened on 8 October, it was unable to take any steps for seventeen days, and, indeed, it did not meet at all between 13 and 21 October. The pro-Arab members of the Council were pleased at the initial Arab success, whereas Israel and the United States played for time to enable the Israelis to regain lost ground. For a cease-fire to be called and for it to hold required not only the cooperation of the belligerents' backers, the two superpowers, which would have enabled the Council to call for a cease-fire, but would also require the parties (Israel, Egypt and Syria) to have come to a stage in their hostilities where a cease-fire would appeal to them all. Inevitably, these two requirements did not coincide for a considerable length of time. With increasing Arab losses the Soviet Union sought a cease-fire and invited Secretary of State Kissinger to Moscow. The result of this diplomacy was a joint superpower sponsored resolution which was virtually forced through the Council on a take it or leave it basis.[133] The resolution simply called upon the parties to 'terminate all military activity' no later than twelve hours after the resolution's adoption and then to implement resolution 242. The resolution appeared to be adopted as a provisional measure under Article 40 and even in the absence of an express or implied finding under Article 39, the superpowers probably intended it to be binding.[134]

Nevertheless, although the Arabs were in retreat, Israel had not yet accomplished its political and military objectives and so there was a time-lag between the superpower sponsored call for a cease-fire and all the combatants accepting it. Non-compliance with the cease-fire resulted in another United States/Soviet Union proposed resolution, which confirmed the Security Council's previous 'decision' and urged the forces to return to the positions they occupied at the moment the cease-fire had been called for.[135]

However, continued fighting brought about threats of superpower intervention and the consequent danger of escalation into a global conflict. The situation was rescued by the seven Non-Aligned members of the Council, who introduced resolution 340 on 25 October. It demanded an immediate cease-fire, decided to set up, under Council authority, a United Nations Emergency Force, and, in the meantime, requested the Secretary General to increase the number of UNTSO observers on each side.

The Secretary General interpreted UNEF II's mandate as requiring supervision of the implementation of the cease-fire called for in resolution 340. He also outlined the general characteristics of the force on a similar basis to UNEF I, in that it must operate with the full cooperation of the parties; have freedom of movement and communications; use force only in self-defence including self-defence against 'resistance to attempts by forceful means to prevent it from discharging its duties'; and 'in performing its functions, the force will act with complete impartiality and avoid actions which could prejudice the rights, claims or positions of the parties concerned'.[136]

The latter phrase suggests that UNEF II was in the nature of a provisional measure, or more correctly would not interfere with the positions of the parties under the provisional measures (cease-fire and withdrawal) it was to supervise. Article 40 would seem to be the origin of UNEF, but although resolution 340 could be interpreted as a mandatory demand for compliance with provisional measures, UNEF II could not be interpreted as an enforcement measure.

For the six-year period of its presence UNEF II successfully implemented its mandate of observing and supervising the cease-fire between Egypt and Israel. In his penultimate report to the Security Council on UNEF II, Secretary General Waldheim repeated his usual finding that 'the situation in the area of operations has remained stable. The force has continued efficiently to discharge its mandate and, with the cooperation of both parties, it has been able to contribute to the maintenance of the cease-fire called for by the Security Council in resolution 338 (1973)'.[137]

UNEF II had the potential to join ONUC as a fully successful peacekeeping force, not only in terms of fulfilling its mandate, but also of contributing to the ultimate solution of the dispute. The Camp David Accords leading to a peace treaty between Egypt and Israel on 26 March 1979 provided for a continued United Nations' presence to oversee the implementation of the treaty. Several factors prevented this, namely the fact that the treaty was negotiated outside the United Nations set most of the members against a continued United Nations' presence,[138] and also the fact that the United States' sponsoring of the talks represented the final stage in Egypt's move away from Moscow to Washington. The Soviet Union was thus unwilling to alter the mandate of UNEF II to enable it to supervise a treaty between two States friendly to the United States. Instead, a United States' backed, Western-in-composition, Multinational Force was created for the purpose.

UN Disengagement Observer Force (UNDOF) 1974-present

Whereas UNEF II was interposed between Egypt and Israel on the initiative of the Council following the 1973 conflict, on the Syrian front the parties accepted the cease-fire and negotiated their own disengagement agreement which called for the establishment of UNDOF to supervise it. The Security Council approved the establishment of UNDOF in resolution 350 on 31 May 1974, again exercising tight control by giving UNDOF short, renewable mandate periods of six months.

The Council approved the Secretary General's report which interpreted UNDOF's functions as the supervision of disengagement and the observation of cease-fire lines. The general principles governing UNDOF would be the same as UNEF II.[139]

UNDOF's constitutional origin is basically the same as UNEF's, namely the supervision, with the consent of the parties, of provisional measures adopted under Article 40 of the Charter by the Council, and in this case embodied in an agreement between the parties.

UNDOF has performed its functions of supervising the disengagement agreement between Israel and Syria very effectively to the present day. The ability of UNDOF to help create a climate of stability has in part led to the current possibility of a solution to the Israeli occupation of the Golan Heights at the Middle East peace talks between Israel and Syria in September 1992. Israel had invaded the Lebanon twice since the establishment of UNDOF, in 1978 and 1982. The fact that Syria was not sucked into a conflict which could, in turn, have drawn in the superpowers, was due, to a considerable extent, to UNDOF's presence.

After the Israeli invasion in 1978, the Secretary General was able to report that the 'situation in the Israel-Syria sector remained quiet and there was no incident of a serious nature'. UNDOF's fortnightly inspections of areas designated as containing limited armaments and troops by the disengagement agreement, accompanied by liaison officers from Syria and Israel, probably facilitated the defusion of the situation by preventing a build-up of arms by either party.[140]

UNDOF apparently had a similar effect following the June 1982 invasion of Lebanon by Israel. The situation was summarised by the Secretary General: 'Despite the present quiet in the Israel-Syria sector, the situation in the Middle East as a whole continues to be potentially dangerous and is likely to remain so. In the prevailing circumstances, I consider the continued presence of UNDOF in the area is essential.'[141]

UN Interim Force in Lebanon (UNIFIL) 1978-present
Israel invaded southern Lebanon in March 1978. The Security Council responded with resolution 425 on 19 March which expressed grave concern at 'the deterioration of the situation and its consequences for international peace'. It called on Israel to 'cease its military action' and to withdraw its forces from Lebanese territory. The resolution also established UNIFIL at the request of the Lebanese government to confirm Israeli withdrawal and then to ensure 'the effective restoration of Lebanese sovereignty'.[142] This remains UNIFIL's mandate to date.

The Secretary General interpreted the Council's mandate as authorising him to establish a peacekeeping force based on UNEF II and UNDOF, with UNIFIL acting only in self-defence, pursuing a neutralist approach of not undertaking 'the responsibilities of the Lebanese government' and being under the exclusive control of the Security Council.[143]

By basing UNIFIL firmly on the consensual-type peacekeeping of UNEF and UNDOF the Council and Secretary General made it clear that enforcement was not contemplated. Resolution 425 contained a non-mandatory call for provisional measures based on Article 40. However, when Israel and various other factions in southern Lebanon prevented the second part of UNIFIL's mandate from being fulfilled some members of the Council referred to Article 25.[144] Even if such references could somehow make resolution 425 retroactively mandatory, such an effect would only make the call for provisional measures mandatory, it would in no way affect the functions of UNIFIL in supervising those measures. UNIFIL's mandate remains dependent on cooperation. The question of whether the provisional measures are mandatory or not only applies to the effectiveness of those measures, and not to the nature of the force set up to supervise them.

UNIFIL was based on other inter-State peacekeeping forces because at the time the situation was viewed essentially as a dispute between Israel and Lebanon. However, it became increasingly clear that Lebanon was in a state of civil war with various factions, including foreign States such as Syria, having more power and influence than the central government. This made UNIFIL's mandate unrealistic, the Council might have considered changing it to deal with an intra-State conflict as ONUC was in the Congo. Although the Security Council had, in the case of UNFICYP, changed a peacekeeping force's functions from being of an intra-State nature to being of an inter-State nature, it has not yet been prepared to change UNIFIL's essentially inter-State structure. This, in turn, has greatly impeded UNIFIL's success in implementing its mandate.

Although Israel withdrew by the end of April 1978, the second part of UNIFIL's mandate, the restoration of Lebanese sovereignty, was almost impossible to achieve given the state of virtual civil war in southern Lebanon and the inability of the profoundly weak Lebanese government to assume any sort of responsibility for the area. However, the Syrian backed government has began to reassert sovereignty in southern Lebanon in 1991–92, resulting in UNIFIL relinquishing some of its areas on 15 January 1992 to the Lebanese army. UNIFIL may have had little direct involvement in the reassertion of sovereignty in southern Lebanon but it clearly is creating sufficient stability in the area to allow this to happen. It cannot, however, prevent the frequent outbursts of violence in the area or prevent the Israelis or their proxy army, the South Lebanon Army, from launching attacks or invasions from their so-called security zone in southern Lebanon south of the Litani river.

Although it did not facilitate a restoration of Lebanese sovereignty, UNIFIL was successful in negotiating a cease-fire between Israel and the PLO which lasted from July 1981 to April 1982.[145] However, this success was shortlived for whereas the PLO regarded the cease-fire as confined to the Israeli-Lebanese border, the Israeli authorities interpreted the agreement as proscribing all hostile measures against Israeli or Jewish targets overseas. So when on 3 June 1982 Israel's ambassador in London was shot by Arab gunmen, the precarious cease-fire collapsed and Israel commenced operation 'Peace for Galilee' by invading Lebanon with the aim of driving the PLO out.

Israel forewarned UNIFIL of its action and passed through the force's lines.[146] Neither UNIFIL's mandate, nor size, nor armaments, enabled it to resist. With Israel pushing further into Lebanon, UNIFIL's original mandate was impossible to achieve. Nevertheless, the Council renewed its mandate, while directing it, during the period of Israel's occupation, which was not ended until June 1985, to undertake humanitarian assistance to the population of southern Lebanon.[147]

Despite the improvement in the situation in southern Lebanon in 1991–92 with the partial restoration of Lebanese sovereignty in the south, the Israelis still deemed it necessary to ignore UNIFIL in February 1992 to launch an attack aimed at Hezbollah guerrilla bases again illustrating that UNIFIL is simply a limited stabilising factor in a region where the prospects of peace still appear to be remote despite the Middle East peace process.

UN Transition Assistance Group in Namibia (UNTAG) 1989–90
During the period of *détente* in the late 1970s, there arose the false hope that a solution to the Namibian problem was at hand. In 1976, the Security

Council declared that the Namibian people should be 'enabled freely to determine their own future' by the means of free elections under UN supervision.[148] Indeed, optimism was so high despite South African non-committal, that Canada, the Federal Republic of Germany, France, Britain and the United States made a proposal for the settlement of the Namibian situation detailing the electoral process.[149] This led in 1978 to the appointment of a Special Representative and a decision by the Security Council to establish UNTAG in accordance with a report by the Secretary General 'to ensure the early independence of Namibia through free elections under the supervision and control of the United Nations'.[150]

The Secretary General's report of 1978 recognised the 'unique character' of the proposed operation, in that it entailed not only a peacekeeping operation in the true sense to supervise a cease-fire between SWAPO and South African forces, but also supervision of free and fair elections leading to an independent State. This resulted in the Secretary General recommending a large military force of some 7,500 with a component of several hundred police and civilian administrators. The mandate of the military component was interpreted to include: the monitoring of the cessation of hostile acts; the restriction of South African and SWAPO forces to base; the phased withdrawal of all except a specified number of South African forces; the prevention of infiltration; and the monitoring of the demobilisation of civilian police forces.

The mandate of UNTAG appeared widely drawn in 1978. Despite its division into military and police components, the overall mandate was for UNTAG to keep and enforce the peace in Namibia during the independence process. As with ONUC, there existed the possibility of a peacekeeping force crossing the threshold and becoming an enforcement action. Nevertheless, the internal nature of the conflict necessitated such a widely drawn mandate.

As with all peacekeeping forces, before UNTAG could be emplaced it needed the consent of all the parties to the conflict. SWAPO had consistently accepted resolution 435, while South African consent was not forthcoming until 22 December 1988 when it signed, along with Cuba and Angola, a tripartite agreement consenting to the UN plan.[151] The plan was acceptable to the South Africans because the accord linked Cuban withdrawal from Angola with South African withdrawal from Namibia. The agreement was also the result of pressure by the United States on South Africa and the Soviet Union on Cuba and Angola. The agreement envisaged the independence process commencing on 1 April 1989.

The Security Council welcomed the agreement while stating that UNTAG's mandate was the same as that envisaged in 1978 following a further report by the Secretary General.[152] SWAPO and South Africa agreed to a cease-fire to commence on 1 April so preparing the ground for UNTAG.

UNTAG's constitutional base remained in the Security Council resolution of 1978 and the accompanying report by the Secretary General. The military component's task was to oversee the implementation of provisional measures necessary for the success of the independence process to be monitored by the civilian component. As has been stated, UNTAG's mandate contained the possibility of it being able to enforce the peace, but it did not do this when faced with a breakdown in the cease-fire. Indeed, the agreements between South Africa and the United Nations on the status of UNTAG foresaw it having a neutral and impartial function.[153]

Although the Security Council decided to implement its plan for Namibian independence in its original and definitive form, it eventually decided to reduce the size of UNTAG to 4,500, following intense pressure from the five permanent members, who thought that the improved climate in southern Africa in addition to financial constraints meant that a smaller peacekeeping force was sufficient for the tasks.[154] The wrangling over the size of the force combined perhaps with some complacency as to the anticipated success of the peace process, may have resulted in the inauspicious start to the UN plan, when on 1 April 1989, the cease-fire was breached. Several hundred SWAPO guerrillas infiltrating from Angola, were met with force by South African troops purportedly acting under UNTAG authority due to the fact that the UN had only 1,000 troops in Namibia with very few in the border area.[155] There was no doubt that the South African forces enforced the peace in a way that the peacekeeping force was not mandated to. On the other hand, SWAPO appeared to be in breach of the tripartite accord which confined the guerrillas to bases inside Angola. However, although SWAPO consented to the UN plan as laid down in 1978, it was not a party to the agreement which finalised the details. The peace process seemed to have ignored the fact that all the parties to the dispute should have fully consented to all aspects of the peace agreement before the peacekeeping force was emplaced.

During the fighting between SWAPO and the South African forces, the United Nations appeared helpless. It required a new agreement on 8 April between the original signatories to the tripartite accord and this time consented to by SWAPO before a new cease-fire could be made effective. The fresh agreement between South Africa, Angola and Cuba with the United States and the Soviet Union overseeing, provided for a cease-fire and a withdrawal of SWAPO fighters to north of the 16th parallel under UN supervision. This agreement was reported to the Security Council by the Secretary General.[156]

The shaky start to the UN plan gave rise to fears that the elections, scheduled for 1 November 1989 might be delayed. However, the Joint Monitoring Commission of Angola, South Africa and Cuba, agreed on 14 May 1989 that the situation was normalised sufficiently for the plan to proceed on schedule.[157] UNTAG then successfully ensured a free and fair election on 11 November 1989 at which 97 per cent of the electorate voted. Full independence was achieved on 21 March 1990.[158]

UN Transition Assistance Authority in Cambodia (UNTAC) 1991-present

The end of the Cold War signified a change in the attitude of the parties to the Cambodian conflict which had raged in the country since the civil war of 1970–75. The communists (the Khmer Rouge) won that war and then subjected the population of the country to genocidal outrages which cost about two million lives. The Vietnamese then pushed the Khmer Rouge out in 1979 and set up a puppet regime which waged war against the Khmer Rouge who were still supported by communist China. The Vietnamese pulled out in 1989 and it appeared that the country might slip back into civil war. However, the UN brokered peace talks, which started in earnest a few months before the Vietnamese troops withdrew in September, took hold in the post Cold War climate, and Cambodia started taking some tentative but positive steps towards a peaceful solution to what had seemed to most observers an intractable conflict.

The four factions involved in the Cambodian conflict, agreed to a cease-fire in May 1991 and then signed the Paris Peace Accords on 23 October 1991. This document contained several agreements detailing, *inter alia*, the comprehensive settlement of the Cambodian conflict which included the establishment of UNTAC for an eighteen-month period as well as a pro-gramme for elections and for the creation of a new Cambodian con-stitution.[159] The Security Council authorised the creation of UNTAC and the immediate emplacement of a UN Advance Mission in Cambodia (UNAMIC) to deal with the initial supervision of the cease-fire and to assist in mine clearance.[160] The Secretary General was asked to prepare a plan for the full implementation of the peace process by the creation and emplacement of the full UN peacekeeping force, UNTAC.

On 28 February 1992, the Security Council unanimously approved of the Secretary General's implementation plan,[161] creating the largest and most ambitious UN peacekeeping operation in the Organisation's history with over 22,000 personnel (16,000 military personnel, 3,500 police monitors and over 1,500 civilian administrators) to be emplaced by May 1992 to oversee the country's transition to a new regime after multi-party elections scheduled to be held by May 1993. The mandate of the force, derived from the Paris Peace Accords, covers a wide variety of matters, many beyond the core peacekeeping function of supervising the cease-fire.

The military component of the force is to verify withdrawal of all foreign forces and to monitor the cessation of outside military assistance; and to supervise the cease-fire and related measures such as the cantonment of the various armed bands and their subsequent disarmament and demobilisation. The civilian administrators are to exercise direct control over the existing institutions in Cambodia to ensure strict neutrality, whilst the civilian police monitors are controlling the local police to ensure that law and order are maintained effectively and impartially. In addition to the election supervision, UNTAC has within it a human rights component along the lines of ONUSAL in El Salvador.

It can be readily seen that UNTAC is in many respects the culmination of UN peacekeeping in that its mandate covers every aspect of traditional peacekeeping as well as the features of the new forces with integrated mandates. The concept behind the implementation plan reflected in the discussion in the Security Council at the adoption of resolution 745 and stated clearly by the Secretary General at the signing of the Final Act at the Paris Peace Conference 'is to encourage the establishment of a neutral political environment in which the Cambodian people can freely determine their future'.[162]

As with the initial demobilisation of SWAPO forces in Namibia, UNTAC has run into serious problems concerning the cantonment of the Khmer Rouge. The process envisaged the emplacement of the peacekeeping force to be followed by the demobilisation and disarmament of the four factions, beginning on 13 June 1992. This would entail the collection of the arms of what is estimated to be 200,000 troops from the various factions gathering in 95 UN controlled regroupment areas. The Secretary General reported on the 21 July 1992 to the Security Council that less than 5 per cent of this figure had been cantoned. In addition the Khmer Rouge has stepped up its cease-fire violations. It spuriously used the excuse that the UN had not properly supervised the withdrawal of Vietnamese troops and had, by controlling the government administrators, conferred legitimacy on the government. The charge was obviously intended to undermine the UN's neutrality, a facet essential to its success in this operation and with peacekeeping generally.

With the UN's forces taking on wider and wider mandates in more and more difficult situations, it will become increasingly difficult for it to maintain its neutrality. Despite condemnation by the Security Council in resolution 766 on 21 July 1992, and a demand that the Khmer Rouge permit UNTAC into the areas under its control, the UN operation in Cambodia is, at present, in great difficulty. The Supreme National Council, the interim body established by the Paris Accords to represent all four factions, is in the process of negotiating pledges from the Khmer Rouge that would allow the UN process to proceed.

UN Protection Force in Yugoslavia (UNPROFOR) 1992-present
The end of the Cold War and the collapse of communism, while encouraging settlement of old disputes, also unleashed new internecine wars, most

notably in Europe with the collapse of the Yugoslav federal State into its various religious, ethnic and national factions. The UN was clearly reluctant to become involved in such a conflict bearing in mind the cost to the Organisation of its foray into the disintegrating Congo in the 1960s. However, unlike the Congo, where ONUC's mandate was basically to keep the country intact, any peacekeeping operation in Yugoslavia would inevitably have to oversee the disintegration of that State and, hopefully, the emergence of stable new States.

The civil war between the various factions, most notably the Croatians and the Serbians, commenced in June 1991, with the Security Council quite willingly leaving any attempt at brokering and observing a cease-fire, and negotiating a peaceful settlement to the European Community, although it did impose a mandatory arms embargo against the whole of Yugoslavia in resolution 713 on 25 September 1991, after determining that the continuation of the situation constituted a threat to international peace and security.

Indeed, it was not until 27 November 1991 that the Security Council was eventually persuaded by international pressure to become involved in a possible peacekeeping operation. In resolution 721, it repeated its determination that the situation in Yugoslavia constituted a threat to international peace and security and requested that the Secretary General's envoy prepare a report on the feasibility of sending a peacekeeping force to Yugoslavia. The Council made it clear that the emplacement of the force would be conditional on all parties complying with the cease-fire negotiated in Geneva on 23 November.[163] The request for the force came from the Serbian dominated rump Yugoslav Collective State Presidency.[164] The Croatian authorities agreed to such a force on 28 November. The sticking points were principally: the numerous cease-fire violations between the Serbian dominated Yugoslav National Army and the Croatian forces, and the federal request that the peacekeepers should be emplaced around the self-proclaimed Serbian autonomous regions within Croatia. Croatia denounced this demand as an attempt to create a Greater Serbia and demanded that the force be emplaced only on the officially recognised internal borders of the former Yugoslavia,[165] possibly in the hope that the effect of this would be to help create an international frontier, bearing in mind the experiences of UNFICYP in Cyprus.

The cease-fire broke down in December 1991 and the Security Council, in resolution 724 of 15 December, agreed with the Secretary General[166] and stated that the conditions for establishing a force did not exist, but did agree to send an advance team of twenty observers to prepare for the eventual deployment of a full force. Furthermore, it appealed to all States not to exacerbate the situation, a veiled, and, as it turns out, unsuccessful attempt to persuade Germany and other States not to recognise any of the breakaway Republics. The cease-fire between Croatia and the remnants of the Yugoslavian State (Serbia and Montenegro) began to take hold more effectively in January, so that the Council was confident in sending another fifty observers specifically to supervise the cease-fire.[167]

With Croatia accepting that the Serbian occupied areas of Croatia and the Serbian enclaves could be put under temporary UN control in so-called UN protected areas, a compromise agreed to by the Serbian leaders of these regions, the final blocks to the emplacement of the force were removed, and on 21 February 1992 in resolution 743, the Security Council unanimously authorised the sending of 14,400 peacekeeping troops to Yugoslavia, their mandate to oversee the cease-fire and to control the disputed areas until the parties, initially under European Community brokerage and then under joint EC/UN efforts, agreed to a final settlement.[168]

Unlike the integrated force in Cambodia, we have a return to traditional-style peacekeeping, with peacemaking occurring separately and so far unsuccessfully, which could lead to a prolonged peacekeeping presence in the former Yugoslavia. Although the Council reiterated its determination that the situation was a threat to the peace, UNPROFOR's mandate was in all respects of a consensual and non-enforcement type.

Indeed, the arrival of the first UN troops in Yugoslavia in March 1992 saw a further deterioration in the situation with numerous and serious cease-fire violations occurring, and a deterioration in the central republic of Bosnia-Herzegovina, with the Muslim and Croatian majority voting for independence, whilst Serbs in Bosnia committed themselves to remaining in the Yugoslav Federation. Violence between the various communities in Bosnia broke out towards the end of March and was heightened in April 1992 with the announcement of a new Yugoslav State comprising the two remaining republics that had not sought independence, namely Serbia and Montenegro, to which Serbs in the other former republics, Croatia and Bosnia, claimed allegiance.[169]

With alleged outside involvement in the conflict in Bosnia in May 1992, principally from the new Yugoslav State in the shape of the remnants of the still powerful Yugoslav National Army (JNA) but also by the Croatian army, the Secretary General reported to the Security Council that UNPROFOR or any other peacekeeping force should not become involved in Bosnia, and that the UN plan for Croatia was in jeopardy because of the failure of the Serbian irregulars in Croatia to demobilise.[170] As a result the Security Council adopted resolution 752 on 15 May 1992 which in recalling the provisions of Chapter VII of the Charter demanded that the parties in Bosnia cease firing and cooperate with the European Community 'to bring about urgently a negotiated political solution respecting the principle that any change of borders by force is not acceptable'. It also demanded that the JNA and the Croatian army desist from interference and withdraw their forces immediately.

This apparently mandatory demand was not complied with, resulting in the Council adopting resolution 757 on 30 May 1992, in which it condemned the JNA and the Croatian army and then proceeded to impose sanctions on Serbia and Montenegro covering trade, oil, sporting and air links, under Chapter VII of the Charter after determining 'that the situation in Bosnia and Herzegovina and in other parts of the former Socialist Federal Republic of Yugoslavia constitutes a threat to international peace and security'.

It appears that at this stage the UN lost its neutrality in the conflict and could be seen to be siding against Serbia by taking mandatory enforcement action against it. One cannot doubt that Serbia, or at least the Serb militia, are the most guilty of the warring factions with their aggression against Bosnia and Croatia, and their policy of ethnically cleansing those areas in Croatia and Bosnia under Serbian control by forcing non-Serbs out despite the presence, at least in Croatia, of UNPROFOR. However, such alignment by the UN does seem to make the task of peacekeeping in the same conflict at the same time that enforcement action is being taken very difficult if not impossible. The blue berets, despite the fact that they remain impartial, are seen to be the enemy by the Serbs.

Nevertheless, the Security Council, appalled by the suffering in Bosnia, was gradually sucked into that conflict. On 8 June 1992, it adopted resolution 758 authorising the Secretary General to deploy military observers to Sarajevo, the capital of Bosnia and scene of the worst fighting, to supervise the withdrawal of heavy weapons from around the airport. It also enlarged the mandate and strength of UNPROFOR with 1,000 infantry to allow for the delivery of humanitarian supplies to the beleaguered city by securing the airport for the delivery of humanitarian aid. The deployment of troops was conditional upon 'an effective and durable cease-fire' being agreed to by the factions in Sarajevo. The parties appeared to agree to a cease-fire on 5 June 1992, and the Security Council mandated 1,000 Canadian troops to secure the airport, in resolution 761 of 29 June 1992, following a report by the Secretary General.[171]

The situation in Sarajevo remains bleak although humanitarian aid is getting through despite many interruptions as the fighting continues in Bosnia. The situation is confused but the recent development as regards UNPROFOR is that as regards the situation in Bosnia, the Security Council has apparently authorised outside States to 'take all measures necessary' to facilitate, in coordination with the UN, the delivery of humanitarian aid to Sarajevo and to other parts of Bosnia by resolution 770 of 13 August 1992. By using the formula of 'measures necessary', which was used to authorise limited and the full-scale use of force in the Gulf, the Security Council has opened the way for third States to use force to secure humanitarian aid to the beleaguered people of Bosnia. This would seem to compromise further the presence of UNPROFOR which is still mandated to perform peacekeeping tasks without having the ability to enforce the peace.[172] Further enforcement action in Bosnia would seem to indicate the necessity of withdrawing UNPROFOR before it suffers heavy casualties.

The bulk of UNPROFOR in the UN Protected Areas of Croatia seems to be having greater success, although there is little evidence that it has reversed ethnic cleansing by the Serbs. It has been authorised to take more 'quasi governmental responsibilities' for these areas in an effort to restore some Croatian authority to them.[173] Although making headway along its neutral tightrope, UNPROFOR cannot solve the problem itself; it is dependent, as is the rest of the UN operation, on the success of the so far unsuccessful UN/EC peace process under the joint chairmanship of Cyrus Vance and Lord Owen.

UN Operation in Somalia (UNOSOM) 1992-present

The overthrow of the regime of Siad Barre in January 1991 signified a further deterioration in the civil war and anarchy in Somalia. The Security Council somewhat belatedly acted to try to combat the conflict which was exacerbating the famine in the drought-stricken country. It imposed a mandatory arms embargo and demanded that the various armed factions within the country observe a cease-fire in resolution 733 of 23 January 1992. A cease-fire in Mogadishu was agreed by the two main warring factions on 3 March 1992, with provision for a small number of UN military observers (about 40) to monitor the cease-fire. The leaders also agreed to develop a plan for the unimpeded delivery of humanitarian aid. The Security Council supported the sending of a limited number of observers in resolution 746 adopted on 17 March 1992.

Further negotiations led to the Council adopting resolution 751 on 24 April 1992, establishing UNOSOM, a force of 3,000 peacekeepers mandated: to facilitate an immediate cessation of hostilities throughout Somalia, to maintain a permanent cease-fire, to provide urgent humanitarian assistance, to supervise the indigenous police force, and to promote national reconciliation and peaceful settlement. As with UNPROFOR in Bosnia, one of UNOSOM's main tasks is to provide humanitarian assistance to the starving population. The Secretary General's plan to provide aid includes the establishment of aid corridors and zones of peace as well as the deployment of UNOSOM, which in part will consist of a security force, to replace the need for the UN aid convoys to hire local gunmen in highly dangerous operations.

This immediately raises the possibility of such a UN security force needing to 'force' its way through the multitude of tribal armed bands in the country, bands which do not appear to be under any central command. In resolution 767 adopted on 27 July 1992, the Security Council did not exclude 'other measures' to deliver humanitarian assistance in the absence of cooperation from all the factions. It also supported the Secretary General's proposal to establish four operational zones in Somalia under UNOSOM supervision. The Secretary General stressed the need for the UN to adapt UNOSOM's involvement there, eventually enlarging the operation in an effort to bring about a sustained cease-fire throughout the country, while at the same time pressing for national reconciliation.

UNOSOM has the potential to be another UNPROFOR or even UNTAC if the factions can agree on a means of settlement, but at the moment problems of gaining cooperation with the various warlords in Somalia has meant that by September 1992 only 60 UN troops had so far arrived in Somalia to assist with humanitarian assistance, although another 440 had been agreed to.

Notes

1 SC Res. 27, 2 UN SCOR Resolutions 6 (1947).
2 SC 390 mtg, 3 UN SCOR (1948). UN doc. S/488 (1948).
3 SC Res. 30, 2 UN SCOR Resolutions 8 (1947).
4 UN doc. S/586 (1947).
5 SC Res. 31, 2 UN SCOR Resolutions 8 (1947); SC Res. 67, 4 UN SCOR Resolutions 2 (1949).
6 SC 390 mtg, 3 UN SCOR (1948), Australia.
7 SC 174 mtg, 2 UN SCOR 1716 (1947), Netherlands; SC 194 mtg, 2 UN SCOR 2191 (1947), Indonesia.
8 R. Higgins, *United Nations Peacekeeping: Documents and Commentary, vol. 2: Asia 1946–1967*, 61–86 (1970).
9 SC Res. 15, 1 UN SCOR Resolutions 6 (1946).
10 UN doc. S/360/Rev 1 (1950).
11 GA Res. 109, 2 UN GAOR Resolutions 12 (1947).
12 UN doc. A/521, (1948).
13 GA Res 193, 3 UN GAOR Resolutions 18 (1948).
14 UN Yearbook (1947–48), 341.
15 Higgins, *United Nations Peacekeeping: Documents and Commmentary, vol. 4: Europe 1946–1979*, 32 (1981).
16 For example: UN docs A/374 (1948); A/1857 (1951).
17 SC Res. 48, 3 UN SCOR Resolutions 17 (1948).
18 SC Res. 54, 3 UN SCOR Resolutions 22 (1948).
19 See UN doc. S/928 (1948).
20 SC Res. 72, 4 UN SCOR Resolutions 7 (1949).
21 SC 1743 mtg, 28 UN SCOR 15, 4 (1973).
22 SC 1745 mtg, 28 UN SCOR 2 (1973).
23 SC Res. 516, 37 UN SCOR Resolutions 8 (1982).
24 UN doc. S/15956 (1983).
25 UN doc. S/628 (1948).
26 SC Res. 39, 3 UN SCOR Resolutions 2 (1948).

27 The Karachi Agreement, UN doc. S/1430/Add 1, Ann 26 (1949).
28 SC Res. 209, 20 UN SCOR Resolutions 13 (1965).
29 On the 1965 breach see UN doc. S/6710 (1965). On the 1971 breach see UN doc. S/10412 (1971).
30 UN doc. S/4029 (1958).
31 UN doc. S/4040 (1958).
32 GA Res. 1752, 17 UN GAOR Supp. (No. 17) 70 (1962).
33 UN doc. A/5501 (1962).
34 UN doc. S/5298 (1963).
35 UN doc. S/5321 (1963).
36 SC Res. 179, 18 UN SCOR Resolutions 2 (1963).
37 UN doc. S/5412 (1963).
38 UN doc. S/5447 (1963).
39 UN doc. S/5794 (1964).
40 UN doc. S/5142 (1962).
41 See UN docs S/5927, S/5142 (1964).
42 UN doc. S/6651 (1965).
43 UN doc. S/6735 (1965).
44 SC 1247 mtg, 20 UN SCOR (1965).
45 UN doc. S/6719/Add 5 (1965).
46 UN doc. S/6710/Add 5 (1965).
47 UN doc. S/6699 and Add 1 (1965).
48 UN doc. S/6719/Add 5 & 12 (1965).
49 UN docs S/19834, S/19835 (1988).
50 SC Res. 622, 43 UN SCOR Resolutions (1988).
51 UN doc. S/20465 (1989).
52 UN doc. S/20561 (1989).
53 SC 2852 mtg, 44 UN SCOR (1989).
54 SC Res. 647, 45 UN SCOR Resolutions (1990).
55 SC 2823 mtg, 43 UN SCOR (1988).
56 UN doc. S/20093 (1988).
57 SC Res. 619, 43 UN SCOR Resolutions (1988).
58 UN doc. S/20442 (1988).
59 UN doc. S/22263 (1992).
60 UN doc. S/20345 (1988).
61 UN doc. S/20346 (1988).
62 SC Res. 626, 43 UN SCOR Resolutions (1988).
63 UN doc. S/22644 (1991).
64 S/22627 Add 1 (1991). 65 UN doc. S/24145 (1992). See also Presidential Statement in SC 3092 mtg, 7 July 1992.
66 26 *I.L.M.* (1987), 1164.
67 UN doc. S/20491 (1989).
68 UN doc. S/20699 (1989).
69 UN docs A/44/921, A/44/927 (1990).
70 UN docs S/20895, S/20979 (1989).
71 SC Res. 650, 653, 45 UN SCOR Resolutions (1990).
72 SC Res. 730, 47 UN S/PV (1992).

73 SC Res. 621, 43 UN SCOR Resolutions (1988).
74 UN doc. S/21360 (1990).
75 *The Independent*, 6 February 1992.
76 UN doc. S/23662 (1992).
77 SC Res. 725, 46 UN SCOR Resolutions (1991).
78 UN docs S/24059, S/24040 (1992).
79 UN doc. S/21541 (1990).
80 UN doc. S/23999 (1992).
81 29(2) *UN Chronicle* (1992), 30.
82 SC Res. 729, 47 UN S/PV (1992).
83 485 UNTS 321.
84 UN doc. S/22454 (1991).
85 SC 748 mtg, 11 UN SCOR (1956).
86 UN doc. S/3710 (1956), US; UN doc. S/3713/Rev 1 (1956), USSR.
87 SC Res. 119, 11 UN SCOR Resolutions 9 (1956).
88 GA Res. 997, 1 UN GAOR ESS Supp. (No. 1) 2 (1956).
89 GA 562 plen. mtg, 1 UN GAOR ESS 296–305, 282 (1956), Canada, New
    Zealand.
90 GA Res. 998, 1 UN GAOR ESS Supp. (No. 1) 2 (1956).
91 GA Res. 999, *ibid.*
92 UN doc. A/3289 (1956); GA Res. 1000, *ibid.* UN doc. A/3302 (1956); GA Res.
    1001, *ibid.*
93 GA 638 plen. mtg, 11 UN GAOR paras 76–77 (1957), Australia.
94 UN doc. A/6730/Add 3 (1967).
95 GA 592 mtg, 11 UN GAOR paras. 13, 111, 79 (1956).
96 5 *I.L.M.* (1967), 595–602.
97 J. I. Garvey, 'United Nations peacekeeping and host state consent', 64 *A.J.I.L.*
    (1970), 241.
98 UN doc. A/6669 (1967).
99 UN doc. A/3568 (1957).
100 UN docs S/3659 (1956), A/3694 (1957).
101 Higgins, *United Nations Peacekeeping: Documents and Commentary, vol. 1:
    Middle East 1946–1967*, 481 (1969).
102 UN doc. S/4382 (1960).
103 SC 873 mtg, 15 UN SCOR para. 18 (1960).
104 T. M. Franck, *Nation against Nation*, 176 (1985).
105 SC 901 mtg, 15 UN SCOR paras. 20–85 (1960).
106 UN doc. S/4523 (1960).
107 SC Res. 157, 15 UN SCOR Resolutions 8 (1960).
108 GA Res. 1474, 4 UN GAOR ESS Supp. (No. 1) 1 (1960).
109 J. Lash, 'Dag Hammarskjöld's conception of his office', 16 *International
    Organisation* (1962) 551.
110 G. Abi-Saab, *The UN Operation in the Congo*, 13 (1978).
111 UN doc. S/4389 (1960); SC 873 mtg, 15 UN SCOR paras 18–29 (1960).
112 Higgins, *United Nations Peacekeeping: Documents and Commentary, vol. 3:
    Africa 1946–1967*, 54 (1980); D. W. Bowett, *United Nations Forces*, 176 (1964);
    Abi-Saab, *The UN Operation in the Congo*, 105.

113 SC 920 mtg, 15 UN SCOR para. 75 (1960).
114 I.C.J. *Rep*. 1962, 151.
115 Bowett, *UN Forces*, 180.
116 UN doc. S/5240 (1963).
117 E. W. Lefever, *Crisis in the Congo*, 181 (1965).
118 UN doc. S/5488 (1963).
119 UN doc. S/5508 (1964).
120 UN doc. S/5526 (1964).
121 SC 1095 mtg, 19 UN SCOR paras. 124–7 (1964).
122 UN doc. S/5653 (1964).
123 UN doc. S/5671 Annex 1 (1964).
124 UN docs S/11334, S/11335 (1974).
125 See for example SC 1779 mtg, 29 UN SCOR 5 (1974), USSR.
126 SC Res. 355, 29 UN SCOR Resolutions 8 (1974).
127 SC 1789 mtg, 29 UN SCOR 11 (1974).
128 UN doc. S/11473 (1974).
129 UN docs S/6102 (1964), S/8141 (1967).
130 UN doc. S/7969 (1967).
131 L. Mates, 'The United Nations and the maintenance of international peace and security', in Rajan (ed.), *The Non Aligned and the United Nations*, 90 (1987).
132 SC Res. 550, 39 UN SCOR Resolutions 12 (1984).
133 SC Res. 338, 28 UN SCOR Resolutions 10 (1973).
134 SC 1747 mtg, 28 UN SCOR para. 11 (1973).
135 SC Res. 339, 28 UN SCOR Resolutions 11 (1973).
136 UN doc. S/11052/Rev 1 (1973).
137 UN doc. S/12897 (1978).
138 See GA Res. 34/35B, 34 UN GAOR Supp. (No. 46) 19 (1979).
139 UN doc. S/11302 (1974).
140 UN doc. S/12710 (1978).
141 UN doc. S/15493 (1982).
142 SC Res. 425, 33 UN SCOR Resolutions 5 (1978).
143 UN doc. S/12611 (1978).
144 SC 2085 mtg, 33 UN SCOR 3 (1978).
145 UN doc. S/14869 (1982).
146 UN doc. S/15194/Add 1 (1982).
147 SC Res. 511, 37 UN SCOR Resolutions 6 (1982).
148 SC Res. 385, 31 UN SCOR Resolutions 8 (1976).
149 UN doc. S/12636 (1978).
150 UN doc. S/12827 (1978); SC Res. 435, 33 UN SCOR Resolutions 13 (1978).
151 UN doc. S/20346 (1988).
152 SC Res. 628, 629, 632, 44 UN SCOR Resolutions (1989). UN doc. S/20412 (1989).
153 UN doc. S/20412/Add 1 (1989).
154 UN doc. S/20412 (1989).
155 *Keesing* (1989), 36576.
156 UN doc. 10 April 1989.
157 UN doc. 24 May 1989.

158 UN doc. S/20967 (1990).
159 UN doc. S/23179 (1991).
160 SC Res. 717, 718, 46 UN SCOR Resolutions (1991). Also SC Res. 728, 47 S/PV (1992).
161 SC Res. 745, 47 UN S/PV (1992); UN doc. S/23613 (1992).
162 UN Press Release, 23 October 1991; SC 3057 mtg, 47 S/PV (1992).
163 UN doc. S/23239 (1991).
164 UN doc. S/23240 (1991).
165 *Keesing* (1991), 38559.
166 UN doc. S/23280 (1991).
167 SC Res. 727, 46 UN SCOR Resolutions (1991).
168 UN doc. S/23592 (1992).
169 *Keesing* (1992), 38848.
170 UN doc. S/23900 (1992).
171 UN doc. S/24075 (1992).
172 See further SC Res. 771, 47 UN S/PV (1992).
173 SC Res. 762, 769, 47 UN S/PV (1992).

INDEX